# LIFE ON THE OTHER SIDE

A personal story on how to live and thrive with a mental health problem, for anyone, at any age and any stage of life.
This book gives honest, realistic, easy to read guides and stories on living with a mental illness by someone that knows. You will read about life in therapy, on medication, in school or work, dating with a mental illness, why motivation means nothing without action and real life tips and strategies to make your life easier. This is not a medical book.

Best wishes

# Life On The Other Side

By Jack Pridmore

# Disclaimer and Copyright

This book is not intended as a substitute for the medical advice of professionals. The reader should regularly consult medical professionals in matters relating to his/her health and particularly with respect to any symptoms that may require diagnosis or medical attention.
All medical and non-medical information within this book are true to the author only and are not intended to be specifically best practice although may be considered so by medical establishments at the time of writing.
This book is considered semi-autobiographical and stories are for illustrative or entertainment purposes only and not in any way intended to be promoting any specific choices or lifestyle, nor are they intended to be read as an endorsement of the actions written.



**All proceeds from this book are donated to OCD Action, the UK's largest charity supporting those affected by Obsessive Compulsive Disorder. Thank you for your support.** www.ocdaction.org.uk

For trade buying requests, details of stockists or further purchasing information please contact info@lifeontheotherside.co.uk

Printed in the United Kingdom
First Printing, 2019 (Cloc Ltd)

ISBN 978-1-9163136-0-6

Otherside Publishing
United Kingdom

www.LifeOnTheOtherSide.co.uk

# Acknowledgements

Firstly, to every single person that has played a role in me getting to the point of being able to even write this. Medical professionals, teachers, friends, all of you. Andrew Bradley, Josh Cannings, Megan Morgan, Olivia Bamber, Imogen Pearce, Merle Currie, Pete Weiss, Dr Travis Osborne and Richard Cooke, each of you played a starring role and I am so grateful. To anyone that contributed towards me living in my version of recovery, it is beautiful and vibrant and challenging and exciting and everything I'd hoped it would be. I hope I haven't let you down.

Towards writing the book itself I would like to thank everyone that has contributed, be that in their words in this book or in its research. Thank you to; Dr Joseph Hayes, Claire Littlejohn, Katy Jade Dobson, Sherelle Wedderburn, Rebecca Dawkins, Laura Thompson, Jake RT Brown, my good friend Chris D'Arcy and Mark Sloan - who made this book possible, we did it man.

A quick shout out to everyone that has inspired this book by being who they are, including; Debbie, a warrior. See you for coffee soon. Oliver Wilson, who continues to impress me every day and Millie H, who I cannot wait to watch smash it as she deserves. This book is also in loving memory of Jo Morgan, a wonderful lady.

To Lils, you inspired much of this book, I can't wait to watch you fly. To Henry, you inspired much of me, you are the best man I've ever met. To Aubrey, until you write your own. I love you all.

To my best friends and siblings, Dave (+ Densmore), Vix and Gary. My heroes. To my brother Bjorn. To my Ma and Pa, for always trying to try. To Nan and Gramps, cockney royalty.

Thank you to the team at OCD Acton, for whom all proceeds from this book goes. You are all amazing. Thank you for everything.

To anyone that reads this, learns from this and meets me on the other side, thank you so much. This is the thing I am most proud of in my life. I hope it is worthy.

This book is dedicated to Olivia.
The best friend I'll ever have.

# How To Read This Book

This is book one of two and is aimed at you, the reader living with a mental health condition. You may be diagnosed or undiagnosed, experienced or inexperienced, a teenager or an adult, it is a book for everybody.

**TRIGGER WARNING: Themes of suicide, drug use and grotesquely impressive swearing feature throughout this book. As do words on periods of particular struggle. Take your time reading it. It's never wrong to stop and put it down, and do ask someone to read ahead for you if you feel it may be uncomfortable.**

On the other side of this book is another book 'for the supporter'. Supporters are the people that help us live as happily and healthily as we can. They can look like anyone. It may be a parent, a partner, a best mate, teacher, colleague, boss or acquaintance that shows an interest.

Ideally you will read your side and then pass them the book to read their side. Once they are done, read their side too and you'll get to see how I have suggested we can support those of us living with a mental health condition. After this is done, let them read your side. When you've both read both sides, I'd love for you to have a conversation on how to make life easier for you both. (Sorry for writing 'read' so much).

Chapters are not in a fixed order so pick this up and put it down as you please.

If you don't fancy doing any of this, the book is pretty thick. Probably make a good doorstop.

# Contents

# LIFE ON THE OTHER SIDE

# The Truth

This seems like the only place to begin.

Make no mistake, this is not going to be easy. Let's agree on that right away. The sheer fact that you hold this book in your hand indicates that you are probably very aware of this already. You've probably experienced rock bottom or have faced it as you fall and are acutely aware of more darkness than you wished to ever see.

Let's also agree on something else very important. The fact that you are holding this book is in itself the very reason you have every ability to turn your life around entirely. And not just because this book is badass.

Your thirst for improving your situation, be it borne from calmness or desperation, is the most relevant thing here. As long as you hold onto that you hold the golden ticket you need to begin your path to recovery. How you got here is less important. You're here now.

People may tell you what they think you want to hear and impress on you that recovery is easy, that it can be fast tracked or that it can be achieved by one method – be that therapy, medication, anything. People may tell you what you don't want to hear and that recovery is an impossible goal, too difficult to truly attain or just not for you. Both statements are incorrect. Recovery is not black and white, nor is it a finish line we all run towards. Recovery, like mental health, is personal.

That is such an important lesson to learn. This is all so personal. You are able to take a substantial amount of control in this. You are in charge here. You.

Seeing recovery in a more appropriate light is a fantastic way to start. As you will come to read, recovery isn't a line you pass or a destination you can name. It is a series of changes, improvements or amendments to your life that benefit you to the point you feel that you are 'in recovery'.

The Oxford English dictionary has a definition for recovery that I think wonderfully sums up how I believe recovery should be seen, it reads; 'recovery is the action or process of gaining possession or control of something stolen or lost'.

Now I think that really hits the point. If you lose your wallet and find it down the back of the sofa, that's an action of recovery – mental health recovery is a little trickier so let's look at the second part, 'the process of gaining possession or control of something stolen or lost'. Bingo. This is what we are seeking to attain, control of our lives and of our health, and as it says in its very definition – it is a process.

When I talk of finding this control, I am not suggesting we try to cheat life and search for an existence that we have a grasp on every single aspect of, this is both unattainable and unhealthy. Control is about being consistent and having a calmer, measured approach to the chaos and finding ways that work for us.

The 'stolen or lost' part is probably something that resonates with you, it certainly does with me. Those of us to have suffered with mental illness will be harshly aware of the things we have lost, sometimes the people we have lost, and that often overwhelming feeling of theft. As if our time, health, opportunity or potential have been robbed from us.

I've lived a chequered life to say the least. I'm 29 now and I have enjoyed some of the greatest highs life has to offer and some of the crushing lows it can bestow. I consider myself to now be in recovery and have often threatened to write this book - and this is actually the second time I've written it in full. I wrote it first without really divulging much of my personal life but reading it back I realised that if I were in your shoes I'd probably want to know the qualifications of the author that is talking via lived experience, so I know it is important you know where my words come from and where they were learned. I'll keep it brief on myself, as this book is about you – not me. You are the main character in this, I am simply a minor part piecing it together. I'm the Neville Longbottom of this book!

Born in 1990 in East London, I grew up (mostly) in Chelmsford, Essex living with my three siblings Vicky, David and Gary, and our parents. Ever since I can remember I knew that Gary wasn't very well. I knew he had had cancer and I knew that he now had problems with his kidneys, highlighted by the fact I learned to change his dialysis machine before I could even spell 'dialysis machine', and that my second home was Great Ormond Street Hospital. I'd accompany Mum and Gary for his many, many appointments. I never really knew how ill he was. As ridiculous as that sounds, because he just always *was*. I remember around my 8th birthday waking up to be told by one of my siblings that Mum and Gary were in the hospital having had to rush there the night before and being completely nonplussed by this news as if it was the most natural thing and the world and not really noticing how often it was happening until I was awoken in the room I shared with Gary, by now 14 years old, to both of my parents now home. They came in the room quickly and the first thing I noticed was their huge smiles. As an adult now I can appreciate grief really makes people act strange and this was obviously my parents trying to show everything would be OK. Mum sat down next to me and informed me that 'last night Gary took a trip to heaven' and I turned and faced my pillow and just cried and cried. It was a tremendously confusing time.

Within 4 weeks of my brother's death my Dad had been diagnosed with a rare condition that was considered terminal but with no real prognosis due to its unique nature. The condition, Von Hippel Landau Syndrome caused brain bleeds for him of which ultimately led to issues with his heart, kidneys, spine and led to a diagnosis of Schizophrenia. His own personal development from a hard as nails Cockney builder to a seriously ill man more interested in reiki healing and spirituality took a lot of adapting for all of us. Mum was diagnosed with cancer twice during my teenage years and both of my living siblings mental health deteriorated as we all tried to come to terms with our loss and the mammoth changes in our lives.

By aged 5, I'd already began showing symptoms of Obsessive Compulsive Disorder and everything that happened in the following years firmly put me in a pretty dark place for a kid. In lots of ways I was doing well, I was a confident little shit that liked to make people laugh and I was a talented footballer – attracting interest and becoming attached to Premiership football clubs.

By 14, however, things had got seriously worse and my life was becoming unbearable. My anxiety levels were dangerous and everyday was a horrible battle that I never seemed to win. I was feeling physically sick all of the time, constantly feeling suicidal and fantasising of running away for good. Simple tasks become gigantic asks and my way of interacting with my mates had become unhealthy. I was caring for Dad as the sole sibling at home and my Mum's health was not good. It was like I had the weight of the world on my shoulders and I hated waking up. I'd feel a devastating moment of realisation every single morning when I'd realise I hadn't died during the night, the disappointment was encompassing.

To combat the physical side of mental illness (more on this later) I began taking all sorts of painkillers to get me through the day which was something I'd not really address until I was in my twenties.

It felt like I was living life as if I was running with a parachute. I had the ability to run and do the things I wanted to do, but the faster I got the more I noticed the parachute stopping me from progressing. During this time I was seeing many different medical professionals and got an insight into lots of different therapies and lots of different therapists. I became an expert by experience.

I was absolutely one of those people that simply could not get better. I was sure of it.

I was wrong.

# Meant For Someone Else, But Not For Me

Not so long ago I was there. I believed that good lives existed, I saw them all around me, but I knew (or thought I knew) that these lives were not something meant for me. One of the most difficult mental challenges to overcome as you begin or continue a journey of mental wellness is accepting that there is even a chance you can live a life you are happy with.

A particularly sad facet of humanity is that many of us naturally see good things as unattainable. So many people miss out on their dream jobs because they simply do not apply. More people believe they cannot than believe they can. If Donald Trump has taught us anything, it is that nearly everything is attainable. You'll not be surprised to know that even I am a bit appalled at myself for using that last sentence.

Alongside this being the natural stance for many people, those of you reading this are also dealing with having your hands tied behind your back in the fact you're also living with mental illness. That makes facing forward and at least seeing some light at the end of the tunnel at best daunting and at worst impossible.

About a decade ago, following some serious market research into their own financial supporters and also those that hadn't donated, UNICEF decided upon a change of direction. As a charity that provides humanitarian and developmental support to mothers and children in developing nations they claim a major role in many countries and have an important and vital place. However, they had ascertained from their research that those paying money to them would answer questions along the lines of 'Do you think your money is making a difference to those Unicef aims to support?' with 'No'.

The people who paid their own hard earned money into a charity they wanted to assist felt their money couldn't make a difference. That's not the people who did **not** donate, that's those who actually spent money on something they felt was futile!

This led to the realization from the feedback that maybe their ad campaigns that showed the horrors and deprivation many of these young ladies and children face was actually resulting in people thinking that their work and donations were ultimately a lost cause. Obviously that is wrong and as we all know Unicef do incredible work. Soon after and in response it was decided that the charity would begin to show 'Beautiful Africa'. Although they would display the message of how bad things can be, they would prioritise highlighting Africa's enormous potential and the many wonderful attributes of the world's second most populous continent.

This example illustrates how our minds can view health. You know those moments when you have a blocked nose from a cold and you almost can't quite remember what it felt like to not be unwell? You feel a bit like you took your snot-free nostrils for granted all of a sudden and remembering a time when you felt fine seems but a distant memory. Many of us do this with our mental health.

We can easily be led by our brains into feeling like we are in a room with no windows and no doors. This is absolutely incorrect. I will be honest, what happens next isn't guaranteed. Recovery isn't guaranteed. Some of us create a door and walk out unscathed pretty quickly, and for others it feels like a lifetime looking out of the crack in the window but for all of us there's at least a potential for improvement and that is something we need to focus on. There is a chance for you.

Ambiguity can be a really dangerous obstacle in the journey towards becoming mentally healthy.

There is a quote from the legendary Major League Baseball coach Yogi Berra that I used to have on my bedroom wall that I think is really important. It reads; 'If you don't know where you're going, you'll probably end up somewhere else'.

Berra's words ring true particularly when we plateau in treatment, when we are beginning a therapy plan or when we feel we aren't moving forward in anything else in our lives for that matter. If we are set on 'becoming well', that is a fantastic dream to have, but as our favourite celebrities will tell us in their autobiographies, a goal without a plan is a dream.

We need something more tangible and relevant to make recovery and health a more feasible possibility. This requires us to be purposeful.

The reason why we absolutely must adopt a deliberate approach towards our goals in treatment is that without it, human nature can naturally make us adopt a stance that we are failing.

If our goal of becoming well isn't being measured by anything, how do we appreciate our own successes? No matter how your therapies go, even if the majority isn't positive, there will be cause for celebration and success to enjoy, but if you do not know what you are looking for from yourself you'll not be able to fully accept when things **are** indeed working. Conversely and equally, it's important to have this mindset for when things are not going as you'd hoped too. There's a personally agreed measure of success so you can judge things a little easier.

Motivationally, without checkpoints for ourselves things can get a little murky and grey. Therapy and seeking mental wellness is a tiring and difficult process so without a journaled and clear set of goals when we begin to consider how things are going, we'll think the glass is half empty.

So, which goals should we set? The best advice I can give you here is to choose things that are practical. Do not set 'no more symptoms of depression' as a goal, it's too fluid to definably measure so even if you did attain it, you'd not be able to see that as one bad day will make it seem like a fail which can be completely crushing. If you do want to set big goals like this, I'd opt for the goal of 'having more good days than bad'. To measure this, keep a journal everyday and write in the good and bad parts of the day (be realistic here so that you don't let your mood at the time of writing dictate what counts as a good or bad day) with a score at the end of the day out of 10. If over a week you see that there are more days between 6-10 than between 1-5 then you can say that you've certainly met the goal that week of more good days than bad. Then try again for a week after that and maybe change the goal to 'more good weeks than bad weeks' down the line, then 'good months than bad months' etc.

If you're looking for something a little more achievable if you're early on in the process or been into it for a while but not really feeling like you're moving forward then set yourself day to day goals that can be a great measure of success.

I previously worked in a primary school as a one to one learning support assistant, supporting children with special educational needs. I absolutely loved that job. Every day was utter inspiration as children really are the best of us. In my last year at the school there was a new initiative called the 'One Plan Project' introduced.

Before term began we had a Behavioural Psychologist and a SENCO (Special Educational Needs Coordinating Officer) come into the school and speak with the teachers and assistants about what this would mean.

A 'One Plan' is a person-centred, outcomes focused action plan that was led by the child (primarily), with their family, healthcare professionals and teachers (secondarily) to establish what the pupil would like to achieve and the support needed to make this possible.

The part I particularly loved about the project was its versatility in its goal setting. Getting an A in Maths is a simple and effective goal and for some pupils the process and teaching objectives would be clear and attainable in a fairly generic fashion.

For the children I worked with, in the main this was not at all the type of goal they were hoping to achieve. One of the mentors of the project explained how during his school's introduction to it he had a One Plan meeting with a brilliant young lady with Downs Syndrome who was going into Year 11 and had her end of school prom that following July. One of her goals, as set in her plan, was to be able to do her own makeup on the night of the prom.

This meant that the action plan involved numerous motor skills activities, some specifically tailored towards a staff member teaching her makeup skills, and some more general learning techniques. It made parts of her learning specific to her and what she deemed successful. She had a regular schooling schedule but no intention to go into higher education so something that was really important to her was her being able to achieve independence on her big night and enjoy the self-esteem that came with the pride of making herself look and feel as she wished.

One of the plans I had a part in was with a young man who is autistic who wanted to 'have more friends to play basketball with', so we worked on that in specific and non specific ways. We developed people skills through social stories together, built trust and allegiances with his peers in the classroom so that the transition to basketball was easier and even did extra basketball lessons with him so that he felt like he was talented at the sport enough (we all need to do things we feel good at regularly) to hold his own around the other boys and girls.

Another young man I supported knew the term 'anxiety' and could communicate 'feeling anxious' quite well. His goal was to 'not be as anxious at school'. As a side point here, as mentioned above those supporting the pupils were secondary in the plan but the importance of their role is shown here. His original goal was 'to not be anxious at school'. We felt this was a little ambitious from the point he was at so explained how everyone feels anxious at different times so to not be anxious at all wouldn't be completely possible, we then changed the goal, together, to 'not be as anxious'.

His plan involved creating time out plans for when things got really difficult for him, having a number card system where he could leave his card deck on the corner of his desk to indicate to me and his teacher his level of anxiety from 1 to 5. 1 meant his anxiety was at a '1' and therefore he was fine, '5' meant he needed to take some time out urgently. It taught him to understand his emotions and really vitally to communicate when he needed support and the number itself would dictate how he needed that support. If it was a '2', he would use his fiddle toys to bring his number town, if it was a '3', we would take a few minutes break, if it was a '4', we would leave the classroom momentarily to calm down, if it was a '5' we would leave indefinitely. We would also work on building better relationships with his peers as we all know feeling anxious around someone you are uncomfortable with or hardly know can make things worse, so we worked on that so that the fear of feeling anxious around others would no longer scare him. There was many other techniques and it was a really rounded approach. We met regularly with his parents, other teachers and anyone involved in supporting him at school and home and would change the plan accordingly and taking his wishes into account as priority.

If you'd like to try the bigger goals above, great. But for some of you, maybe even most of you, setting more specific smaller goals may be the more comfortable steps on the ladder you need to feel comfortable enough to consistently move forward.

It's impossible for me to write this without thinking back to my Mum's sneaky way of getting me to eat vegetables as a kid. She'd try the whole hiding them in mash routine, a staple of every deviously kind mother in the land, which wouldn't work. I soon realised, when threatened with not being allowed out to play football unless I finished my carrots, that I could finish the food much easier if I cut it wafer thin. And by wafer thing, I'm talking into millimetres. It would take me longer but was so much easier and more manageable than big bites that I got the job done – just in quite a few more steps. Silly analogy aside that can actually be quite a good way to look at achieving smaller goals.

To use myself as an example, I'd often use goals like 'be comfortable enough to plan and follow through with meeting a friend once per week publicly'. I could then either consider the act itself as the goal achieved, or understand that if I was finding this action easier over time that therapy was working generally as to do so I'd need to be feeling calmer. It can be anything really. Even much smaller. Maybe if your mental health is affecting your school attendance a goal could be 'to have a full week attending each day'. You can then make the goals smaller if needed to a day, or bigger once improvement begins to a month. The key here is you lead the goal setting. Certainly speak to your family and Doctors about the goals too, they may be able to assist practically but will definitely be able to assist emotionally with support.

Once you've established clear and relevant to you goals, your plan provides you with a reason to keep going and evidences your success in terms that mean something to you. A big reason why gyms are so full in January but so empty in February is that fitness goals are often not specific. If your goal is just to 'get fit', motivation wains and failure seems to be the course you are on, even when you're not. If your goal is 'to be able to run a 10k', you deem success in a more measured and clear way. It works much the same here.

With your plans in place you also now have something to look forward to, even if you're looking forward with a little bit of trepidation and fear. You're at least future focused. I can testify that once you achieve this, all of a sudden the lives you see each day that are the sort you hope to live become possible. You now know the steps needed, however big or however small, to get there. Now you see some sort of light at the end of the tunnel. You do not need much, but having just enough light to shine the way you want to go allows you to accept that believing you simply cannot, is simply wrong.

I'm going to give the final word here to another quote, this time by the Roman Emperor Marcus Aurelius. A timely reminder that you absolutely can; **'Do not think that what is hard for thee to master is impossible for man; but if a thing is possible and proper to man, deem it attainable by thee'.**

# Being Famous For Five Minutes

In 2013 I sat at home in disbelief as Channel 4's 'Obsessive Compulsive Cleaners' did its very best to belittle the very condition that had destroyed my life.

The show is a light-hearted (!) entertainment programme that shows 'OCD sufferers' taken to homes of hoarders or to public buildings with less than favourable hygiene standards and tasked with using their 'skills' to clean up the area. We'd often see the participants very sad or anxious in the situation but they get out some cleaning products and go at it and that's the basic crux of the show. Some of the 'sufferers' are shown as enjoying the task at hand. For the record, I'm not disputing at all that some of the participants did have OCD.

At the time of the show going out I was very heavily dictated to by OCD rituals that included cleaning so this had a very close to home feel. This condition has already been trivialised and ridiculed beyond being understood as a serious health condition (one the World Health Organisation points to as one of the top 10 most debilitating a human can suffer from) and shows like this do nothing to help, in fact they take us much further away from being understood. The OCD community was collectively up in arms, both national charities condemned the show highly, the top hospital for OCD (The Royal Maudsley) condemned it and more enlightened members of the public condemned it but sadly ratings are ratings and to date Channel 4 have commissioned several more series of the show.

As I sat there pulled between seething anger and acting franticly on compulsions (many OCD sufferers spoke of how this show negatively affected their health) I realised I wanted to do something more to illustrate just how big a mistake this was. I wrote to Channel 4, Betty TV (the production company) and many different media outlets. I also decided to speak to both national charities for the condition and in doing so read the advert that changed my life.

OCD Action had on their media section a call from a production company, Watershed TV, for a new documentary on Obsessive Compulsive Disorder. The first thing I liked was that the language used in the advert was serious, honest and not in any way aimed at promoting sensationalism or soap opera. It was clearly researched and the very fact the charity had it on their website showed the people behind it had been vetted. Secondly, it was for the BBC who I appreciated were making huge efforts and big strides towards raising awareness of mental health.

I watched the Channel 4 show and didn't see my condition. I saw humour and relatable quirks but I didn't see debilitation. I didn't see the meltdowns I recognised in myself and fellow sufferers. I didn't see the anger, aggression and negativity that pulsated through my body. I didn't see the tears, the screams, the desperation to not wake up. I didn't see the bleeding hands from washing, the exhaustion of completing a 17hour single compulsion, the countless wasted money buying things you 'needed' to help ritualise. I didn't see the loss of earnings, loss of potential and loss of life. I wanted to scream about what I was going through. The pain was so intense and all-encompassing and beyond my eloquence. But no one showed that. It wasn't sexy or exciting or interesting, so they thought.

I wanted to tell my story. My story wasn't even just my story, it was our story. It was relevant for thousands of people and I knew they were hurting like I was watching these types of stigmatising shows so I decided to try and see if I could tell my story. I put my name forward to take part.

The show itself was for six British teenagers and young adults to go to the vast and powerful American wilderness, away from all distractions and enabling comforts of home to take part in a 10 day long ERP course (Exposure Response Prevention therapy, more on that later) led by two renowned US based therapists named Pete Weiss and Dr Travis Osbourne.

I wasn't getting any therapy at this point due to a monstrously long waiting list in my home town of Chelmsford and was desperate. If I could get involved in this show I could show my real story and get therapy quickly, filming started in 2 months. It would mean I would be showing my rawest self to millions of people on the BBC but the worry of embarrassment or ridicule didn't really exist, it was simply enveloped by sheer panic about the future.

A day or two later I received a call from a lady named Merle Currie who was the producer of the show and also came up with the concept after learning of Pete and Travis' successful OCD Camps for kids that had gained quite the interest abroad.

Merle was lovely. Calm, honest, educated as to how she should talk to someone with OCD and just a brilliantly intelligent, funny lady. We just spoke for a little while and that was that. I basically told her what I had written in my application email and we chatted in general. Whatever happened, I was pleased the project was going ahead as she and the team had clearly done their research and wanted to honestly portray the condition.

A week or so later Merle asked if I'd be interested in chatting on Skype with Pete and Travis, separately. I said I'd love to. They seemed really interesting and I wanted to pick their brains.

I had a wonderful hour long chat with Pete who provided a really calming influence. We talked about lots and I remember being a little awestruck by how well he understood what I was trying to say. I had a real fear of people not understanding me when I spoke of my mental illness and explained to him how I didn't get that fear of being misunderstood with anything else, but I did with that – he immediately pointed out, 'well, that's just OCD, right?' and a weight fell off my shoulders. He understood even that fear of being misunderstood, that obsessive fear of being misunderstood, was this dog on my back and nothing else. I really wanted to be a part of this project now.

I spoke with Travis who like Pete was warm and charming and kind and I saw right away why they were so well respected in their field.

A few days passed and Merle asked if the director of the show, Richard Cooke, could come by and film a little of me at home so they could meet me and put a name to a face. I agreed and they were with me filming a few days later.

Richard is a confident and focused man. A consummate professional he is well respected in the film and TV industry and I understand why. He was a little different to Merle, Pete, Travis and Itamar (the camera operative) though, but I felt comfortable with him and happy to have him there. As an Aston Villa fan he completely empathised with immense pain and suffering so he was obviously perfect for this show.

The next thing I knew Watershed had arranged for me to see a top Psychiatrist in London (in the most ridiculously plush offices I have ever seen. I imagined it being the GP of the Royals, it was that grandiose. There was no Take a Break magazines on site, just Tatler. I was there in case I was asked to be part of the show as the producers understood their care commitments and wanted to have it verified that my taking part would not do me damage.

Now that's an important point. As discussed elsewhere in this book, the media are becoming more and more intrigued by mental health stories as matters of human interest. It's worth noting some production companies do not take their moral responsibilities as seriously as they should. As a warning, if you are contacted by a company wanting to share your story and they've advertised via twitter and facebook but not bothered seeking validation from a charity that represents people of that condition – avoid them. Watershed TV had sought advice and counsel from several major OCD and mental health charities, numerous healthcare professionals, sufferers of the condition and did everything right to make the whole process safe and exploit free. I couldn't rate the experience highly enough. Having established my eligibility for the show, Merle called me on a Monday to say 'if you'd still like to take part, we'd love to have you'. Just like that. It dawned on me immediately that in a few weeks' time I'd be having the most intense therapy of my life, meeting six new people and experiencing the beautiful but unforgiving Washington wilderness – all in front of the cameras of the BBC.

I wasn't at all nervous. I took the show in the right spirit and saw it purely as a fast track to the therapy I so needed. The cameras being there to film what would hopefully be insightful and helpful as a documentary was fairly secondary. I was more interested in getting better than getting on TV and I think this helped me take the experience for what it was.

The BBC and Watershed arranged for our first meeting as the six participants to be in Shepparton, London, on April 24th 2013. I was the first to arrive at the hotel and that meant I had about 4/5 hours of being holed up in my room waiting for everyone else. Richard wanted to capture our very first meeting on camera, over dinner, and so I had to wait until it was time to go down and film. The whole team was brilliant with me throughout so it wasn't nervy or worrying at all and I looked forward to meeting the people I'd be sharing such a surreal and hopefully beneficial experience with.

As I sat alone at the dinner table, alone with a big camera in my face, I cracked a couple of jokes (some were belters, if you're reading this Richard you really should have included them) and jumped up to greet the first person to enter the room as Olivia arrived.

To somewhat do her a disservice and simplify her rituals, Liv's most noticeable compulsions centred on smells and how people perceived her. Funny and down to earth I immediately liked her. It was obvious later on why Richard chose us as the first two to enter the room, we were clearly the gobby bastards that wouldn't shut up so the camera could actually film conversation! That's still the case. Olivia is my best friend and I love her dearly.

Next up we had Andrew, like Liv another Northerner, who was quiet, shy and reserved. Andrew clearly lacked self-esteem and was dominated by obsessions to do with numbers and counting rituals with technology. Following Andrew was Megan, a bubbly and confident girl plagued with intrusive thoughts that are a part of what is known as 'Pure O', a particularly horrible form of OCD where the compulsion is mental rather than physical. Rather than compulsively touch something, for example, Megan ritualised in her mind. After Meg came Josh, a wonderful, kind, beautiful man that I shared many common interests with. Josh was hilarious and just lovely to be around. Lastly, to complete the group, we had Imogen. Imo was the youngest and had obsessive compulsive rituals around tapping led often by her intrusive thoughts to do with her family, often involving food.

I've given very simple examples of their different versions of OCD above but as the show highlighted very effectively – every single OCD sufferer has a different story from the last. This is the case for each and every one of us battling a mental illness. There are many linking themes and symptoms but ultimately all of us have a different mental health journey.

The next day we flew to Seattle where we were met by the affable and kind faces of Pete Weiss and Travis Osbourne.

It's no exaggeration to say that these two men changed my life.

Actually, let me rephrase that. We changed my life. It was always a team effort with them and like all good therapists it was a collaboration between them and myself. I took control when I needed to and they guided me when it was needed. Anyway, we headed back to the ranch we were staying in where we would have a few days of work within a more comfortable setting before heading off to the great outdoors. I was enjoying the ride so far but I knew the real work was about to start and if I'm honest, certain parts of the process petrified me. All I could think was, what if this didn't work? What if I didn't benefit as much as I need to here? What do I do if they push me along too far and I do not cope? Fear made me question myself, desperation to live a better life made me continue.

The first day the therapists presented to us; 'OCD 101', lesson one. This probably sounds a little dull but I actually recommend learning the basics of your condition, and that's exactly what we did. We spoke about how the condition manifests itself differently in people, how it's treated in different ways, what is happening in our brains during bad days and good days and so on. It wasn't what was going to make us better but it was vital to understanding. I was glad we did.

We were put into two different groups that would be our groups for the week – myself, Imogen and Andrew with Pete and Olivia, Megan and Josh with Travis.

Off we went to our first exposures and my very first experience of ERP. Exposure Response Prevention therapy is an effective linked form of Cognitive Behavioural Therapy, a standard treatment for OCD.

ERP, in basic terms, is a therapy of 'facing your fears'. It works well as a treatment for OCD sufferers as it aims to make you become anxious whilst going towards the object/subject of your OCD and then trying to prevent ritualising for as long as possible to slowly reduce the level of anxiety to the point where the more you do it the lesser you feel the anxiety. An example could be someone who has an obsession with tapping something, an ERP 'exposure' may be to try to not tap for five seconds when they feel they should, to sit with the anxiety until it reduces and to later on try to extend the time. It needs to be done in a safe and realistic way so if someone can only hold off their ritual for 5 seconds, trying to get them to hold off for 1 minute is reckless, dangerous and not beneficial. It's about slowly and effectively building up a long term tolerance and in turn acceptance and further in turn comfort with the level of anxiety.

For the 10 days we were encouraged to ask the question 'what's your number?' to find out where someone is on the anxiety scale of 1-10. It meant we could subtly ask each other how we felt without making us have to use words that would get us further anxious. It also made us develop a really strong feel of accountability and togetherness for each other which built trust very quickly as we were really all in this together. This is another reason why I am such a huge advocate of peer support to combat mental illness.

My OCD (at the time) was hugely dominated by obsessions and intrusions based around germs and illness and being ill. For someone that grew up around so much serious illness it's no wonder this is how my OCD latched on to me.

Obsessive Compulsive Disorder is a bully. It feels your weakness and fears and capitalizes on them so at the time I was handwashing for 30 minutes at a time, not touching anything directly with my hands, eating only certain foods and all via plastic cutlery and spending hours and hours per day ritualising. It was grim. I was in a horrible place and my life was diminishing a little more each and every day.

My first exposure was in the toilet of my cabin bedroom I shared with the boys. As my team of Imogen and Andrew watched on Pete and I discussed what could happen, should I choose to try. That's an important thing to remember. Pete didn't tell me and I didn't tell him. He proposed an exposure and we discussed it. Initially I think he may have been taken aback by the speed at which I told him to f-off but he put his case to me and we decided I would touch, with my bare hand, part of the wall in the toilet. The wall in the toilet in which people used. The wall in the toilet in which people flushed and of which germs could get on the wall. The wall in which I was about to touch. Realisation and reality hit home. My voice cracked, my already pasty skin paled, my hands trembled and my back was drenched in sweat. I couldn't do this. Obviously I couldn't do this. I was hot with the glare of the lighting and the camera and I was standing 5000 miles from home in a toilet trying to work up the courage to touch the wall and it felt like I was being asked to jump off of a cliff. Some of you will relate to this and some of you won't and that is absolutely fine. We spoke more and I decided I would try under condition I could touch as far from the toilet as possible. Pete said to me 'Well that's great, I think you've made a great choice'. Which was lovely to hear. He understood my pain and appreciated my efforts and so I tried. And I did. I felt an incredible wave of exhilaration, anxiety and fear smother me as I stood staring at my hand. This was a foreign feeling and I didn't feel comfortable but felt pride in myself and my dogged determination to improve battled out the negatives enough so that I could go along with Pete's suggestion to maybe not wash my hands until Imogen had completed her exposure.

Even attempting exposures is an incredible win. It is a big achievement and every one is a step in the right direction, even if the exposure itself doesn't go right. It is also a cause for celebration and results in people championing your commitment and courage, rightly so. However, during these moments you do not really take in the gravity of your actions as you're so focused on the task at hand or dealing with the anxiety, but seeing someone else do one really hits home how important and mammoth your own attempts are. Watching Imogen complete hers with the limitless bravery and awe inspiring strength I'd grow to know and respect in her made it all very real as my pride for her and Andrew during our exposures was reciprocated as we built, as we did with Olivia, Megan and Josh, a wonderful team.

In the evenings we would sit around a fire (I mean, this was America!!) and talk a little more about our lives at home and who we were. It had been such a rollercoaster I felt like these 5 people were the best friends I could ever wish to have and a 10 hour flight and some very intense bonding through therapy had made us know each other deeply, but the first few evenings gave us a chance to find out a little more about each other. During the first evening around the fire Pete asked us all to listen up and gave us a speech I wouldn't be able to do justice in my writing. He explained his admiration for us to leave our comfort zone, home and country and to come so far to attempt to make ourselves healthier and complimented us on our ability to accept the unknown, embrace the unpredictable and go from 'yes and no' to 'maybe'. This was a key point and remains so.

This point is very relatable to those with OCD and those without, it's actually a great life lesson and something I use every single day now. Pete explained how from a young age all of us had, via our condition, tried to take full control over every aspect of our lives. Control is obviously a good thing, with things you can actually control. But there's so much in life you cannot and I and the rest of the group had spent so many wasted hours seeking assurances on things no one could assure us on, so we developed our own. 'Well, if I perform this task using this action, everything will be OK' and so on. That's how the brain of an Obsessive Compulsive Disorder sufferer deals with anxiety and life and that constant search had led us here. We all agreed we were in dark places and couldn't continue this way.

Pete gave us one assurance for the programme and that was that assurance itself was well and truly out. From now on in, 'Maybe?' was our focus. Could I become ill from eating here rather than my well prepared and OCD 'friendly' home? Maybe. Would my relentless and horrific intrusive thoughts that I'd kill one of the girls actually come true if I didn't ritualise when I thought I needed to? Maybe.

Would this whole thing not work and I'd go home in a worse position? Maybe. The pursuit of this assurance and control was not only holding us back but making us worse and it had to end to regain our lives. Pete presented us with some temporary tattoos of a question mark to put on our hands and wrist so we could remember all week; maybe.

We eased into the system of quizzing each other with a simple 'what's your number?' to assess our levels of anxiety. On a basic 1-10 scale we would let the other know how we were feeling and this was important before, during and after exposures and as a general check-up of how we were feeling. It provided a small nod of support when you needed it.

After a few days we were on the road to the main part of the journey and the beautiful but unforgiving American wilderness of Washington State.

The car journey was a mixture of nerves and excitement. Josh, Andrew and I spoke of how much we were relishing seeing the sights of such unspoiled beauty, the girls were up for an adventure and were ready to get moving having had a few days stuck at the lodge and the therapists were ready to make the time count.

On the way we stopped off at a high ropes course in the middle of nowhere, which was a staple of the camps Pete and Travis held, and allowed the cameras to film how we dealt with a more mainstream fear; heights. I've always loved things like this so I was in my element running around 100ft in the air. Which is I suppose says it all about fear really – it's uniformed but not specific. I didn't think twice about being that high, but I was petrified of touching the dirty ladder with my bare hand. I'm sure of a thousand people climbing that high, half would be scared of the height and maybe one of them would be because of the dirt. Fear is a funny thing. It packages itself in many different ways but what's inside is often the same.

We enjoyed the company of ropes course leader Bernie who told us a story of dragons. He spoke to us about how sometimes dragons are going to be there, and sometimes we can't face away from them. Sometimes we need to look our dragons in the eye and kiss them on the nose. It was an odd expression, and being the young and sarcastic bunch of Brits that we were, we could easily have rolled our eyes at that. The thought stuck with me throughout the week though.

We got back on the road and headed to the ferry that was going to take us into the unknown. As someone that is emetophobic (vomit/vomiting) this was actually the thing I was least looking forward to as I was incredibly nervous I may get sea sickness. Thankfully I'd brought this up before so was given some tablets that actually ended up making me drowsy and with five teammates supporting me so wonderfully we had a few hours to mentally prepare for Lake Chelan.

America is blessed with insurmountable beauty and Chelan was no different. A tiny community of 4000 people, everywhere you looked was stacked with incomprehensibly stunning landscape. I was hooked.

Right away, Pete, Travis, Jordan and Caroline asked us to begin gathering logs for firewood and to start making space for camp that night armed with only a tarp. Without wanting to be stereotypical here, I grew up in East London and Essex – I didn't know what the fuck I was doing.

Negotiating snakes, the rain and our own trepidation as to what was about to come we set up camp and began dinner. This was not something I was looking forward to.

I knew it was coming, of course. I'd built up exposures around utensils I perceived as unclean over the course of the stay at the cabin and had actually started drinking from glasses I hadn't personally cleaned. That was something I hadn't done for as long as I could remember.

Now though, I had to cook and eat food from camping utensils and all my brain was thinking of was those uses it had before. Was it cleaned properly after? Will I get sick now? Am I overstepping the line of what I can handle? It was a big step.

Olivia was cooking and had prepared some hash browns for me and as I looked into the pan it honestly felt like I could actually see the germs crawling all over it. My mind was playing so many games with me and my anxiety hitting uncomfortable levels I seriously felt I was holding a bowl of illness.

Pete oversaw all of this and made sure my number didn't go so high that I would be in a dangerous position. He kept me at a manageable level and slowly my anxiety began to decrease. With a full support act around me I decided I was going to try the food and to my immense pride (much later!) I did it. Throughout this period I was stood alongside Imogen who was holding my hand throughout. My trust and admiration for her evidenced by this as I never held hands with anyone, but as my team mate she did a wonderful job and would often do this – not reassuring me, as this was off limits, but just letting me know she was there.

Sometimes I think that's all we need from the people that support us. Their presence. Sometimes all it takes is a little nod or a wink and a reminder that 'yep, if I'm needed, I'm here'.

I began to feel a worse and turned to her and said I needed to walk it off as it was feeling a little intense so we walked the 200 yards or so down to the lake and she just calmly spoke to me and everything started to feel OK again. I felt a huge wave of pride now, but also utter exhaustion.

We laid down for the night in our new makeshift home with just a 10ftx10ft plastic tarp to keep us sheltered and the promise tomorrow of a several mile hike through some tough terrain.

The beauty of being so far out of your comfort zone physically, as we were out in Lake Chelan, is that it really sets the tone for trying. For attempt, at least. A long day hiking up and down the mountains in the blistering heat and then downpour of rain really promotes a culture of accepting (or adapting to) whatever is thrown at you.

Throughout the hikes we supported each other through a series of exposures. Mentally and physically we were pretty much shattered. We didn't have masses of food and we had big, heavy bags to carry with all of our things in it.

I'll always remember how when we stopped to eat the atmosphere would turn to fun. We were six OCD sufferers going through intense therapy under the glare of the BBC and a sometimes unforgiving general public but more importantly we were Jack, Andrew, Imogen, Olivia, Megan and Josh. We were some people's most important people and we were all individuals. We weren't just numbers or people making a TV show we were our own people with differing ambitions, interests, passions. I found those times really important as it reminded me that after all this I was going to go back to my everyday life so it was a refreshing reminder of who we were. I urge you to look at your own diagnosis in this way. Yes, you might have a mental health condition on your medical history file, but you're someone special. Many things make you and contribute to who you are and your diagnosis is a part of that, but it isn't the defining part of that.

As we faced down the final two miles on the last night we had to walk around a tight cliff edge for about half a mile. We had to walk slowly and mind our feet as falling 500 ft. down jagged rock edges wasn't the sort of ending the BBC was aiming for.

Walking along I began to be haunted by some seriously overwhelming intrusive thoughts. All OCD was telling me was that I was going to hurt the girls. I was going to be the reason they fell. I was possibly going to cause it.

Images began intruding my brain like parasites as the unwanted thoughts played out in my mind like my own personal horror cinema. Hurting people was one of my biggest fears and now OCD was telling me unless I ritualised constantly by the way I walked I would cause someone's death.

In my tired and emotional state, this was all a bit too much and I began to get very angry when Richard the director asked for us to slow down so he could get a shot. I reminded him, more aggressively than necessary, that we were cold and tired and in the middle of fucking therapy and that I had to keep moving. Everyone sensed I wasn't going down the right route mentally and did their best to pull the reins in but by now I'd gone a bit too far to be helped, I thought. We were close to the new camp and I began to walk faster, then jog, then run. I ran down to the water, threw my bag to the ground and clasped my hands on my ears to drown any sounds out. I closed my eyes and paced the boardwalk and tried to shut the world off.

All I could see was these tremendously upsetting images of me doing exactly what I didn't want to do and my rituals weren't being done quick enough to accommodate the evolving intrusions. It was hell. I honestly wouldn't wish the feeling on anybody.

Pete came and busied himself near me but made the right choice to not come and interfere. He knew this was my battle to win. He respected the situation and me enough to allow me the opportunity to fight my way out of it and his immense abilities as a man and therapist shone through here. I sensed him close but he didn't get in my way. Slowly, as I had done all week, I began to settle into the anxiety. My number reduced from 10, to 9, to 8. My eyes opened, my pace slowed, my heart rate normalised and Pete and I spoke. He convinced me to come and sit with him by the camp as the others washed in the lake and prepared dinner and we had a conversation that was just between us but that relieved years' worth of emotional trauma in one honest, frank chat. By this point I was crying my eyes out. I was apologising (I don't even know what for) and Pete spoke calmly, purposefully and empathetically with me as we discussed the situation and spoke more honestly than I'd probably ever spoken to anyone before. As a fact for those of you that watched Extreme OCD Camp, this incident was the only thing Pete and Travis vetoed from the BBC and Richard. The therapists played their cards as the ranking officers here and Pete spoke with Richard to tell him this wasn't something the world needed to see. It was personal to me and a milestone in my life I probably didn't need to share with 2 million people. At the time of the show, I was disappointed in this decision as I felt, later on, it was an honest and realistic portrayal of OCD but in the position I am now and with the benefit of hindsight I'm actually really grateful Pete made that decision for me.

On one of the first days I'd made the declaration to the therapists that I was so ready to be well I would attempt anything they gave me to try, I was ready. At the time they said to me 'we know, it's not motivating you we'll focus on, it's calming you down' and that proved so true.

Within your own therapies it can be so easy to go a million miles an hour sometimes. You're desperate for change and if you can sprint before you can walk, you will. This highlights the importance of working with professionals that understand you, and for them to do that they need to be let in a little. If the team in Washington hadn't wisely calmed me down when they needed to, it would have been a detriment to my therapy. Bear in mind for some of you this will be the case, and some of you may need coaxing a little to try. Motivation works both ways, listen to your therapists. They are there to caution or inspire, to help you and you only. Be honest with them and promote your point when you feel you are right but know they are sometimes there to guide your over/underambitions.

We slept out under the stars the following night and said goodbye to Lake Chelan. It had been a shattering week but in the most brilliant way. I was ready for a bath, an actual toilet and a pillow and we enjoyed one final night in the solitude of the Northern Cascades, made s'mores, drank hot chocolate and congratulated each other on 'kissing our dragon on the nose'.

Arriving back at our 'home' in Seattle, we had one final evening together the next day. I was really, really sad to be leaving. It had been such a horrendously difficult 10 days but the most important of my life. I didn't really know if I could face the world back home without my team.

On the final evening we had a campfire debrief where we spoke about each other. We shared our admiration for each other and took it in turns to hear back from everyone how we had impacted each other's week and lives. We sat there for hours. We laughed and we cried and we prepared for the trip home and back to make what we had learned count.

A few months later we were preparing for the show to be released on BBC3 (when that was just a TV channel) and it all went a bit nuts really. The day of the first show Imogen and I were interviewed by Susanna Reid and Charlie Stayt for BBC Breakfast Live. It was a surreal experience promoting the shows and we knew a lot of young sufferers of OCD were looking forward to this. It was probably the first really big show just on OCD to have such a platform so there felt like a bit of pressure. This wasn't alleviated by Stayt's dry sense of humour as we were about to be interviewed. He followed Reid's comment to 'not be nervous, it's just us in the room' with 'Yeah, and 2 million people'. It made me laugh. At the same time Olivia and Josh were on This Morning and all of us did radio, TV and print nationally, regionally and locally. It was pretty full on. The whole way through the team at Watershed supported us wonderfully and we tried our best to put across the important points of OCD to raise the right kind of awareness. I'm happy to say I think we did just that.

To my Nan's immense satisfaction, *Inside Soap* magazine referred to me as having 'boyband good looks'. I think that was her favourite part.

The show went out to a few million people over two weeks and has amassed millions of hits on YouTube since. It is used to teach students about OCD in colleges, universities and even medical environments and being wholly honest I am completely proud of what it did in the UK for OCD awareness. I'm still contacted about it every single day by parents, children and adults as they negotiate their own mental health. The countless times I was told the show was the reason they sought help makes me so happy and I'm immeasurably proud of each and every person that played a part in it. It is for that reason this book is even being written. I have so many questions sent to me every single day from parents wanting to know how to support their children, husbands asking how to support their wives, best friends asking what to do to help their mates and young people wanting to know how they can seek help. This book was a natural way to piece those answers together in a way that will hopefully help.

7 years on, I'm about as far into recovery as I ever hoped I may go. Some days are really hard, of course, and I will continue to have battles daily but I'm winning far more than I'm losing. I love my life now and the experience of that TV show is a huge part of why I am healthy and happy. I really probably should buy a TV licence now, it's only fair.

# Coming Out.

One of the biggest milestones for anyone with a mental illness is their coming out story. For me personally having been unwell from a young age this wasn't ever anything I worried about as people 'just knew'. Over the past few years I've spoken with and met hundreds of young people that have told me their next big step is telling their mates and people around them. Although I had so many people around me that knew my condition, every so often there would be someone I'd meet or a group I'd join that wouldn't know and I'd have that inevitable dread of feeling like I had to explain myself or make excuses. First things first, you control who you tell, when you tell them, how you tell them and why you tell them. You are not obliged to. Although I certainly recommend doing so, I wholly advocate doing it entirely on your own terms. Hopefully this gives you a bit of an idea of how it may well go and some things to consider.

I was talking with a good friend of mine recently about his coming out story for his sexuality. He is a very wise and worldly friend and put something to me that struck a chord. I was asking his experience as I was writing this chapter and was interested in learning how his coming out went. He reminded me that in general people are very nonplussed about something like that. He said, quite correctly, that when you come out you are simply 'giving people a bit of information about you'. Nothing more, nothing less. Before he spoke to everyone he was petrified. He went over and over the ramifications, agonized over the consequence of telling them, debated if he even should and had to really push himself to.

Finally he committed to doing it and told me in the reality of it the word best used to sum it all up would have to be 'underwhelmed'. He appreciated the fact that people have their own lives and this facet of his that doesn't change who he is really, isn't as big a news to anyone else as it is to him. He basically sighed with relief and carried on living exactly as he had before, except now people knew a fact about him they didn't know before.

Obviously 'coming out' about mental illness is very different and the two can't be compared as one is illness and one is the sexuality you are born with but both are things that have a story of which you tell the world and both are significant enough information that you tend to have times you inform people of them.
Everyone is different and all group dynamics are unique so how things go with your friendship group will be different for you as it was for me but hopefully the below is of help for the things I've noticed as someone that has had this conversation many times.

**People can be confused and that can be frustrating.**

Having built up the courage or overcome the nerves to finally say something I think we can all be forgiven for hoping for a little bit of a lightbulb moment for those around us when we do say those words. Sometimes though, people will not quite understand what you are telling them and this can be tough to take right away. If you're telling them you have depression, there is certainly a chance they will confuse 'depression' with 'sadness' or 'being down'. I think it is important here to not react too emotively and to try and calmly explain why that isn't correct. In preparation for this conversation, it is certainly worthwhile having some information to hand that is relevant to whomever you're speaking with. You may just want this to be general information on the condition itself or it may be worth having info that relates to how you know them. For your boss it may be how this may affect your working or extra support you may need (something employers have to provide within reason). For a teacher it might be discussing how you can work together to make deadlines, examinations and participation. For friends it might explain how the condition can or does affect you socially.

**People can say inappropriate things**

When telling a former boss of mine about my OCD, (having spoken for a minute already about my mental health in general) when I explained what my exact diagnosis is my boss sat down in visual relief (literally saying 'phew!') and explained their alleviated fears by saying 'Oh thank god it's only OCD! I thought it was something serious for a minute'. Needless to say, I put them right! But some people are going to say things you aren't going to like, again, this needs to be something you take calmly and then explain as best you can. If you aren't calm and lose your rag with them, they'll not be inclined to listen properly, or worse will always fear upsetting you so spend the rest of their time awkwardly tip-toeing around discussing it. If you do not tell them why they are wrong if they say something inappropriate, it can quickly become fact. So my advice would be to be clear, be calm, be honest and be informative.

**Pity, Compassion, Apathy Or Respect**

From the many, many people I've spoken to about their coming out story, most seem to find people react in one of the above four ways. For the record, I'm not really sure any of them are wrong or right, but some certainly feel nicer than others!

Being pitied for your illness is not something anyone wants but it's a reaction people will give you. Unfortunately, for some people – particularly those that have no personal experience of mental illness, being unwell is something to be pitied. Some people will see it as an inferiority and offer a safe bout of pity. These people are more likely to be acquaintances than anyone you are close to.

The reaction you'd like to have from someone who pities your situation is instead compassion, something you will absolutely experience. Compassion implies tangible, real support. These people are great because they are the one's likely to offer genuine, practical help. They are the ones that will, when they know what will help (hopefully after you've told them) offer real assistance like 'Can I give you a lift to your appointment?' 'Can I cover you at work?' 'Where would you like to eat?'. Some that pity you may well graduate to compassion, once they have gained understanding, knowledge and experience of your health and how they can play a more positive role.

Apathy sounds like a negative reaction but for some it can actually be the most comforting reaction, depending on the circumstances. If it comes up for me in a professional environment with people I do not know very well apathy is my favourite reaction! I just want someone to say 'Oh, ok, fine' and then carry on with my day. I wouldn't necessarily want a loved one to act this way but for you maybe, this could be ideal. It's a real personal thing. As my friend wisely said above, for these people 'it's just some information about you'. Apathy doesn't necessarily indicate a lack of care and some people may seem apathetic when in reality they are just processing the information so do be aware of this.

For others, and these people tend to be those that have personally experienced the effects of mental illness – the first reaction you receive by these people is respect. This reaction can be humbling and appreciated but can make you feel a little awkward too but it's a loving and kind reaction. Often these people are the ones that will offer emotional support through their own lived experience and will be the sort you can talk openly with.

**People will try to identify with you, wrongly**

We all know those people that are waiting to talk, rather than truly listening. People who like to do 'one-upmanship' and better your story with their own, and these types of people do tend to try and pipe up with their own identification that will likely be something very different to something that you know. I've actually been present when a friend was telling a new friend of ours that they have bipolar disorder. This condition, previously referred to as 'manic depression', is described by Bipolar UK as being 'a severe mental illness characterised by significant mood swings including manic highs and depressive lows'. It is a very serious condition that affects between 1%-5% of the population. It is something that friend has experienced throughout their life and has hospitalized them, led to suicide attempts and devastated those around them.

As you can imagine – he is pretty sensitive about it, quite rightly so. After explaining his condition slightly, our new friend came back with 'I'm a bit bipolar. I've definitely got it, some days I feel really bad and other days I actually feel brilliant. Isn't that just emotions?' Genuinely word for word how that exchange went down. Some people will, normally through awkwardness or ignorance, try to turn the conversation around to them and how they see it. This isn't helpful but it's also not uncommon. Especially for the 'stereotyped' conditions like OCD, Bipolar, Tourette's and Autism. These types of conditions have become so diluted in certain aspects of a media that is often intent on creating a story rather than actually telling a real one that you'll find people respond with their own sensationalised version of what they think they know.

I promised myself and I promised you that this book would be honest, and I don't plan to turn around on that now.

Some people will react negatively to you when you come out to them. You may well lose some people in your life.

For those of you that haven't begun this process yet and are nervous by my words, as a 29 year old with two decades worth of experience in this I can tell you now that although I have indeed lost people – everyone I need and want in my life is now in it.

Explaining this important factor of yourself to someone and having them change their opinion of you for the bad is devastating, absolutely. But as I explained at the beginning of this chapter, the captain of your ship is you. If you have had the bravery and the desire to tell someone about your mental health, then you have done so as you've decided they should know, need to know, or that you simply want them to know. Therefore it is important enough to you that you initiated that conversation.

If you have been so bold and they now feel a change in you or them or their opinions on you that they shall now be unsupportive, then these are the types of people that hold you back anyway. My advice here is to be grateful that at this crossroads in your life they have revealed themselves truly and offered you the opportunity to move on from them with only the people who have more of an interest in your health and happiness.

We all want people to like us. That's just a part of being human. But have the courage to have people like you for you. Whoever you are, reading this, you are someone's vision of spectacular. You are someone's hero and someone's inspiration. You may not know it yet and they may not even know it yet but the true you is able to take someone's breath away. When you do, make sure it's you that took their breath away, not a version of you that you have to act.

Telling someone you are mentally ill is not fun, but it's done for purpose. It is done to improve your life, progress your relationship with that person and ultimately it contributes towards your potential health.

You are completely and utterly in charge of this aspect. You can give them a little look through the keyhole or you can open the door and invite them into your world. Some will enter, some will turn and walk away. But those that do come in will make for one hell of a party. Everything will be OK.

# Self Care (And How To Do It)

Let's be honest here – I bet you brushed your teeth today before leaving the house, right? Even if you woke up half hour after you were supposed to be at work or school, I bet that even if you didn't grab breakfast you still found 2 minutes to clean your teeth.
That is because for something like that, we make time. Even when we think time isn't there, we create it. Why then, have we as a society got into the position where we do not make time for ourselves as standard? Where is the cleaning and maintenance of our mind?
Each day has 1440 minutes in it. If you cannot find 20 minutes within that time (1.4% of your day), it's time for a schedule revamp. The gloriousness of taking the time to purposefully care for ourselves and water our personal plants is that the dividends it pays off often outweigh the time spent.
Of course we all have a limited amount of time to spend per day, but if there were stockbrokers for things we spend time on, they would all choose to invest in self-care. The returns are just so good. For that percent and a half of investment in your day, you will definitely feel an improvement and a profit greater than 1.4%. Often ten times this. Not only can self-care help alleviate some symptoms of your mental illness, it can actually go some way towards preventing further symptoms. Self-care is an important but all too often forgotten part of a mentally healthy diet.

Now reading this I'm pretty sure you fall into three categories. You're either a) agreeing with me, you've already began enjoying the benefits of this b) thought about it but never considered it important enough to start with or c) see no benefit at all, your eyebrows are firmly raised and you feel your mental illness is far too powerful for a bubble bath and some candles to sort.

If you're c) you're absolutely right, some Ben and Jerry's and a Judd Apatow film isn't going to cure you. But, if it moves you forward even slightly, is it worth dismissing? If you believe in the potential benefits of therapy and medication (which I hope is the case), do you think one CBT session or one pill is going to get you where you want to be? Of course not. Sadly. But consistent sessions and a course of medication may well get you there. Self-care works in exactly the same way. It is a simple, cheap, effective way of progressing in an environment we can all handle, under terms and conditions we write, at times we choose. Reading this sentence can count as part of a good self-care routine.

I find it frustrating and upsetting that this is a therapy so many people so readily dismiss. I think a large part of this is often the perception people have on it, or the expectance they believe others have on it. I'm yet to meet a medical professional that has told me that a good self-care routine will be the sole reason for mental wellness, but I've met hundreds that advocate it alongside conventional treatment options. It is not expected to rid you of a mental health condition, but it can absolutely release you from some of its symptoms, even if just for a while.

There's a perceived feeling amongst some people that self-care is some cuddly, new age, hippie initiative that mistakes emotions for illness. These people see it as some lovely idea that's not really laced with reality. To be clear; it is certainly not a case of advocates believing that depression is simply sadness or a lack of acknowledgement of the severity of your diagnosis. It is experienced medical professionals and lived experience peers appreciating that recovery is best achieved by a rounded and full approach to treatment. We all know we need protein and carbohydrates to survive and thrive, but we also need good fats.

For me, it begins with early morning walks. There is nothing better at calming my mind than getting out as the sun is coming up and walking out in nature. It slows the world down for me and starts the day off right and just seems to make things seem all the more manageable. Not only does it calm me mentally in an almost meditative sense but obviously it has physical benefits too. It makes me look forward to the mornings, which for those of you out there that are not morning people – a self-care activity may be a brilliant way to change that and begin the day positively.

Making time for you and only you is a vital component of feeling well, which is a step on the path to recovery.

Defining what self-care actually is can be open to debate– but essentially self-care is the deliberate, regular and personal actions (or attitudes) that positively influence or enhance our physical, mental, emotional, social or spiritual wellbeing.

Everyone can appreciate that looking after your body is a valued part of taking care of yourself. It's important to understand that you do not need to chisel the body of an athlete to be well but keeping an eye on the basics, good nutrition, good sleep and good exercise will go a long way towards making you feel well. Don't cut out all treats, late nights with friends or a film marathon in the place of a run from time to time, but do invest in yourself a little by adopting some healthy living tips. As part of mine, I drink tons of water. It's often the only drink I'll drink throughout the day and it just makes me feel fresh. I don't eat fast food takeaways anymore but I absolutely bloody love a Victoria sponge cake. I run most days, but when I'm busy or life gets in the way, that's fine too. It's simply changes we can all make at any time that just start moving our ships in the right direction.

There are many ways to combine a pursuit of physical health that are forms of self-care too, these can include; walking, jogging, taking the dog for a walk, swimming, yoga, joining a sports club and so on. Some of these provide a wonderful social injection too if you can join a local sports team for example so are doubly beneficial but all of these are linked in that they are something that you do purely to make you feel like yourself and feel happier and healthier.

Things I have tried over the past few years include learning a language (I'm currently learning Norwegian), boxing on my own followed by boxing in a class, experimenting with different kinds of art from drawing to painting to sculpture, joining our local cinema club meaning once every other week I had something new to look forward to, learning to cook (well, sorta!) and meditation. I also try to go for a calming walk every day, earphones at home, and just take in the sights and sounds of everyone and everything moving around me. Any and all of these things may be for you but decide on something you think is specific to you. If you're creative or wanting to be more creative, make art. If you're sporty and feeling you could do with having more friends, take a class in a sport you've never tried. If you feel your mental illness or life in general has made commitments with friends fall to the wayside, arrange a mate date and as you've planned it as a specified time for self-care you'll feel less inclined to cancel it. Taking a bath or taking your time over a shower can be examples too, as can a time before you leave the house where you simply have a little Netflix session uninterrupted and not rushed. Anything that works for you. Sometimes they will be planned, sometimes you'll need to take one as an emergency session when things feel rough, and either are fine and good. I like to make one or two of these sessions things I know I'm good at, because that gives a little self-esteem boost and is obviously easier to enjoy. So if you're a bit of a badass chef, get in the kitchen. If you're a talented basketball player, set 30 minutes aside every few days to shoot hoops. You decide.

An important point to remember is that it won't always be successful. Some days you'll not feel up to it or time will beat you but that's not cause for concern, simply opportunity to make the most of the next one. As this is a scheduled and consistent thing, there's always next time.

Yet another benefit of engaging in a self-care programme is the familiarisation it provides for the actual process of therapy in general. By recognising what you need/do not need and then actively and purposefully planning it you become accustomed to your responsibilities and potential to improve by your actions and engagement. It teaches you how to do therapy. It shows you why it is important to be methodical about treatment and to read yourself better to help those around you help you. If you can get the confidence and understanding of yourself to be able to say to a loved one 'listen, I need space for an hour' you'll hopefully develop the intuition and ability to say to a therapist 'I feel like this right now'. Sometimes self-care will fail session to session, and sometimes you'll need to change the type you do, when you do it or your own goals when doing it to feel the full benefit - just like in other therapies and treatments.

Talking of the time you do it, another positive of understanding and implementing self-care is that it can be used between other therapies. As it can be done at home and at times that suit you, if you are on a waiting list that is taking some time to access treatment you need – this will offer some mild to medium relief in the meantime. It's certainly not a replacement for a talking therapy, medication or other course of treatment your psychiatrist may recommend – but it's a truly great side course.

Too often we spend our lives tunnel visioned on things that are purely long term goals rather than creating short term benefits that support us in being healthy enough to accomplish those long term goals. School, work, passing our course or paying our rent are valid and important parts of life but if these are all you are doing – you can get lost in them and neglect doing things that make you feel good. And really, that's the point, right?! We want a nice house and a good career as we feel these will make us feel happy and fulfilled, but neither of those things come in one day. So do we simply forget about feeling content and nourished on the way to achieving these long term aspirations?! Not at all. In fact, practicing feeling healthy and well ultimately plays a part in leading to being healthy and well. Positive lifestyle changes are not the sole contributor to becoming mentally healthy and do not promise to banish a mental illness, but a positive lifestyle change can provide light and relief during even the darkest hours. So learn to look after you today and you will look after yourself tomorrow. It works hand in hand.

# The Importance Of Honesty

Ever since I can remember, I have lied to myself.

I think we all do at times, sometimes it's as simple as letting ourselves believe another hour awake binge watching a TV series won't hurt in the morning, sometimes it's when we're working out and we tell ourselves we've reached our limit and sometimes it's a little more serious.

Being honest with ourselves is often the scariest thing we can do, but it's the only way to really, truly, unapologetically live.

As a young man I battled with what I knew was addiction but I never really saw it as so. I told myself it was a minor problem or just part and parcel of having mental health issues. It was always something I told myself I could control and something I 'knew' wasn't as bad as it was for others and therefore it wasn't something I really needed to address – I had bigger fish to fry. I'd go online and search for cases of addiction where people died and read their stories and validate to myself that these people died, I'm nowhere near this bad so obviously I'm doing OK. Really.

I was completely and utterly wrong but the worst part and the part that fills me with regret each and every day is that in reality I knew something was wrong, I'd just got incredibly good at silencing myself on its severity.

This chapter is probably the one I least wanted to write but the one I know was most important to write. In this spirit of this chapter I am going to tell it exactly how it was, but appreciate this isn't a pretty read.

Aged 14 I began to seriously spiral with my mental health into a dark place no child should ever see. My world was falling down around me. My Dad had not long had two near fatal heart attacks, Mum was being treated for cancer, OCD had started to become the biggest companion in my life and on top of that I was 14. That's never easy.

My old man had so many pills to take if you'd have shaken him he would have rattled.

Our medicine cabinet put Boots to shame. With anxiety cloaking my day every day I found myself in quite a lot of physical pain that derived from my stress and anxiety. I'd constantly have a stomach ache or headache and many trips to my GP confirmed it was the physical side of my mental illness revealing itself and truthfully it was a horrible time. I got into the habit of pre-empting the pain but simply keeping myself on constant painkillers. I would see how often they could be taken and diligently keep to that. If it was every 4 hours that I could have them, I'd have them to the minute 4 hours later. Soon I realised I was still in pain despite the constant medication so I began doubling it. I would also find myself stealing medication. Now seemingly fancying myself as some sort of amateur child chemist I understood that I felt ill without medication and I knew medication had the potential to change how I felt. I was kind of right, but obviously medication has to be taken properly and with specific cause or need. Counselling wasn't working, my psychiatrist wasn't working and anything else seemed to be failing so I felt that pills would be my best chance. Painkillers mainly but I loved sleeping tablets too, particularly in liquid form. I realised not only was it masking my symptoms but if I took the sleepers and stayed awake long enough I'd experience a buzz and as someone that was only used to feeling like shit 24/7, that was worth the effort.

If you're just 14 and ingesting as much medicine as I was, you're going to be rumbled. I had no serious physical conditions so people would question my overuse of medication if I didn't learn some tricks. It didn't take long for me to start stealing medication. I didn't really do this from my Dad as OCD was controlling me there that if I touched his then he would die and it would be my fault, so I worked out where my local pharmacies were and would often bunk off school to go and learn their layouts so I would know where the good stuff was. I became quite the thief, which I'm obviously not proud of now – but I never saw it as stealing. In my head I'd always explain it away to myself that if I was ever caught, I'd explain to the shopkeeper that I was in pain and needed this and he'd be so understanding and everything would be OK.

So I began a dependency on painkillers that would follow me for nearly a decade. When I was playing football in Finland in my early twenties I broke my hand quite badly and had to have surgery that night as I really had mashed my hand up. I was delighted to see the nurses and doctors at this particular hospital didn't speak much English, so I just complained and complained about the pain that wasn't even there and scored myself some morphine. As I was playing football, I convinced them pain management was key so left the hospital with my own private stash of morphine. With everything else I was taking I went back to the stadium of my team and watched a game I think ended 4-1. But then I don't remember any of it. Or getting there. Or speaking to anyone that weekend. It was a weird time.

But, the word 'addict' never once hit in my brain. No chance. Alcoholics are addicts. Not me. I'm a sportsman. I'm healthy. I understand mental illness and I've been around addicts before. They die. I'm not. I'm fine.

As is not uncommon in addicts, I was under the spell of multiple addictions. I was completely in limbo with what they were though really because I didn't fully accept it about myself. That was a huge mistake. Addiction feels like you're carrying too many plates but as you're doing so you genuinely think you can take more. You can always carry one extra, you think. One day you'll drop them all. And that's your time to get well or get unwell again, there's no in between really.

I do not blame myself for being an addict and equally nor do I expect sympathy for being one. It is so very much misunderstood still. But, like all addicts, I can think of so many things I regret that was borne from addiction. I take full responsibility for my actions and my words, of course, and I'll be forever devastated at the things, opportunities and people I have lost through addiction.

Someone wiser than me once said that it's better to learn through other people's mistakes than our own and I couldn't agree more. I'm hoping that for you this book is giving an insight into the roads you may go down for good or for bad but it is also a tale of caution. There have been periods in my life where I have had absolutely everything I had dreamed of. The job. The love. The respect. The physical health. The opportunity. All of the things we look for and hope to attain I've been around or had in the past and sadly I have also lost each and every one of those things. I have some of them again now and I'm completely grateful but the sole reason I believe I will keep them is because I am now honest.

Lying (or not telling the truth) is your first class ticket to fuckery. If you want to know how to royally screw your life up, it's by not being honest. Take it from me. I've basically got the Oscar in Best Self Sabotaging Performance.

Why do we lie anyway? It can be for own versions of self-protection. It can be to exaggerate who we are or our abilities, as self-promotion. Self-promotion and self-protection are both absolutely fine, as long as we know the truth ourselves. It's often to mislead others to a perception so they see through our camera and not their own so they see a situation as positively or as negatively as we do. A favourite of mine would be through omission, by simply not giving a detail or details that truly paint the picture. It can simply be habit.

We all know lying, or not telling the truth, is wrong. It hurts people. But I can guarantee you without any shadow of a doubt whatsoever that the person you have the most ability to damage by your lies is yourself. Lying to others has the potential to be incredibly damaging, lying to yourself has the promise of it.

During my days incarcerated with addiction I would be pained by something that I now refer to as 'the flicker'.

In my mind I'd developed such an almost impenetrable ability to mask the reality of my condition and the truth of it that I had actually got to the point I forgot I was doing it. It was almost real. I was telling myself things weren't so bad and I'd told that lie so many times it began to feel like the truth. I'm certain now that if I'd taken a lie detector test on anything to do with my illness, I had become so focused on not being truthful with myself that the test wouldn't even pick up the lie. Now it was lifestyle. It had gone beyond a lie here or there to my life.

Sometimes though I would feel the flicker. It was reality and truth tapping on my brain with a little reminder that this wasn't right. I genuinely did not think I was an addict and didn't think what I was doing was wrong or unhealthy and I'd got so bad I actually didn't realise I was doing it. I'd go through the motions and be in the throes of addiction without even realising I was doing anything. Once in a while I would have the tiny flicker try and pull me away, but I shut it down. I lied to myself.

You may or may not deal with addiction yourself but it is a lesson in honesty.

The truth isn't this shining light of loveliness we can all stand around and bask in. The truth can be fucking horrible and it can make situations practically/logistically worse at times by making those around us look at us differently or think of us differently. But my biggest life lesson thus far has been to be truthful, always, no matter the consequence. One trick I use now in my everyday life is to try my best to empathise how my words and actions appear to my peers or those I'm talking to and if they'd deem it trustworthy and honest.

Do you ever do that thing where you'll be in the shower or in bed and have a pretend argument with yourself? Or you'll run a play in your head of a situation and how you'd handle it? Like 'what would I do if my neighbour hit my car tomorrow?' and then you'll daydream over if you'd be angry or calm, the words you'd say, how you'd win the argument? Assuming you've done this, as I think we all have, I try to tap into that mindset.

I'll go into the courtroom of my mind and preside over the conversation I'm having and if it's an honest one. If I realise that I could argue for the other person that it wasn't, I realise I need to modify myself and up my integrity.

To give a practical example I was on the phone with my sister not too long ago. She lives in Norway so most of our communication is on the phone unfortunately. While we were talking I was enthusiastic about how I'd not had a bad day for about two months and how happy I was. This is pretty much true. And when someone says 'pretty much true' of course they mean; 'not true'.

I'd rung her up about three weeks before complaining about a horrible day I'd had at work and something personal I was incredibly frustrated with. I wasn't feeling good that day and even the most generous of people would struggle to refer to that day as anything other than a bad day so although generally I was right, I hadn't really had any bad days for a couple of months – I had. Realising this in my head I did follow it up with 'well, nearly a perfect two months' and recalled my bad day. That may seem meticulous but that's the level of openness and honesty I think it is vital to live with to truly understand yourself mentally which in turn throws you the keys to becoming mentally healthy.

The problem with lying to yourself in particular is that it is utterly inescapable. You simply cannot run from your truth, it lives in you.

Approaching your own truth and fully engaging with where your mental health status is can obviously be overwhelming but know that trying to run towards recovery whilst withholding the truth is like running on a treadmill. You'll get nowhere. You may feel you are for a while because you are simulating movement, you'll go through the motions and do the right things and feel the tiredness and exert energy on it but one day you'll stop and realise you've worked incredibly hard for no reason.

My advice here is to embrace the flicker. Do not settle for the flicker. Turn that light on and everything becomes immensely clearer.

If reading this you feel that feeling like this chapter is written just for you and like I'm talking directly to you, please know that I absolutely am.

That thing or those things that you are lying to yourself about. Say them now. Literally. Or grab that pen and write them down. Even if you do not write them down exactly, write yourself a contract right now that when you're next sitting in the right setting be it your GP's office, psychiatrist, counsellors room or just with the right ears to listen, you'll say it.

Be someone of integrity and be someone you can trust. When people lie to us, we begin to lose respect and trust for them. When we lie to ourselves we lose self-esteem and trust in ourselves. That is a path not worth treading. Be so truthful about who you are that you begin to trust yourself properly.

The truth can be uncomfortable and difficult like the imperfect world around us but this is your opportunity to have the strength to be the authentic you. We all want to be liked and we all want people to have a good opinion of us. It's one of the things we are most curious about; 'What do they think of me?' The quickest fix to a good answer to that question is to commit to being the most honest version of ourselves we can be, as this guarantees that any opinion of us is formed over the real us. Including the opinion we have of ourselves.

For those that feel they simply cannot handle their truth, have the confidence in yourself to know that you already are. If it's that small flicker or a shining light, you already do have it in your life. Acknowledging it simply allows us the opportunities to learn the skills to make it work in our lives.

Why live the life of the best version of someone you are not, when you can choose to live the life of the best version of someone you are?

# What I Wish My Patients Knew

Some time ago I began thinking in detail about the various treatments I'd had and the many different therapists I'd seen. I began dissecting the 'why' behind the lack of success I'd had, and it was some serious lack of success, to try and piece together exactly what had gone wrong. Or, to be more accurate, what hadn't quite gone right yet.

Knowing what I know now I'd have approached therapy very differently but it may be a surprise to know that I'd probably not have changed anything about the things I actually said during those unsuccessful sessions. I was in most cases blisteringly honest. I could build rapport and answer thoughtfully and listen in to what was said in response.

Hindsight paints a much clearer picture than the present does and the answer to why I didn't come as far as I'd have liked is plural and broad. There are many reasons a treatment may not 'work' and I know the importance of understanding these things before, during and after treatment to give yourself the best possible chance of making the time count. We do not need to be experts of the ins and outs of therapy but having a realistic idea of what is about to come can be very helpful.

What I hadn't accounted for was what the time in those sessions actually meant. I had an expectation that wasn't correct and I never took the time to address that issue. I was aiming towards a goal I didn't really have in place. I had no measure of what I wanted from the sessions and ploughed on talking deeply and intensely about anything and everything without talking about why I was actually there and what I wanted from this.

Similarly, it is important that the medical professionals we work with have their own aims and expectations as although they are not experts in us, they are in their chosen fields and therapies.

For them to work out how to facilitate our therapies, they need to learn from us. So the clearer the idea of what we want to be achieved, the clearer the means of achievement

may be. It is a very collaborative process and benefits from not being heavily weighted on the expectation that the professional will just tell us what to do in full.
Working together before or at the very beginning of a course of therapy to establish how you can both achieve agreed goals is an absolute must for truly life changing therapeutic intervention. Making these goals more specific than 'to be happy' or 'to not have anxiety' can be helpful. Maybe for you this will be 'to be able to enjoy my free time at weekends more easily' or 'to learn to be less anxious at work'.

Over the years since I was a part of the TV show 'Extreme OCD Camp' I've been invited to work alongside many fantastic therapists across the UK and in the research for this book I spent time talking with these professionals on the things they wish their patients knew before beginning a course of treatment or during treatment. This is quite a broad outlook as I'm sure they would also agree that many go into it without needing their expectation to be explained, and in certain cases having an expectation may be a bad thing, so as a disclaimer not every professional would agree it is helpful to know much pre-treatment and should all be established when you commence. However, I believe you can gain from knowing a little more so have included some testimony from a couple of medical professionals I respect. I hope it is useful to you and allows you to learn from my and many others mistakes without having to make them yourself.

Claire Littlejohn has worked for 7 years as a Cognitive Behavioural Psychotherapist in Essex. Holding an MSc in Mental Health Nursing and a Post Graduate Diploma in Cognitive Behavioural Therapy, Claire works predominately with anxiety disorders and depression and worked for The Priory providing individual outpatient CBT and inpatient group therapy. With a vast experience and progressive and measured outlook towards treating those living with a mental health diagnosis her daily interaction with children, adolescents and adults allows for a revealing and invaluable insight into the possible issues that may arise.

I sought advice from a number of professionals to give a big consensus of opinions and one I knew I had to speak with was Dr Joseph Hayes, someone I have an immense amount of respect and admiration for. In possession of an MSc in Epidemiology from the London School of Hygiene and Tropical Medicine and a PhD in Psychiatric Epidemiology from UCL, and with professional experience as an Honorary Consultant in General Adult Psychiatry with a North London trust, he has held fellowships and positions across the field.

Dr Hayes encapsulates exactly what I would hope for if I had to design the optimum type of person we can benefit from working with. He is experienced and impressively qualified but is also incredibly personable and so easy to talk to. Both are quoted throughout this chapter and I thank them for their important insight.

**Myths and Misconceptions**

*'A common misconception is that the therapist will direct all of the session and give advice. If undergoing a course of CBT your therapist may teach you strategies and offer psycho education around your condition, but they do not advise you what to do. They help you to find your own answers by asking you open socratic questions and you will reflect on situations together, to help you think about what you could do differently the next time'* Littlejohn explains.

My own definition of socratic questioning (named after Socrates) would be focused questions or communication that is aimed at gathering data and may be used as a teaching/learning opportunity. This is a way of a professional being curious to clarify thoughts and conclusions we have come to and to maybe be self-critical, in a positive way, about how we came to these conclusions.

Dr Hayes knows that there are a number of things people may believe to be true before they begin therapy and has helpfully listed some below that you may be thinking and that are worth dispelling.

**'Therapy is something that is done to you**. *Therapy is a collaboration between you and the therapist. You will be very engaged in whatever agenda you set.*

**My therapist can read my mind** - *If I share my thoughts, my therapist will think I am an awful person.*

**Therapy will dig-up the past.** *The types of therapy that have proven effectiveness for OCD focus on the here and now, and the future. Sometimes there may be important events in our past that have contributed to our current situation, but these will not be a central part of the work that you do with your therapist.*

**My therapist will make me leave my partner, blame my parents, change my life, change my personality.** *Your therapist can't make you do anything! You will be working towards establishing more helpful patterns of thinking with your therapist as a guide. Hopefully this will change your life for the better.*

**Focusing on my problems will make them worse, not better** - *There is no evidence that this is the case. CBT offers practical solutions to addressing unhelpful thoughts and behaviours and moving towards helpful thoughts and behaviours'.*

**OCD and CBT are used as an example here as this is the condition and the therapy I personally know and have used, hence Dr Hayes' examples.

Particularly with therapies like CBT the bulk of the work you do will actually be outside the therapy room and the hour itself. Homework and challenging yourself within your regular setting and personal life is not only a must for keeping consistent with improving your mental health and your ability to learn to take some control of your symptoms and condition, but an expected and vital component of most therapies. Essentially we are all there to learn something. We're not there to just hear information about our condition, but to learn and discuss how to live with it or recover from it. Learning to use the tools and strategies we learn within therapy during our regular lives is the most important thing. Being taught how to do something in an office with our therapist is great, but that's not why we arc here. We need to know how to take it, or its lessons, out of those confines.

When I knew less than I do now, I'd be present for therapy but not ever really there. I'd answer and interact in an abstract and sterile way and was completely matter of fact

without really ever changing something or exploring beyond my preconceived ideas. It took a long time to realise I was there to change, but not really doing anything to action the change. I was talking but not saying anything and agreeing I needed to change without ever doing the things to make the changes I knew I needed. I wasn't lacking commitment, I was lacking understanding of how therapy works.
For an example; at the time when therapy wasn't working for me I wasn't sleeping for more than 2 hours a night or eating well. My therapist spoke with me to say that if I continued the way I was I'd be too exhausted to really function to make my contribution to getting better beneficial. I couldn't give it my all as I was constantly fucked.

Obviously I agreed. That's common sense. But was a nap and a biscuit going to change me, really? Nah. It was only going to be something like a serious therapy intervention and not something as simple as eating and sleeping better.

Of course I was far from correct. As I now know, to my massive benefit, I needed both. And more. I needed a balanced mentally healthy diet. I didn't need to change one thing and neglect the others, I needed to take a considered and proactive approach to my whole health. Maybe the therapy wouldn't have worked for me anyway, maybe the therapist wasn't right for me. But would 9 hours sleep and eating healthy have helped? Undisputedly so. Now, firmly in recovery, I place a premium importance on my all round health. I keep fit, don't smoke, don't drink, mostly eat right and sleep as well as I can. That didn't and doesn't cure me, but it gives me a far better chance. You've got double the chances of winning if you buy two lottery tickets.

The commitment factor is huge with overcoming the effects of mental illness. As loose as it sounds I always advise people to commit 'mentally and physically'. By that, I mean it is important to not only say you are going to make changes but to also make the actions happen that begin or continue those changes. If the actions are too great for you right now, don't just stop them. Discuss them with your team and scale them down to more manageable actions. If you have a plan to help combat social anxiety by meeting 5 new people a day and this is beyond you right now, don't stop the work, change it. Speak to 3, or 1. Bring it back to manageable.

Talking through the changes you want to make in therapy is the beginning of recovery, but the work you do between sessions is the vehicle.

*'Another misconception is that all the work will take place during the hour session. For most types of therapy this is not usually the case. You will learn tools and strategies but in order to make the most of your treatment you will need to monitor symptoms in between sessions, log situations, practice thought challenging and tasks'.* Claire explains the relationship between what you do in session, and the importance of what you do out of session; *'If undergoing an exposure and response prevention programme, you may complete live tasks (in vivo exposure) in session with your therapist, but in order to habituate (get used to) a situation it is recommended that you practice the tasks for 3 times per week to learn to feel less anxious about the trigger/ situation'.*

Elsewhere in this book I talk about the fact that nothing feels as we expect it to. The feeling of being over or underwhelmed in nearly every scenario is one we experience because we build up an idea of the feeling before that moment to find that when we get there it's totally different. Think of leaving a dentist appointment and thinking how that was actually totally manageable, or the reality of feeling fine giving a speech but uneasy beforehand. That is because we set a picture of different scenarios within our mind that is almost never actually achieved.

One way to control this is to practice it. The way we feel before, say, singing in front of someone – feels completely different the 50th time to the way it did the 1st time. Some things may stay the same, but our ability to tackle it is often wholly different. What we learn (or unlearn) in therapy is much the same. We use therapy to learn helpful tools and we use the time outside of therapy to learn how to use those tools in a way specific to our lives.

One thing I never took into account before I headed into therapy was how I would feel after. I believed I'd leave a session and feel better right away, calmer, more relaxed. This is something that can come later on but is very probably not something you are going to experience right away – in fact, it's probably going to be the opposite.

Claire agrees that *'Initially you may feel very drained and anxious after sessions, as you will be focusing on difficult thoughts and behaviours in the early sessions and the therapist needs to go through an assessment period to look at what is maintaining your condition before a treatment plan can be put into place. You will experience discomfort in the short term to free yourself in the long term'.*

There's no escaping the fact that therapy is difficult. You are probably there to try to make the biggest change in your life so that's going to be mentally, physically and emotionally taxing. But we must remember why we are there. This is all part of a process that may allow you to finally live your whole life, or give it back to you. This is understandably a time for nerves, frustration, fear and worry but do not neglect the fact that is also the time for excitement and hope.

I would always worry, and still do actually, that I wouldn't use the time properly. I would get anxious thinking about if I felt unwell on the day or had a headache or another ailment and it distracted my learning or something similar, this would be hugely distracting for me.

I asked Dr Hayes about this fear and how to make our therapy as beneficial as possible.

*'Be open. It may be a challenge, but you should feel comfortable talking about anything with your therapist, like any relationship this might take time'.*

This point answers my own anxieties in fact and is exactly why I tell my own therapists that I am concerned I'll not make the time count. In my example, they'll often help me develop a bit of a framework for our therapy with clear recaps and adequate time to discuss the previous and the next session so that I can understand where the development is. I asked Dr Hayes to bullet point some potentially helpful ways of making your therapy time count if you share a similar worry.

**- Spend time reflecting.**

**- Ask if you can record your sessions** – *'Some therapists will be happy for you to record all, or selected parts, of your therapy. This can help maximise the benefit of the session as often lots is discussed and you might feel overwhelmed during sessions. This is also helpful for homework and after therapy has finished'.*

**- Do your 'homework'** – *'The work you do outside of the sessions is as, if not more important, than the work in the sessions. It can be hard to make time for tasks, but you'll benefit more if you are able to'.*

**Before your first appointment**

Having been referred or self-referred for a treatment programme, you'll be asked to fill in a few different kinds of paperwork depending on the condition you are being referred for. This paperwork is often sterile, non-accommodative of you as a person and often a prospect many will feel wary about. Some of you, me included, may actually find the questions helpful or illuminative to a part of you you'd not completely considered until this point. Sometimes it will be things like the GAD-7 (anxiety measure) or the PHQ-9 (depression measure) and it is used to determine the type of therapy you'll be put forward for, so it is important we take that seriously and answer it as honestly as possible.
Going into our courses, it is helpful to have an idea of what our goals are from therapy, as Dr Hayes points out; '*Think about what your goal is. Where would you like to be by the end of therapy? What will have changed? – your therapist will help you set realistic goals'.*

.

These tips are good for you beyond just your first appointment, but this may be specifically helpful if a first appointment is approaching for you or even if you're experienced at this but changing therapists or therapies, there may be some points here to note.

**Write your own paperwork to explain how you feel at the moment –** As discussed in this very chapter it is very difficult to accurately recall a way we have felt in the past, the 'feeling' behind it can be tough to describe so if you have any particularly good, bad or important days be sure to write down how you felt to share at a session. It can also be helpful to do this if you have a day you would describe as 'typical' so your therapist knows how an average day looks for you.

**If you can, choose a time you won't be too tired -** Therapy is hard work and physically and mentally taxing. If you sleep badly, a 9am start may not be for you. If you struggle in the afternoons, avoid them.

**Allow yourself adequate time to get to your session –** As Dr Joseph Hayes says *'Give yourself enough time to get to the appointment. You may already be anxious about meeting your therapist for the first time. If you can, give yourself some time in the waiting room or outside to relax and prepare'*.

**Choose the rest of your day wisely. –** Similarly it can be an overwhelming experience so do not sandwich an appointment between two big meetings, an exam or when you know you have something anxiety provoking after or before session. Afterwards, rest up, eat well, do something nice for yourself.

**Don't go in hungry –** You can see the theme here! Everything we can do to give ourselves the best possible experience is worth it. Eating will make you feel better, stronger and more energised. Don't neglect it. Maybe take a glass of water in with you.

**Take notes –** Everyone leaves the Doctor's office wishing they'd said more or remembered a specific part of the conversation. Therapy is similar. We know the things that will be important to us later on in most cases, so take a notepad and if something comes up you think you need to devote some time to thinking about or discussing later, save it. This also takes a little pressure off of you to remember everything.

**Know that you aren't expected to give it all away first session –** Some people charge in to therapy sessions and say everything they've wanted to say to a therapist in one go, and that's fine. Maybe difficult to manage (!), but fine. Equally, if you need to build trust and confidence in a calmer fashion that is both expected and common.

**Be prepared to be consistent to help the therapy 'flow'! –** Claire Littlejohn summarises why this is important *'I would say if you can try, and attend your session every 1-2 weeks. Weekly if you can in the earlier sessions, as this will help your relationship with your therapist to grow more quickly and you will be likely to remember sessions without large gaps which helps the treatment to flow'.*

It is often said that personal experience makes for a better therapist and I think this is actually not true. We know developing a good therapist-patient relationship is key so that is a much more important measure of if the therapist is for you than if they have a diagnosis. This theory can actually be a little unhealthy as it can set unrealistic prerequisites that are in many ways cosmetic.

If this plays a role in your own comfort, that may be a fair point. But if you judge a therapist on if they have had your symptoms, you will be narrowing down your choices and possibly losing a great therapist. I asked Dr Hayes about this and he unsurprisingly explained it better than I ever could!

*'I think this ties in to concerns that people might have about not being understood by their therapist. Whilst there can be benefits to seeing a therapist who has personal experience of mental health problems, it is by no means necessary, and wouldn't necessarily mean having a better experience. Many therapists will have worked with people with a range of problems, and people who are affected by these problems in different ways. Your experience of your mental health problems is very personal, but your therapist will have experience in applying some relatively standard techniques to these problems. Maybe it's too simple an example, but we don't need the doctor fixing our broken leg to have a personal experience of having a broken leg, it's enough that they understand that it would initially be painful, then maybe frustrating as it*

*takes time to heal. Most importantly they would know the best way to fix it'* I think this sums it up perfectly. Your therapist's experiences as a therapist are more important than their experiences as a person. If you have a therapist with personal experience, great. But don't let it be the be all and end all.

We have been over the process of before therapy and beginning therapy itself, but what about at the end? How do we prepare for this? Should we prepare for this?
I think this is something we are wise to prepare for and is something therapists will be thinking about, even early on in our courses of treatment. If you are accessing therapy with the NHS there is a strong possibility you have a number of sessions rather than a rolling agreement to continue weekly or monthly until otherwise decided. A continuing and undefined quantity of sessions is either rare, or normally something that comes with private treatment.
Bringing up this part of the therapy may make you feel sad or frustrated and maybe even really scared but things can be put in place to alleviate that feeling, including by openly discussing it with your therapist. Many will offer/highly recommend a follow up session a few weeks or a month after completing a course of treatment so you'll have a chance to debrief and discuss life after that particular therapy with your team or therapist.
There is a natural grieving process for some people when they leave therapy. If you've been at it for years with the same therapist it is likely you will feel uncomfortable at times and probably a feeling of 'loss'. These are all normal and can be spoken about before therapy ends and followed up after. If you are completely discharged and struggling with this feeling, speak with your GP/General Doctor on how you feel and it will be a process you are helped through or if deemed as necessary you may be referred again for other/similar therapies.
As written, the way things feel in the present and the way things feel looking back on them can be vastly different. You may feel no affiliation or affection to your therapist now but miss them greatly when you part ways or you may have an almost intense bond with your therapist and dread leaving them, but once you do you may realise you are fine without and enjoy being out of the commitment. You may also still feel the same way

about your therapist but recognise and accept this as a good step so are focused on enjoying the fruits of your hard work. There is no uniformed way of leaving a therapy and coping afterwards, but this is something we must address during the therapy itself to adequately prepare.

The process of therapy and working with medical professionals may feel daunting or foreign to you or it may seem exciting and positive, either way please remember that a bad experience of a therapy does not necessarily mean that therapy is bad, nor is a bad experience with a therapist indicative that all therapists are bad. These experiences are probably isolated and unique to your circumstances and health at that very time. If your experience isn't positive first time round this does not rule you out as being someone that could dramatically improve their life with consistent and quality medical professionals supporting them.

# The Medication Myth

It seems that a culture has developed where the general public now seem to see medication for mental illness as a completely bad move. It's said by these social commentators that we are 'too quick to prescribe' and that if we 'rely on medication we'll never fix the real problems'.

This is, quite frankly, bullshit. Not only as it quite the impressive lie but it's dangerous, too. It has almost become accepted as fact and I'd like to address that a little here. It has got to the point where people are not trying or entertaining the possibility of antidepressants or the like through being almost conditioned to believe they are bad for you.

While medication for mental illness certainly isn't for everyone, for some this is an absolute life saver and sometimes quite literally so.

In 2008, having begged for years to be given something or anything, my medical support team of my GP and psychiatrist at the time decided it may be beneficial to try some medication to see if it may arrest the symptoms I was currently feeling. At the time OCD was putting me into a very dark place and I had fallen into depression like I hadn't really before. It wasn't a place I never wanted to be and I was open to new options.

Having tried a course of a certain antidepressant and having given it the right amount of time I felt like it wasn't really having the effect I had hoped for. I was still very anxious, sometimes a little more so than before, and my stomach felt bloated and uncomfortable all the time after medication. I felt sluggish and slow and like I wasn't really 'in the room' so rather stupidly, just stopped. Predictably this gave me some side effects and I chalked the experience up as being unsuccessful and decided to agree with the train of thought that medication wasn't a benefit.

As I hope you're seeing from this book, our recovery stories are entirely unique. They need to be based upon evidence backed medical research (what we know works for people) and to some extent educated theory (what we know may work for us). The good news is that the options are vast. There isn't just three options of medication or therapy and that's that, crippling mental illness forever – there are genuinely hundreds and thousands of ways forward. The key is to filter than information to make the perfect cocktail for you, so to speak.

Medication is one of those options and shouldn't be dismissed. Medical fact backs it up and although some conditions tend to have a better success rate with meds, they are worth a try.

In 2010, having basically just become more and more unwell my psychologist recommended another medication, Fluoxetine, which tends to be a good option for OCD sufferers. With little faith in its ability to help but complete desperation to try anything to feel better, I reluctantly gave it a go.

It would be lovely to now move on to saying that this medication changed my life in one go, but it didn't. Instead, alongside cognitive behavioural therapy it slowly gave me the platform to be able to function better day to day. It was described to me at the time as being able to 'take the tops and bottoms off of the mountains' (basically, keep you somewhere in the middle, not too up, not too down) and I think my experience with it seemed to live up to that analogy.

One thing I've always been fascinated seeing is the way some mothers speak to pregnant women expecting their first baby. They'll wish them luck and talk about how much motherhood has changed their life and then they'll tend to ask 'how far along are you?' When they find out how long they have some will then tell a long and gory story of how horrible their own childbirth experience was. They'll go on and on about how painful it was, how the midwife didn't listen, how the hospital was dirty and the drugs did nothing and the poor pregnant woman will be standing there looking at their pregnant belly feeling complete and utter terror! People also do this with; root canals, injections, job interviews, experiences with companies, exams, driving tests, presentations and they do it with taking medication for mental health. They'll tell you their horror stories, but they won't tell you the success stories. It's a weird facet of human nature. The Tripadvisor affect in action. Many people will rush onto a ratings website to condemn a hotel for being bad, but they'll not rush to do give praise for a good hotel. So take these horror stories with a pinch of salt. For some people medications will be a huge positive, that is medical fact and not anecdotal.

There are side effects and often these can be led by a feeling of heightened anxiety for a small period of time and they do not work immediately, but medication should not be dismissed and is a sensible option for many of us. I'm actually not on any medication now having decided to come off of Fluoxetine a couple of years ago, very slowly and over the watchful eyes of my medical team, but I'll always be very happy with the decision to give it a go. Medication is also not the only way to get better. I obviously advocate and agree with its benefits, but bear in mind for the majority of you this will need to be backed up with good therapy too.

# What To Do If Therapy Isn't Progressing As You'd Expect

Firstly, this is something we all feel in nearly every single course of therapy. It is wise to be calm and not too hasty with any definitive assessments of your therapist or the therapy itself, as worrying you aren't moving forward or that previously successful work is now starting to not be as effective is something we all feel at some stage during treatment. But if you truly believe you are giving the sessions your all and things are not progressing as you feel they should, do not be afraid to ask your therapist why. Any competent therapist will be ready for this question. If you can say you are giving it everything and nothing is progressing, then maybe a change is needed. I'm not for changing medical professionals/therapists constantly as consistency can be a great asset to recovery, but if there is no development and no reason for this – just maybe this therapist isn't the one for you. That does not mean that the therapy isn't. That is really important to know. I had tried various kinds of CBT before it worked for me. I had the perfect cocktail of the right therapists, the right therapy, the right peers and the right time. I was motivated and it all fit into place.

Anyone with an interest in fitness will tell you that often our bodies need variety to ensure we do not simply plateau. A bodybuilder will not just stop lifting weights because they are not seeing results as quickly as they did when they first started the process – instead they'll mix it up a little and lift different weights, in different orders, using different techniques to maximise results and we do similar when we are engaging in mental health treatment. Using the analogy above, if you're going to the gym and performing what you feel is a great workout, eating right at home, sleeping well and taking care of yourself – surely you'd ask your personal trainer why you aren't seeing more benefit? It's exactly the same with therapy. All good professionals undertake a wide variety of different courses and experiences to be able to be armed with the arsenal required to help you so will all (or should all) have the ability to work out different ways forward for you. Therapy should really be a partnership and a team game so make sure if you are putting everything you can into making it a success, that those involved also are. Try to remember that therapy only needs to work once for the catalyst to recovery, or your version of recovery. And therapy is hard. It's really fucking hard. So sometimes the most successful courses of therapy start off by disguising themselves as unsuccessful therapy but you need to be the captain of your own ship as much as possible and no therapist will be offended by you asking if things are going as they should be. Often this question leads to revaluating the way things are going and can be the springboard to turning the therapy into a success – if it doesn't, you know it may be time to change. Asking your therapist to help you choose realistic therapy goals, or to help you devise a set of goals together into a plan may be a good way to both simultaneously audit how things are going and for you to keep track of your own therapy development - or to know when to ask why things are not moving forward how you'd wish. It gives you something to go off of.

The biggest takeaways here need to be that just because the therapy isn't currently working for you does not mean it never will. Just because the therapist relationship isn't currently working for you doesn't mean it never will. And we are completely entitled and should be encouraged to ask about how our therapy is going and to feel complete comfort in questioning where we are with it.

# Wanting To End Your Life

This book is a book of positive realism (hopefully!) but I have promised myself it is going to be open and frank throughout rather than just unrealistically positive, and I do not want to shy away from the scary parts. You've had the courage to pick it up and see if it'll help, so I'll have the courage to write it honestly. Let's both have the courage to discuss something that not so long ago was a word not mentioned in some circles.

Suicide is one of the most complex parts of human life. Not so long ago it was actually considered a crime to 'commit' (hence the outdated term 'commit suicide') and it is now common enough to be the number one killer in men under 45 in the UK. For that reason, it must be discussed and it must be something we look at straight in the eyes.

I wouldn't claim I have ever been truly suicidal. I have wished I was dead and did have a period of my life I regularly felt disappointment each morning that I had woken up, but I've not felt more than that.

I've glamourized suicide in my head many times, I've thought about how it could be an easier path than living.

You may well hear the near-cliché that 'suicide is a permanent solution to a temporary problem'. I grew up hating that phrase. It is meant to inspire and add perspective but it forgets the audience it is intended for. For those suffering with chronic illness 'temporary' is not particularly 'temporary' and for those that are suicidal it would be naïve, or even arrogant, to think that they would not see their pain as permanent. To be in the throes of this feeling and feeling ready to end their life pretty much denotes that they DO feel the pain is permanent. I disagree that it is, or disagree that it always will be but in that moment or time it is immensely difficult to see, appreciate or accept this. Of course I can write this and say 'there is another beautiful side!', but I'm sitting on that beautiful side. When you are in the grips of it, it's hard to see out. But it is true that it is a final answer. One particularly bad day, a matter of weeks before I began the steps that ultimately led me to this point of recovery I am at now, I sat alone in my third floor flat looking at the ground outside and the knife in my hand as I cooked dinner, contemplating if I wanted to go on. Both the knife and the hard concrete below began to look irresistible to me. I weighed up the 'pros and cons' as I stood there – something VERY difficult to do in the moment, and I ultimately decided I couldn't do it and shouldn't do it, and I'm so pleased I reached that decision. However, many do not. In that very moment, consumed by fear, depression, frustration and hopelessness you need to look deeper to find that actually this isn't the way to go. Some people are overcome by the desire to end their life before they can find that deep hidden want to continue.

Two things struck me that day and both of them have prevented me from ever going that close again. Firstly, if I did this right here right now and took my final breaths, it could never get better. At that moment it felt like it was 99.99 percent certain I couldn't recover, but that tiny, minuscule, ridiculously small percentage of hope had me thinking 'Well, what if things DO get better, doing this now, I won't ever know a good life'.

It took a considerable amount of time that day to get myself to that point. Due to this, I made myself a promise to write my Dear Jack letter.

This letter is something I've only actually read twice. Just now, to write it out for you, and once more when things got particularly bad. The letter is one to myself that reminds me ending my life prevents the possibility of anything good happening ever again for me. I didn't write it there and then but instead around two months later. Having been through some intensive therapy and having got myself into a much more manageable position, I was able to experience some good days again. At first they were only few and far between, once a month maybe. On one of those days I got out the paper and pen and wrote to myself. Those exact words are below;

'Dear Jack,

Today was a good day. A few months ago, today seemed impossible.

Since then you have worked incredibly hard to understand your brain and yourself and to make the tough decisions you needed to make, and be forced into some tougher actions.

Some actions you chose, some you didn't. Either way, you're here today.

When you feel like there is no tomorrow for you, please remember to read this. If you are reading this, you are currently not your best self. You currently feel pain, or anger, or fear – or all of them and they are all legitimate feelings. Something may have happened to make them come to the surface, or maybe they just did anyway. Either way, don't beat yourself up for feeling this way mate. You don't need to be on your own case, you need to be your friend right now.

I want you to remember you are so many of the things you appreciate in others. You are kind, thoughtful, brave and filled with potential. You love life really. Right now you do not, I'm sure, but you love its endless opportunity, vast options and limitless adventure. You love meeting new people that feel like old friends. You have experiences that are unique and too important to kill. You've loved, and lost. You've achieved some of your biggest goals and lived a fascinating life. You've got a great message to share that you've not shared yet and you've been through so very much – do not make it all in vain.

You are young and physically healthy. You are a good friend and family member and your heart and morals are right, it's just sometimes your brain needs a little bit of maintenance. Think of all of the wonderful things you've seen and all of the incredible moments you've had. There are simply more of those to come. You've made a decision to be well and you are doing the actions required to be well. You deserve happiness and you've made leaps towards it. Today you felt it and you decided to write this letter to yourself to remind you when you forget. If you're reading this right now, your life isn't all bad – you've just forgotten some of the good bits. Do not give up today or tomorrow and create a life where your good days outweigh the bad. Trust yourself today and you'll thank yourself tomorrow,

Head forward mate, JPx'

And there it is. This is a different kind of suicide note, this is to me for anytime I may need reminding that suicide is not the answer. As I say, I did read it once after this when I needed to – and as I held it in my hands I remembered. It helped me tap into enough of what I needed to divert my crises, or at least calm it down. I'm forever grateful for this letter.

I urge you to write your own. At the end of a good day (they are there, keep looking) get out a pad and pencil and write everything within you to remind you of just how good things can be. If you can't quite extend that far, simply create a diary of the good day. As humans we sometimes struggle to truly remember a feeling after it has passed so describe the good feeling in vivid detail. Be colourful and passionate and bold and put it an envelope with your name on it and keep it in your bedroom. Maybe you'll need to look at it often, maybe you never will. But remembering the feeling of a good day is never a bad thing, so take the time to do this as soon as you can.

The Samaritans here in the UK, who are absolute angels, summarise suicidal thoughts and suicide really well I think when they say; 'The majority of people who feel suicidal do not actually want to die; they do not want to live the life they have'.

That I think provides incredible clarity into the mindset of anyone who has experienced suicidal feelings, attempted taking their own life or even succeeded.

We do not feel suicidal as we purely wish to die. We feel suicidal as we wish to live, just not as we are. The feeling of hopelessness feels too great to overcome or the feeling that life has become so grey there could simply never be any colour.

That is why I suggest a 'Remember' box. This isn't a memory box as those can often feature things like photos of passed relatives or memories of ex's that could cause us to feel sad, but a small box you keep under your bed to be opened when suicidal feelings become too strong for you.

Including a letter like mine above, include a few things that make you happy and remind you of the absolute magnificence of life. This can include photographs, concert tickets, a favourite childhood book, a DVD of your favourite film, something collected from a trip, anything that when you look at or use you remember what you need to remember to move past.

There's a stigma around suicide and this does mean some people feel they may not be taken seriously if they confess feelings of suicide. Charities like the Samaritans have a policy on taking your feelings seriously, as they should, so if you call them – they will listen. No validation required. I do urge you to speak to your medical team though and your family if you can. An increase in suicidal thoughts can indicate many things during treatment and include the times when you start a new medication for one example. Speaking with your Doctor may provide you with techniques and advice needed to avert a suicidal emergency (or even just getting past the feelings themselves even if there is no desire to act upon) and speaking with your family and friends may provide them with the tools and support options needed to assist you when you are there.

7 years ago I was living day to day in a world that felt a little too harsh for me. I was lonely, outcast, constantly in pain and although I hoped for a wonderful future my vision was blurred by a brain I felt utterly betrayed by. Everything felt sinister. Days and weeks would pass without me smiling once. I enjoyed nothing, even the things I was supposed to enjoy. I took no care of myself and I was angry. So fucking angry. I was bitter at the world that had shown me the opportunity of my best life but constantly taken it away from me. I was diagnosed with a condition most likely to be with me until my terminal breath and the more I thought about it the more I hoped that last breath would come soon.

Somehow I mustered up the strength to continue and soon realised it wasn't about how big the leaps were, but how often I tried to make them. I didn't need to go from the first step to the last, I just needed to keep attempting the first step itself. One day things started to move. Then I got momentum.

Soon I felt things improving and this gave me the confidence to seek out other ways to keep improving. I got to enjoy the feeling of progression so much that when I fell or went back a stage, I craved moving forward so much I picked myself up once more and didn't let any setbacks ruin me. I lived by the saying 'a setback is a setup for a comeback'. I chose to celebrate the successes and learn from the failures and now I live a life I'm proud of. But more importantly, I know that if (and 'when') any sort of bad times or big challenges come my way, I've now got the experience to conquer them all over again. Hopefully I'll never have to, but if it comes to it, I did it once – I can do it again.

If you're suicidal yourself, chances are you've already got some of the experience you need. To be at that point you've probably taken more hits in life than you think you can handle but the vital fact there is that if you are sadly at that point, you are also at the point where you know what makes things bad and what it feels like. Now you know that, you can find out how to turn it all around. You have the experience but you do need the medical support. Whilst you feel motivated or able, contact them. Reach out. If you're reading this (a self-help book!), you have the desire. With so many varied, tested and potentially efficient therapies around, you have the opportunity. All you need to do is keep yourself alive and kicking and you've ticked all the boxes you need to begin a recovery story.

# The Thing We've Lost - Fuel or Fire

It's always train journeys for me. I love train journeys, I always have. I'll have my headphones on, my laptop out or a book in hand and I'll just glance out of the window at the beautiful British landscape and think. Just think. I find that time so relaxing and in the midst of busy times in my week I really enjoy letting the train take the strain, I just find it slows life down a little.

Also, if you're anything like me, you like to look out of the window and pretend you're in some melancholic mid 2000's music video on MTV as the main character travels to meet someone and the music paves the way.

Even if you're not that odd, there's many opportunities throughout the week for contemplation and one thing I find myself musing on is the things I have lost due to my mental illness.

Not so long ago this was something I couldn't do without breaking down. It would tear me up inside. I felt like my life was a huge sand timer that was constantly upside down. As each day passed and with me not living my best life I would focus on all I could have had, or all I have had and have lost and my world would feel very lonely and incredibly unsuccessful.

I would constantly think about the people my illness had alienated, the bad choices I'd made, the youth I'd misspent in the worst possible way and it all felt like irretrievable loss. We are never younger than we are in this very moment and that transfixed itself in my conscious and I began to lose sight of what was in front of me by obsessing what I had or hadn't left behind.

This chapter is not about looking forward and discarding the past, for what happened or for what did not happen. This chapter is about recognising how we use this loss for fire or fuel when we do look back.

There is great truth in the saying 'we do not regret the things we have done, we regret the things we haven't done' and I relate to it completely.

7 years ago, whilst engaging in therapy with Pete Weiss and Dr Travis Osbourne I was asked to recall the things I had lost. I was horrified at the thought but worked through them and ultimately began to realise the importance of how we use this information can play a very relevant role in our lives today.

Many of my school friends have big friendship groups now with other school friends, even though we left 13 years ago. I never did as I was so unwell at that time and therefore I spent more time off school than at school, sometimes I will look back and see pictures from a wedding or a night out involving my old classmates and feel a little envy and a little sadness at these long term friendships they've made that I've lost out on.

I think regularly about losing my career in football to my mental illness and I am guilty of obsessing over the relationships I've ruined or had ruined by illness. Some of these things are things I did that caused loss and some of these things are things that were lost without my control.

Under the tutelage of Pete and Travis I began to develop the ability to sift through each of these losses I was holding onto and divide them into those I used for fuel and those I put on the fire. The fuel is the things I recall to remind myself to get healthy and stay healthy, the things I use to motivate and inspire me to work hard and smart to be healthy – I use their memory or impact to benefit me now. At the time of this therapy, I was in a particularly dark place and these things became the ropes I used to hoist myself out of the hole. I used them to say 'enough!' I remembered how they made me feel and how much pain they gave me and from that my determination rose and it provided me with a focus and drive to move forward. It was mind fuel.

Then there is the things I put on the fire. The feelings, subjects or examples of loss that I gain absolutely nothing from – the ones that make me feel bad, offer me nothing good and do not hold any relevance in my search for recovery. These things I put on the fire, they are of no use to me.

I can't advise you on which to use for fuel and which to throw on the fire but this is something you can decide for yourself and be as picky as you want to. It doesn't need to fit into any box or be acceptable to anyone else bar yourself. If you find it useful, use it. If you find it negative, fire it.

The great thing you will find here is that when you start to do this, you can find a place for the majority of it as fuel. The more you learn to do it, the more you gain from it. The more you gain from it, the more you want to find more things for fuel.

In the past I've missed many professional opportunities, but not anymore. I came up with a business idea that I loved and that had some real mileage to it during my dark days. I simply couldn't do anything big with it. I wrote a great business plan, fully costed, and began designing the brand. I knew exactly how I was going to make it happen and the route I'd like to go down with it and then I hit a seriously bad patch and stopped working on it. It's since been done several times over and in most cases has been completely successful. I know of a company that is doing exactly what mine would have done and turns over tens of millions of pounds a year now. For a while I was gutted about this and it impacted me badly – I then learned the power of fire or fuel and now when I think back to that opportunity missed, that loss, I see fuel. A motivator to make things happen today. A reminder to be confident and courageous in my ideas and go forth boldly.

Earlier this year I set up a company for an idea I have had growing that back then I would have not been able to do anything with. That's the result of that fuel. I look at the feeling of loss and I take something from it.

My football career is another story. I use that very differently. This is something I do not talk about much and is quite difficult to write, but in a previous stage in my life I was developing a good football career. I had experienced playing at a professional level in various countries across Europe, taken one of the highest coaching qualifications available at just 17 and I genuinely and completely believe even now I'd have one day managed a football club at the highest level. I had already begun climbing there.

Illness struck and I lost myself. I became unfit and unwell and the football industry is one you need to keep moving in or one you inevitably end up having to start over in. I stopped playing and coaching and found myself basically back at the start and I made the decision to leave football as a career and find something else to realise my ambitions.

When I think about this loss there's not much in it I find comfort in. I had some incredible memories and achieved some childhood dreams but I also lost out on the real rewards of my graft and lifetime of dedication so looking back I feel mostly negatives. I feel pain and anger and bitterness and all three of those are things I do not need, so I put this loss on the fire. It's lost and gone now and I cannot change that. I can't learn from it (right now) and do not gain from it so I choose to put it on the fire.

The way you place these losses normally depends on the status of your recovery. If you are taking your first steps then the vast majority of the feeling or actuality of loss can be attributed towards fuel. If you are at the beginning or in a bad way then all of it can be fuel. If you are already feeling terrible about what you've missed out on or what you've had and lost and are reading this in a bad way, you may as well gain something from that experience! If you are going to feel terribly about it anyway, why not at least use it to help fuel recovery? You're already hurting, you may as well use that powerful feeling to move forward. But make motivation mean something. When you feel motivated; do. Otherwise it is wasted emotion.

Desperation actually teaches us a great deal. Rock bottom has its potential. It's often feeling at our very limit that forces us to make positive steps, to pick up this book, or tell a friend, or call your Doctor. It's the overwhelming frustration that sweeps us up and makes us have to change. When we have a small toothache, we rarely go straight to the dentist. We mostly say 'I'll give it a few days' and then it either goes away or it's gotten much worse and made us realise we should have done something about it right away. Mental illness can be much the same. Most of us can appreciate a symptom not feeling at all right but we tend to wait and see and often that's a bad move. However, if you are feeling that you're as low as you can go already, the harm in addressing these feelings of loss to ignite you towards positive change is a good thing. Do not use the thought of them to beat yourself up, but certainly use the incredibly powerful feelings that come from loss to improve your situation today.

If you're in my position and in recovery, headed towards it or feeling your best then the way you look at loss does change a little.

For me, now, I put more on to the fire than I ever did when I was engaging in intense therapy. I don't need to remind myself of loss or things missed as much anymore as I'm so involved in the process of recovery/working towards recovery that I no longer need anything to convince me to engage, I see the everyday benefits of my engagement already so for me it is more about continuing this and maintenance. I have made peace with these losses and only now look towards a bright future, rather than holding onto the demons of my past.

Mourning aspects of the past is a really tricky subject. It's something we all do and it's also something we all do differently. I'm not telling you to ignore your past or your worries about it, or to forget you are upset about it. I am also not telling you to constantly force yourself to remember it and how it makes you feel as both are extremes that have potential to damage your today. What I am advocating is healthily working towards understanding how you approach loss in your past and understanding it can directly affect your today. It is either helping you or hindering you and either way you have (or can learn) the ability to harness its potent power for serious benefit.

You might be reading this and thinking I'm being over the top so let's make it a bit more practical. Choose something you think about often or that bothers you and that is something your mental illness has impacted by making you stop or changing its course. A relatable example is 'my depression has meant I've not been able to go to University this year like I wanted to, so I'm a year behind my classmates'. Write whatever it is down.

Now it is as simple as this to decide; is this thought inspiring you to make sure you are definitely ready for next year and motivating you to be your best and seek the right support so that you can enjoy Uni? Or, is it painfully swiping your legs away and making your self-esteem and confidence disappear as you think about what could have been?

If it has the potential to be a positive motivator for you, put it in the fuel category. If it only leaves feelings of sadness and has no spark of inspiration, put it on the fire.

Sometimes it may change and your approach to how you see those losses will be different with time resulting in something you feel useful now may not be so in the future, and vice versa – and that is absolutely fine.

# What I Wish My Employees Knew

This chapter is one of the most important subjects I am going to approach for you in this book.
I've tried to be honest, realistic and passionate throughout and there's not many things I feel more passionate about than being a small part of ushering in a revolution in the way we deal with mental health at work.
I, like many others, have this insatiably powerful drive to be a part of making the professional lives of those living with a mental health condition better, safer and more prosperous because the current position we are in, quite frankly, is outrageous.
I have known from the first time I thought about writing these books that the evolution of rights at work for people living and working with a mental health problem should be a big part of the discussion.

I work in the private sector and have been a part of leading companies and consulting for different businesses in a broad range of industries, so have been in a position of huge privilege to be able to take an active role in influencing policy. I am also able to do this as someone that has experienced both supporting and being supported in the workplace. Within this position and the media work I have been a part of, promoting mental health understanding and action, I've often been asked to go and speak with company leaders and their managers and staff on mental health at work and I'll be honest with you, I'm usually not impressed. But, all is not lost.

Throughout the past two decades we have brought great awareness and development to the public perception of mental illness and there have been undoubted leaps made like never before.
Originally the default position from the population started as 'that person is crazy' and

this agreed consensus was fairly universally dismissive of accepting mental illness.
After this we reached 'that person needs help' and an understanding that this is genuine illness. Largely though, this awareness was without a desire to be an active part of helping this cause, and so businesses and individuals had an attitude of 'leave it to the Doctors'.
The next milestone achieved; 'that person isn't crazy, I understand they need help' brought a wider general understanding that mental illness is a possibility for everyone and began the process of bringing more compassion to the subject.
Now we have arrived in the current position of 'I want to help this person'. This means we now have great awareness, but do not yet have enough great actions professionally to back it up into meaningful change. But it is coming.
The next step, and the most important stage to reach in this social uprising is getting to a point where the general position feels 'I want to help this person and I KNOW how to help this person'.
This extends from friends and family to employers, teachers, medical professionals and colleagues – everyone now needs to be educated on mental health and know how to signpost to good support and appropriate action when needed. We cannot simply have those that personally experience it to be leading all of that process. Mostly because we are really fucking tired mate. Everyone must be held accountable as a civic duty to proactively seek answers to provide an inclusive world for any position of accessibility for mental and physical health. We are past needing awareness now. We need change. It is no longer time to talk and absolutely time to do.

In the research for this book I spoke with hundreds of business owners, employers, managers and private and public sector leaders to establish just where we are on a) the understanding of mental health in the workplace and b) the actions and provisions put in place to support mental wellness in the workplace.
This informal research (I asked similar but differing questions in person, on the phone, in email, on record and off record) is still emphatic. The understanding of mental health, in general, is absolutely accelerating in a rapid and meaningful way – however, the actions and plans made to support that level of understanding in the workplace are not

developing as fast as the understanding is and therefore people are unsure how to look after themselves at work.

To appropriately use a business example – if you use analytics, personal testimony and financial facts to ascertain a change you should make or a position to hold for the company's benefit and THEN you spend years saying 'yeah, we should absolutely change something!' but never actually do, you'll not commercially succeed. Businesses in the UK are currently doing this very slow response to facts with appropriately supporting the mental health of their staff and therefore we are not yet compassionately succeeding either.

Bear with me though. We're not going to lose here.

The most encouraging and the most relevant indicator of the positive change long term we are heading to, is that what I found throughout was that companies and bosses were **unaware** of how to support you but not **unwilling**. That is a huge difference.
Breaking unhelpful mindsets is a vital first step in conquering unacceptable environments. Companies are not incompetent through desire, but ignorance. And as I have written many times, ignorance is something we can change far easier than we can a lack of desire. Education will provide the antidote to poor practice and this desire will keep it firmly in place when it arrives.
One such example of this is phoning in sick. Too many people feel they cannot ring into work on a particularly bad mental health day and say they are unwell with their mental health. One of the horrible parts of this is that nearly 100% of the population would rather have a bad cold than a bad mental health day, yet we sometimes take a week off sick with the common cold but don't feel comfortable taking the morning off because our brains are unwell. Does that make any sense?
I've done it myself and called in sick and claimed I had a bad stomach whereas really I knew I needed to rest my head a little and maybe even seek some support medically with a trip to my GP or a support group.

This is an example of a mindset shift we all need to make both as employers and employees. It's not easy coming out and saying how we feel truthfully as employees but this will be achieved with employers creating an environment that will make the employee feel safe enough to be honest and open.

Not only is it good for us mentally to be occupied and feeling purposeful but the economic and social factors of staying in work are huge. And not just for us, for our employers too, don't forget. It costs them for us to be off so it pays for them to help support keep us in work. Try not to think of the responsibility of an employer to be obliged to put things in place to support you as something to feel guilty or burdensome about, there's no need to put pressure on yourself here – illness happens, we never want or aim for it. Their responsibility is a positive thing. It also serves as a reminder that we need to take as much personal responsibility as we can for keeping in work – but we can and should be supported in that pursuit for everyone's benefit. Those living with a mental health problem account for around 12.1% of the UK's GDP, or £225billion per year, so no one can claim we are not contributing here!

The ways we can attain support at work are varied and depend on you, the type of job you have and the business itself. The bigger companies with the larger workforce and budget have different means and resources to support you than the smaller ones do, but they wouldn't necessarily be better as such.

Some companies are now employing people specifically in person/wellbeing focused roles that are often extensions of HR leadership positions and tend to have a vote in company strategy, which is a good illustration of the way I think we are headed.

The first part of this chapter may seem negative, but I promised you honesty. Vitally though, there are very good initiatives and changes coming in that I want to highlight for you to give you some ideas of the ways you may well be supported now and in the future.

Nuffield Health, who employ over 15,000 people across all platforms have a Head of

Emotional Wellbeing, Brendan Street, who told *Talk Business*; *'At Nuffield Health we offer emotional literacy training to all our employees to help them recognise the signs of emotional distress in themselves and others. Employees are also taught different coping strategies to maintain good emotional health. For example, the learning module identifies the signs of emotional distress like changes in appetite; disturbed sleep; avoidance behaviour; feelings of guilt or anxiety and negative thinking'.*
This type of self-recognition can go a long way towards early understanding/intervention at work and as pointed out allows us to look out for each other – with small but meaningful ways to cope taught.

Tesco, who work with Nuffield Health on their own commitment to making the supermarket chain healthier have supported 1000 colleagues' access mental health workshops in 2019.
They also work digitally on their colleague health alongside Mindapples e-learning platform. Mindapples, a London based non-for-profit have developed a rigorously academically and clinically tested programme, independently evaluated by the University of York, that has been found to improve wellbeing in participants by delivering masterclasses and talks amongst other things. Tesco alone have reported colleagues accessing the platform at least 20,000 times. This is a good way of introducing and developing discussion and person to person understanding of mental health but must be followed up with actions and provisions.

Internationally, Regions Hospital in Minnesota, an award winning healthcare provider, have established a Center For Employee Resilience. This is an on-site, dedicated space with a spa-like feel for hospital employees. Open 24/7, they have sound therapy machines, places to do yoga and meditate and colouring pencils and doodle paper for the creative minded. A researcher for HealthPartners found that *'Stress happens, and it happens to everyone. If workers do not have skills and habits to help support them when they're stressed, their productivity declines'.* Which is of course another reason companies WILL be willing to support you, it makes no sense for them to not support you. They do not lose out.

I spoke briefly with Claude Silver, the Chief Heart Officer at VaynerMedia, a digital agency based in New York and made famous by the brilliant and person-centred, kindness-first entrepreneur Gary Vaynerchuk. A veteran of Fortune 50 companies and a speaker at Wellbeing @ Work events, Silver has been invited in to speak at Google and agrees with the virtues of specific modern platforms for supporting wellbeing as she tells me; *'As of now we offer Life Coaching (Guided.io) as a benefit to all employees with meditation apps also available'*.

One more example a little closer to home is innocent drinks. The British based drinks firm has around 300 staff members and has become known for its innovative and charitable ethos with a clear social conscious and from my experience, a very genuine and calculated desire to support its staff as fully as possible. I spoke with Laura Thompson from innocent, who filled me in a little on just some of the initiatives the London based company have in place to support staff mental wellbeing at work.

The thing I was most impressed by with innocent was how their actions were dictated by a well thought out process that in infancy involved forming a Mental Health Policy; *'This is the first thing we did when we set up our mental health plan. This clearly states where innocent stands on mental health, and is available for everyone to read'* Laura explained to me. This is awareness at work. And they back it up with action too.

innocent invests in its staff via Mental Health Training. Through research I was aware that the company had previously overseen training programmes where managers would have their own, support-specific version and colleagues would have a more general version. I actually supported this idea and definitely see the benefits of ensuring management are aware of different ways they can be more efficient at supporting colleagues. This has, however, since changed for the recognisable better. *'We have made the conscious decision to stop doing this (separate training). We decided that every employee at innocent should receive the same level of mental health training, no matter how senior. We worked together with an external company to create a training session that was suited to everyone, and specifically designed for our needs here at innocent. This is a half day training session that incorporates various different activities. This has proved a lot more effective than our original set up of manager and non-manager training.*' This tailored and company specific way of training makes the conversation employee-relevant and by being regular ('*this happens once a quarter in the office and is open for anyone to go to*') enjoys the added bonus of being able work as its own refresher course.

Again, this is super important. Many companies invest in quality mental health training, but once every other year is not acceptable and should not be considered 'enough'.

Some businesses offer bland means of measuring success of wellbeing initiatives like this and will be happy to just tick a box to say they've done it and move on. Thankfully innocent appreciate the role in staff feedback, which in itself helps develop the type of culture that keeps mental wellness within the daily conscious of staff members and hopefully banishes any taboos about speaking up and making changes. '*We send around a survey after every training session to get some feedback from our employees on what they thought of the session. We have a very open culture for feedback here at innocent, so we welcome feedback from everyone in all aspects of our mental health plan.*'

Other ways of keeping in touch with staff at the company include a bi-weekly mindfulness class, amongst other subsidised classes to facilitate higher participation levels. '*We also have a series of 'mindful moments' that our creative team made. These are weekly emails that are sent around the office of tips and tricks people can use to help look after themselves and keep their mind active at work*' Laura informed me. Again, 'keeping in touch' should not be something we just do with people away from us. We can be more in touch with colleagues that are working remotely than those working one desk away if our engagement isn't correct. It seems innocent has this right.

I asked Laura to confirm how colleagues may seek out support directly at the company and was pleased to hear that not only is there a current process in place but that they are still actively seeking ways to develop their current strategy; '*We have a few avenues of support available for those who would like to discuss their mental health. We signpost to managers first and foremost, and also our people partners (every team at innocent has a people partner; a member of the people team who they can go to for any people related queries). We then have our external avenues of support for those who would like to keep the matter confidential. We're looking into introducing either mental health first aiders or 1:1 coaching sessions with our mental health trainer as a next step.*

*Our EAP (Employment Assistant Programme) is with Lifeworks, this is available to anyone that works for innocent and has a variety of support tools, from physical health to mental health, financial issues and relationship issues. We then have 'Stronger Minds', which is specifically for those who are on our private healthcare. This is specifically a mental health support line.'*

It is important to share the success stories of good practice within these bigger companies, the successful smaller companies or the big chains because often they lead the way for other businesses. With 99.3% of companies in the UK being classes as 'small', positives examples will have far reaching impacts. We need to champion these cases, as I have above, to have very clear, evidence-based 'role models' for other firms.
In 2019 we are well aware of the importance of corporate footprints (including and beyond climate responsibilities). It is paramount that these companies, with their global reaches and media interesting campaigns use this position to promote a new and progressive mindset to how we treat mental health and wellbeing in the workplace.

Whilst researching these books and having spoken with literally hundreds of employers, managers and leaders with ideas ranging from refreshingly innovative to downright terrible (in my opinion!), I have put together some general examples of the most commonly reported things employers would like their employees to know about how to help them support you in your mental wellbeing.

**'Tell me exactly how I can help'** – This one I heard time and time again. Most employers I spoke to felt like they were underqualified to know enough about your mental health to be able to support you adequately. This one they are half right on. They do not know you as well as you do, but they can be proactive in offering support – they just may lack the education and experience to lead this. A statement like this shows why it is a good idea to spend a few days or hours writing down exactly what you would like to speak to your boss about, be that about reasonable adjustments longer term or day to day support.

**'I'd prefer for my employee to give me their ideal scenario for 'reasonable adjustments' and then we can work out how feasible it is from there'** – Truthfully, most employers did not have things in place as reasonable adjustments for their employees living with a mental health condition. As part of the Mental Health Act 2010, employers must be able to offer 'reasonable adjustments' to you to make sure you are able to complete your job. This is most known for the adaptions within premises like ramps, lowered shelves and ground floor work spaces. But it can also be flexible working, extended/staggered break times and specific task redistribution for health purposes. The employers that did already have experience of supporting people with reasonable adjustments, nearly all noted that their employees actually under sold what they needed in order to appear more reasonable. They would ask for half of what they needed and consider it a negotiation. So, rather than asking for later morning starts every day as they really needed, they'd ask for it just twice a week. The understanding employers I spoke with said this could sometimes cause inefficiency in their support as they would end up modifying their adjustments to accommodate this anyway – so felt not knowing exactly what was needed from the beginning made things more difficult for the person they support. This is, again, a great example of why we should work out our best case scenario for support and aim for this first. Ask for what you want and need, not what you think your employer wants you to say.

**'I'd like to be guided by my employee to know when they need a chat and when they need to be left alone'** – Another regular comment repeated by managers was that they felt unsure when to approach a colleague about a potential mental health problem and when to leave the person alone. To everyone I met and spoke with I obviously suggested more training/education can help this but ultimately this comes down to improving relationships with your staff either informally by the culture developed or slightly more formally by an agreed Wellness Action Plan as explained in the 'How To Support Colleagues And Staff' chapter on the other side of this book.

**'I do want to be a good support, but I also want to make sure any absence, temporarily in the day or for a longer period can be covered to make sure everyone else does not stress more than needed'** – This is a tough one but I've put it here as it is something I have heard many times. I'll be honest as well, some companies say this to cover themselves first and you second, but lots genuinely showed me they meant this in a way to be inclusive of their support to all employees. I do think putting a pre-sickness plan in place is a good move but I think that is efficient if you have employees living with a mental health condition or not. We all get ill from time to time. My suggestion here is to have this put into your/a Wellbeing Action Plan but if this does not exist, having a separate policy, ideally designed by you on how the organisation can handle your absence may be a really good proactive move, just how you would redistribute workload when going on holiday.

Firstly, it'll reduce your stress levels knowing that should you need to leave suddenly, gradually or for any period of time things are in place to cover this and it also allows your boss to know you are thinking of everyone. It can be a stressor for colleagues to cover so having something in place before an issue is just good safeguarding.

**'I would like them to know that I have personal experience of a mental health problem but don't want to make it all about me'.** – This also deserves inclusion and was a theme throughout. Most of the time I spoke one on one with leaders, managers and bosses and within the confines of an anonymous research query, many spoke openly on how they've noticed someone in their organisation displays similar symptoms to them but that they do not want to offend them by bringing it up. So if you are at work and thinking your boss doesn't have any clue about mental health, there is a fair chance they do. No one in this day and age is completely unaffected by mental health problems – be that by personal experience or very close second hard experience.

I would also note that a fair and common reason many do not disclose their mental health status at work is a fear that this will halt progression at work. Of course any discrimination of this sort is illegal, but I believe actually bringing that fear up ('I'm worried my disclosure may affect my long term aspirations within the company') shows a great deal of professional maturity, self-awareness and I would even call it a clear sign of ambition. Your fears should be alleviated and this may even extend the conversation on how you can attain advancement.

I would certainly suggest investing some time in the parallel chapter to this one on the other side of this book, I mean – I would say that, I wrote it. But reading that chapter and this one should hopefully give you a little bit of a 360 degree view of how to support yourself and others at work. Both chapters were written with each other in mind so to get the full feel of this chapter, please do flip over to the other side once you have done with this one.

At the beginning of this chapter I wrote that my biggest takeaway in my research was that employers are **unaware** of how to support you rather than **unwilling** to. This may sound a bit depressing and in some ways it may be, but it should serve as a very big and very real indicator that if you are sitting there now thinking 'I really need more from my employer', be comforted and invigorated to know that further meaningful support is probably available to you.

This book is about making motivation count. If I motivate you in these pages and an action is not made from that motivation then I would consider my job a failure. Please pick up the pen now, make a note of the things you've learned or thought about whilst reading this chapter and its fellow on the other side. Write down what you are going to do next, be that make an appointment with your manager, read up on reasonable adjustments or even hand this book or chapter over to someone at work if you think it may be helpful. Make it count for something and let that motivation be the starting line towards change.

# The Bad Good Days

My God I used to hate the good days.

I had absolutely no idea what to do with them. They were foreign and uncomfortable and weird and they felt like climbing to the very top of a rollercoaster without a seatbelt on. Somehow I just knew I'd come crashing down.

Amongst the many hugely relatable feelings those of us living with a mental illness can agree on, the familiar inability to enjoy what is classed as a 'good day' is one we have all experienced.

I refer to it as 'stalking anxiety'. This demotivating and often fast accelerating feeling produces an anxiety within me that leaves me feeling almost watched when I'm having a great day – stalked by the very potential that it may all go wrong. There will be this tiny (and not so tiny) little nag at the back of my mind that is just sitting there waiting, anticipating things going wrong. Preparing for them, and not in a good way. It's the opposite of a safety blanket, it's a well versed and very obvious banana skin.

When things were at their very worst I actually got to the point where I feared the good days. I wouldn't want bad days, but I couldn't handle the good one's either so I would hope for a 'not-so-bad-day', something where it clearly wasn't good so I didn't need to fear it going wrong, but was instead manageably bad. I actually hoped for those sort of days instead of the good.

During bad periods in our lives, good days are heavy reminders of the potential of loss. When we are in a good place mentally, we actively seek the activities and opportunities that may make us happy as that's ultimately the end goal all of us should have for our lives. We are open to them and go with the flow of them when they arrive. If things are not so good though and we are mentally spinning plates, we become uncomfortably too aware that our fragile mental health may effectively change that day to a bad one so the thought of having dinner with a friend, a night out, a fun trip somewhere or a day to ourselves all of a sudden becomes a golden noose. It can leave us looking around trying to spot where it could all fall apart – and as we can also agree on, if you go looking for a negative, you'll probably find it.

I was on holiday in Lanzarote a few years ago in the middle of the summer (a perfect opportunity to experience a bad good day) and looking out at the absolutely glorious sea. There was a little island not far out from the beach that I realised I could swim to - that in itself being quite miraculous as my swimming technique is a mix between a doggy paddle and a gentle drowning, so I began swimming out. I've got a few uncommon fears and one of them is jellyfish! All I could think of as I started swimming was that whilst I was researching things to do in Lanzarote the week before, I'd come across an article that was about how in the same water former PM David Cameron had been stung by jellyfish. Now you're absolutely correct, of course David Cameron deserves to be stung by jellyfish, but this thought took over my mind and now my swim became frantic and hurried and nervous.

I wasn't stranded or needing to get to that island, I just wanted to purely for enjoyment. It was a lovely day and I wanted to go and sit there and look back out at the beach and enjoy my surroundings so it certainly wasn't a life or death situation to get there but it turned from a positive to a negative. I didn't allow myself to enjoy my time because of a 'maybe'. I started at 0 and aimed to get to 1 but ended up at -1. How? All because I was worried about something that hadn't happened, might not happen and ultimately didn't happen. There is notifications put up when jellyfish are spotted in the area so it's actually pretty difficult to even come across them but as I set out to do something enjoyable I found a reason to not enjoy it. I created the bad good day.

I think about the 'White Bear Theory' a lot. Known professionally as ironic processing, this is the psychological process that occurs when you try to suppress certain thoughts and in turn make them more likely to surface.

Try now to not think of a white bear. How long can you last? I'd be shocked if you could do 30 seconds. But now think of nothing BUT a white bear. Much simpler.

Ironic processing has a few associations with mental health but I believe the antidote for dealing with this potentially negative psychological process is using another clear psychological process to combat it. The basic core principles of mindfulness and meditation.

As explained elsewhere in this book, for some, mindfulness can be a vital tool towards achieving mental wellness. Aimed at practicing our ability to be present and truly experience the current moment, becoming fully aware of our thoughts and feelings as well as the world around us at that very time, mindfulness is a heavily researched and medically accepted method of treatment/prevention. It's basically the action/s of 'being in the room'. It is the art of not letting the world run away from you.

What I love about mindfulness and meditation is that its practice is not exclusive to feeling good. You do not need to just do it when things are great, and if things that are not good begin to flood your head – they do not need to be ignored. As mentioned above, that's impossible. They are accepted and then processed as being either important or part of the moment, or something to move past in that moment and revisit later, or not at all. I think of it as a 'sorting' session.

To put it more practically as I can feel some of you finding me sliding towards something a little less productive for you, here's an example of my own.

When meditating last week (there was no yoga mat, no incense, no tie dyed t-shirt or wholefoods, just me sitting on my sofa) I started thinking about a stressful meeting I've got coming up. I was trying to relax but beforehand had been doing some work from home and now all I could think of was this meeting. At first I tried to suppress it and ignore it and focus on the sounds I could hear outside, the smells from the kitchen, the warmth from the radiator brushing my arm and just be in the moment but instead this meeting kept cropping up. The more I tried to ignore it, the more it became something conscious. As ironic processing is accepted as being more prevalent under stress and anxiety, which this was now causing me, this wasn't a surprise.

Therefore, I thought of the meeting directly for a short while and rationalised that yes, that's something I need to consider soon but that no, it does not need to be now. This allowed me to walk past it and realise the meeting was simply a 'mental event' and not a 'physical event'. The meeting wasn't happening now and nothing I could say, do, think or prepare at that very moment could change that meeting – so I discarded its importance and moved on. The thinking of the meeting is a mental event, the going to it is physical. I'm not physically going to that meeting in that moment, so it's importance when I'm trying to relax, meditate and focus on today does not need to be there when it occurs as a mental event. To simplify mental and physical events, sometimes when we feel happy (mental event) we smile (physical event). Mental events are essentially thoughts, realisations, feelings, dreams and decisions, physical events are our actual reactions and actions to them. Overthinking and anxiety are often led by a huge amount of importance being put onto mental events, understanding how to process them and recognising which are important to us right now and which are something to work with later can be a big key to a clearer mind.

During a good day we can spend a vast amount of time trying to leave our mental illnesses at home and I think for most of us, that's not realistic.

Of course we all want days where we can step out of the shadow of the illness and are just ourselves, simply enjoying our lives and never looking back at the illness, but unfortunately this illness is a part of you so it goes where you go. That's the truth but you already know that, deep down.

What also comes with you though is an infinite amount of techniques, approaches, therapy learning points, mental tools, experience, understanding and opportunity to be able to change bad days to good days or to keep the good days great. As they should be. If you are reading this and thinking 'which techniques?! I have none!' then you know that therapy is absolutely for you.

The first thing to do is focus on the day – use the white bear theory to be in that room. If you're at a football match and feeling 'stalked' with a dawning and overawing feeling that this may all go bad, start finding things you've not noticed yet about where you are. What sounds can you hear that you've not taken in so far? The wind around the stadium or the bustle around the hot dog stands. What can you see that you've not yet appreciated? The programme seller walking along the stands or the animation of the coach on the sideline. What smells are in the air? The deep heat spray on the player's legs or the burgers being cooked. There is so much going on right in front of us that most of the time we only really take in a small part of whatever we are doing. Try and connect with as much of it as you can and that will force you to be incredibly present which can be really effective at dispelling the anxiety that isn't necessary.

As you'll have no doubt know or been told, anxiety plays a vital function in keeping us safe as humans. It's why we just know to not do certain things, if we didn't have it biologically it would make us extinct pretty quickly. This is necessary anxiety.

On a more day to day basis it can also be necessary towards our own understanding of the important things. We feel an anxiety the day before a big presentation to remind us to be prepared, that is a helpful and useful anxiety but unfortunately most anxiety that we recognise is not necessary.

If, as you attempt the above mindfulness techniques, all you can feel is the rushing blanket of anxiety washing over you then do not try and pretend it doesn't exist – but do rationalise, prioritise and process it.

When I'm either meditating or using mindfulness as a technique to calm anxiety I think of my brain as being like a train station platform.

I visualise myself standing at Liverpool Street Station and trains are arriving and departing regularly. Metaphorically of course, these trains are thoughts. Like trains, we do not need to hop onto every thought that comes by us. As I sit there thinking of this train station, I can start to sift through the thoughts and choose which of them I just let go through until I find the train I want to get on board. On a train station platform waiting for your desired train to arrive, do you stand there with your eyes closed, hands over your ears pretending there are no trains whizzing past you? Of course not. You have your eyes and ears open as each train approaches and decide if that's the one for you. Some of those trains you let pass are not the ones you need today, but may be the ones you need tomorrow, but that's the beauty of facing them and taking the time to choose which needs your attention in this moment.

So, at the football match, what could the anxiety triggers be to ruin your good day? The journey home will be a nightmare after the final whistle? Well that's not now and nothing you can do or say or think or feel changes that right here. Next week I've got a test at school? That's not now, and that anxiety can only make right now worse, it isn't helpful and the test shall come around if you worry or not. What if I become anxious now, while I'm out of the house? Then you'd deal with it, using this technique or any/many others you have available to you. What if I get a headache and feel unwell so need to leave quickly? You don't, so thinking of it isn't preparation, it is anxiety. Preparation is good, but over preparation for every possibility is a control that will only cause anxiety long term.

As you can see with the above common examples of a good day becoming a bad good day, nearly everything that turns bad or feels so comes from our inability to simply connect with what we are doing – instead focusing on what could happen and looking as hard as we can to find something that is wrong or could be wrong. None of the examples mentioned in the paragraph above should make any difference towards your current enjoyment, but of course they do, if we do not treat those triggering thoughts properly. Think each of them through and establish whether the anxiety they are giving you is warranted, and you'll find that in that moment – they won't really be legitimately important and that you are making them important for no helpful reason.

Some days are obviously tough in what they entail. Some days are horribly difficult appointments, really stressful at work or school or a bad day with your partner or family, and those days all have ways of being approached.

But good days, days where we have something we are looking forward to, an activity we enjoy or a day that has become great as it's happened are not red flags for something bad. They do not need to be the start of something bad or the end of something good.

One great lesson to learn is how to approach these days using some of the steps above. Finding an acceptance of the good day even. Recognising the importance of simply just allowing yourself. If for you, a good day is sitting around in your pants whilst watching TV and making some horrendous food combinations that'll make your belly ache then let yourself, do not judge or guilt yourself into finding fault, then anxiety and then easing into the familiarisation of 'a bad day'. Take the good days for what they are worth and sprint with them. If you are in the middle of a day and realise 'well this is good!' that isn't a signal to start freaking out, that's a signal to start celebrating it. Do so by enjoying it to its fullest and find every little detail of that good day that you can. If you begin to wobble, do not hide. Do not stop completely and become as involved in what you are doing as you possibly can. Let the thoughts come and do not fear their presence, you know how to sort through them to remind yourself that every single 'reason' you have for today turning bad is not even a reason, it's a fear that you have the power and ability to discard. Good days do not just have to be about maintenance, they can even get better. That good day can be a great day.

# You Are Not Your Mental Illness

Identity plays such a huge role in all of our lives. How we see ourselves or how we feel the world sees us often dictates how we act and can often affect how we think, too. Suffering with a mental illness can feel like the most all-encompassing part of our lives. It can feel like it defines us and that it is who we are, it can feel like this mental illness IS us. Sometimes it can feel almost like a safety net, to identify so highly with the way we are due to our mental health conditions.

This is something you and I need to realise and appreciate is not fully the case. We are more than our mental health. We are more than a diagnosis and we are more than an illness.

Each and every one of us has our own identities and all of us are unique and wonderful and whole people in spite of our illnesses, not because of them. We may have learned a greater deal of empathy to others in adversity, but the brilliant people we are is us. The illness we have as a part of us is not.

Advice that I have really learned from in my twenties is to ensure I do not fall into the easy habit of revolving my world around my illness when I do not need to.

As a teenager I was absolutely guilty of being 'that kid with the OCD'. I didn't even see this as a negative really. It wasn't like I was playing the role for attention, it was certainly not that – but I saw I was different and knew others saw me as different so being the guy with OCD made it seem like people would understand me easier.

It meant I'd sometimes give a story of my condition that wasn't true just to save an awkward conversation but giving people an idea I was unwell at the same time. I vividly remember a meeting where I explained at one stage that I had OCD and when the person I was meeting admitted ignorance, I came back with 'it basically means I like my hands clean all the time'. I regret it so much now. The condition is so much more than that and the way it affected me was so much stronger than just 'liking' my hands to be clean. It was constant, horrendous intrusive thoughts and a complete disruption and destruction of my life. But I told the story that way because the identity factor became more important that the reality at the time.

There's a big difference to being honest enough about your mental health so that people know the parts of your condition you want them to know to it being the thing you accept as the most prominent part of you.

I think social media, for all of its many wonderful connections and opportunities it provides, can be the platform for people suffering with mental health issues to cover themselves in an identity that purely relates to their illness.

I'll often be contacted by people online whose whole profiles are centred on their mental health. They'll have thousands of followers, all of whom are in similar boats, and their whole timeline is focused on their condition. Now I am a massive advocate of peer support, as you'll read elsewhere in this book, but I urge you to be very considerate of how much time you're spending engrossed in social media when it comes to mental health.

I'm certainly not saying to not do it, nor am I suggesting when you need to that you should not take the opportunity to but do not sacrifice who you are for what you suffer from.

If you find your timeline, your streaming watch lists, your bookshelves and your mates are all linked by illness you may investing too much of your identity in what is ultimately a negative.

For those of you reading this that live with a chronic illness, mental or physical or both, there's every chance you're looking at me and thinking 'another person patronising me with how I see myself' and I understand that concern. There's nothing more condescending than telling a permanent wheelchair user that their disability shouldn't define them, for example. Of course it will if it is one of the most obvious facts in their decision making (or forced decisions) in their lives. Chronic illness is going to possibly be the biggest part of your life, but it's not your interests. It's not your passions, your goals, your loves. It plays a major role in all of these and I can appreciate that but the dangers of over identifying are clear. There is great contentment in being comfortable in who you are, and that includes your illnesses. But the importance of finding and enjoying the side of you that is not your illness is so vital to finding your own happiness.

Illness can feel like it is taking layers of you away. It can feel like it is making you lose yourself and the person you are and that is very difficult. But, remember you. Take the time to remember who you are. Remember who you were before this, or if you do not remember that time, remember who you are when things are good. Focus on this. Be what you like about yourself. If you are proud of your own creativity, be creative. Write. Paint. Tell stories. Make things. If you love being active, go outside. Swim, walk, run and play. If you're a musician, be a musician. Even if just for a short while, play the instrument, sing the song. Never ever let this become the biggest part of you as I can absolutely assure you, it does not need to be. When it has to be, nourish the parts of you that are not.

If you're reading this and thinking you've dealt with this for so long now that you don't remember who you really are exactly – you're the lucky ones. You get to find it out all over again. Make that your mission, find what you like and what you love and reignite your passions. Reclaim who you are. Find out, if you do not know. Actively choose to spend any moment of wellness indulging in you and the side of you that you like, not the part of you controlled by your diagnosis. You are not your mental illness.

# Why Learning To Filter Information Can Be The Key To Recovery

All of the information you need to reach mental wellness is already out there.

This theory is one I have long subscribed to. I didn't always believe this and on bad days sometimes I forget it, but I can tell you right now, it is true.
One of the scariest and most overawing aspects of developing or discovering a mental illness is the vast amount of information that is already out there on the subject and knowing what to believe or which advice to buy. In the digital world we live in you can be forgiven for being completely bowled over by this info and to sit there thinking 'Where do I start?!'
This book itself is another outlet, so that's a case in point. A valuable lesson you can learn, and this is possibly the most important tip in this book, is that learning to filter this vast array of information to you and your condition is the key to living the best life you can.
It is also a source of great hope. How wonderful is it to know that the keys to driving the car that is your own health are already out there? You just need to locate them.
Now here is the catch. Finding those keys is the hardest thing you may ever have to do.
A promise I made to myself before I began writing was that I would be positive, but honest. I want you to read this and be invigorated by the thought that everything you need to know is yours to discover. But I would never say it is easy, it certainly is not.
By the time I managed to enjoy life I had seen over 40 medical professionals and tried various evidence-backed therapies over many years. From GP's to psychologists, psychiatrists, diets, exercise regimes, mindfulness, alternative therapists – I'd tried the lot, I thought. I'd been on all manner of medications, most prescribed, some not – and with

limited success. My library was beginning to resemble that of a PhD student in their final year and I had clippings of so many different articles that my family thought I was taking up journalism. Then it happened.

I met two therapists, namely Pete Weiss and Dr Travis Osbourne that led me in a group ERP (Exposure Response Prevention) therapy and I started being receptive to what they were saying. I'd also never tried group therapy of this type before and it seemed to really work for me. Within a 10 day intensive residential therapy I came back with the tools to handle situations I couldn't handle before, but even more vitally the understanding that I could, and should, recognise the need to filter my own therapy.

By 'filtering' I am referring to the ability to learn and accept that you are unique and therefore your recovery and treatment is too. There are many 'educated guesses' in medicine but it is not an exact science because the test is always unfair as we are all different. An example being that group therapy is something that is highly successful for me in the right instance, but maybe it wouldn't be for you. This illuminates the need to never, ever give up on making yourself mentally healthy but also the vital need to be the captain of your own ship. Do not accept failure as the end of the line but as success not yet being reached.

Here is how I filtered this information for my own good; I realised that not all medication was helpful for me but that the one I was currently on did have a positive effect. Thus I had filtered that medication can be good, and this one works for me. I knew I benefitted from feeling like I was being understood and therefore knew group therapy was good for me. Thus I had filtered the type of therapy I felt would be most impactful and how it fitted for me personally. I then found a therapist that worked for me and thus filtered to a great therapist that I could have a good relationship with. The extra bonus part of all this is that if it doesn't work when you filter like this, you can try a whole other combination. You can change the medication, the therapy, the environment, the therapist. Each part of it can be changed (filtered) until you find the right fit. Think of it as unlocking a safe with a multi-number combination. If you just keep going, one day you'll get the door open.

What this combination theory means in practice is that it is absolutely likely that everything you need already exists. A therapist that works for you will already be working, the therapy that will be most beneficial already exists and the medication you may do well on is already in use. Add in the right other lifestyle choices and it's not a stretch to be confident everything is already out there for you. How exciting is that?!

Everything is difficult until we learn to do it. It took me 22 years to learn how to filter the advice and information being thrown at me and turn it into my recovery. But then for context, until I was 22 no one had actually taught me the importance of filtering, and in that sense, as soon as I was told – it took me a moment to take the first step on the road to being well rather than 22 years. That is how important I believe this to be.

Therapy is already a bit of a concept to get your head around. You are sat in a room with a complete stranger that you need to learn to trust but also someone you are about to tell things to that you've never told anyone. Sometimes you'll tell them things in the spur of the moment you've never even really told yourself. This can be daunting and they have an incredible responsibility to you. The whole purpose of this chapter comes into play in therapy as your honesty is the only way of unlocking the information you truly need. I'm not saying you should necessarily go in there and delve completely into your brain until you feel ready to, but it's important to understand that giving the right professionals the information they need will allow them to also filter information in a brilliantly effective way. It will allow them to realise what tools they need to provide you with to help you, and what tools of their own they need to use to aid this recovery.

Filtering information for you isn't simply good for your health, but good for your whole life in general. We can all relate to learning a skill and not knowing how to nail it, but then being given a simple formula to remember it or a new way of approaching it and all of a sudden it fits into place and just makes sense. You may revise for a GCSE by flash cards only. You may need little, quick nuggets of information that are easy to manage to remember what you need. You may not need to look at anything at all, you may need to listen to a recording of yourself reciting your revision for it to stick. Maybe you need to do practical experiments to remember. None of these ways are wrong, but I bet one of them is right. It's not often that we cannot, it is just often that we don't know how to yet. This is the crux of it for therapy and getting better. Maybe 99% of therapy and therapists will not be for you, but you only need one to pay off and you reclaim your life, or indeed start it.

Educators and scientists agree that we all learn, develop and mould in our own highly unique manner so why would this challenge be any different?

The sooner you stop looking at your recovery as only possible by one or two means, the sooner you can start finding the right outlets for you. If it doesn't work once, that doesn't mean it never will. That means it didn't work once. Try again.

There are so many means and methods of learning available to you, one of them will change your life. Never ever give up on this. Never ever give up on the potential of you and the absolute reality of your ability to find what is right for you.

# What I Wish My Students Knew

Ah, school! The best years of your life. It's just carefree fun, mucking about with your mates and enjoying the world growing with you. You get to learn and explore, find yourself, find your passions and make lifetime lasting friendships. We are challenged. Provoked. Inspired. Enthused. We are moulded into the people we are destined to be and we are on a one way rollercoaster to adulthood that is thrilling and laden with exciting, magical moments.

Except for many of us that's just not the case.
For some of us schooling becomes something very different to the idealistic version we are sold and when it isn't as we were promised it can be a pretty painful conclusion. Worse than that though is when those around you force upon you their own positive experience and invalidate your own as just not being true.
You may find yourself telling people you are not enjoying school and feeling frustrated when they dismiss this by telling you it is the 'best years of your life'. For many, it just isn't. It's worth remembering most of the time those that say this to you are simply trying to be a support even if they are just a bit awkward with it. But, it doesn't have to be this way.

I think there are two ways to look at enjoying school. Either you already do, and happy days, it can be a wonderful experience and hopefully you have that Hollywood experience of school we all hope for. If that's the case that will be a brilliant start before college or university or work, or whatever comes next for you. You'll go into that period energised and excited and hopefully with a developing support system of good mates.

If that does not sound like you though, the good news is that adult life is much more exciting. Some adults will say that the 'real world' is horrible in comparison to school but this one-size-fits-all approach to adolescence may not be true for you, just like it wasn't for me.

I wrote that this post-school period is more exciting and I truly believe that. You are bound by far less. When of school age you can rarely move schools with the same ability you may switch jobs as an adult. Your geographical world is far smaller. Your autonomy to make big decisions is more collectively led, usually by your family. I love the complexities and endless possibility of adult life. The ability to start over, reinvent and refurbish yourself, stand by your choices or go towards a goal or desire undeterred by any other person is an unparalleled luxury to that of school life. And we can eat chocolate for breakfast.

But if you're still in school, that doesn't mean we cannot turn around our educational career. We may never love school and may feel shackled by it, but we can definitely feel happier, safer and much more heard.

These books have three chapters aimed specifically at giving advice from both my personal experience living with a mental illness and the professional experiences of others. There is a chapter about support at work that has inputs from industry leaders ('What I Wish My Employees Knew'), there is a chapter on building a relationship with your therapist ('What I Wish My Patients Knew') and this chapter has some input from teaching and support professionals that has been the basis of putting together some hopefully helpful advice from the voices of teachers packaged as; 'What I Wish My Students Knew'.

To get a full picture of the things teachers and educational professionals wish their students knew about mental health support, I spoke to a good number of teachers, learning support assistants, sports coaches working in schools, SENCo's (Special Educational Needs Coordinators) and former educators. I am also going to give you some examples of interesting initiatives I have found along the way that hopefully give you some ideas about different means of accessing support as a student. Please note, just because these initiatives do not exist at your school, college or uni in their exact format here does not mean they cannot or will not in the future. If you can bring them up with the appropriate staff member there is definitely scope for change, there always is. If you, as the person most likely to benefit see a potentially brilliant way of working – bring it up.

One of the education professionals I spoke with was Sherelle Wedderburn, a Safeguarding Mentor at a London based school who gave me a brief overview of the way she and colleagues work with children at her primary school; *'In terms of what we do to encourage mental wellness – we partake in mindfulness at our school. We are currently training a staff member to be an internal counsellor at school. 3 members of staff have been on youth mental health first aid training so far.*
*When we have a child with a potential mental health condition we will often do a referral to CAMHS (Child & Adolescent Mental Health Service) for a more specialist service. We continue support by having regular meetings with the professionals involved. We also have regular mentoring sessions with children.*
*Waiting times for mental health services need to be improved. We need more services to support parents with how to cope with a child with mental health concerns.*
*Many parents still have a negative perspective about mental health and use negative language towards children, which impacts their self-esteem.*
*Mental health is finally being recognised in schools and children are being diagnosed from a younger age so if affects all of us. We still need to do more to remove the stigma'*

These books do not have a particularly focused target age group but I'm aware this is probably a book that will most resonate with the 14-35 age demographic for those living with a mental health condition and 35+ ages for those supporting.
Including examples of primary age support may seem a little redundant. However, I think

they are important to include as educational establishments do have an expanding approach to supporting those living with a condition, that, although important to be tailored to the age group, do have similarities throughout. I'll explain why, but firstly here is a great insight into secondary school support from one of my former English teachers, Kristy Mee. And she must be good. I've only gone and written a book.

A course tutor for trainee and newly qualified teachers and a current secondary school teacher, I asked Ms Mee to give some examples from her present school and some advice for young people accessing support in secondary education gleamed from her already acclaimed career;

*'At my current school, we employ a counsellor (and lots of schools do now) who has 1:1 sessions with those most in need, and also drop in sessions once a week. To access 1:1 students are usually referred by their tutor or head of year.*

*For me, I tell my students the door is always open and I try to ensure I've forged a relationship with all of them quickly, so that they know it's true (I remember a little 14 year old who would often pop in to my office many years ago*...). As a teacher, I think we learn to read people (not all teachers do- some could be better at empathy!) and the student that takes a little longer than everyone else packing away, or who seems a bit quieter than usual are the ones I'm going to say 'are you okay, fancy a chat?' to. However, for safeguarding purposes, I always have to say I can't promise I won't need to tell someone else. It's nothing innovative, but it's human and that's what I believe helps.*

*For me personally, it's about reading people. Most teachers see their tutor group every single day first thing. If things are happening at home I can tell from how they are as they enter school. Often we are the bridge between home and school so a little empathy goes a long way. Again this is only my personal ethos, but it's about never being too busy to find time for someone and making them feel valued.'*

*It's not an M Night Shyamalan worthy twist to point out that 14 year old was me. One of the reasons I was keen to ask Kristy (Yeah I can say that now, I'm 29. Deal with it) to contribute was that I always found her approach to just be incredibly human. I had a vast amount of need at that age and this was the period my life became untenably difficult and

she played a key role in my first experiences of talking openly with a teacher. Not by offering me the world, but by offering me two ears.
(As an important aside, at this stage I was wearing £30 NHS glasses, had slug-like eyebrows, the physique of an 87 year old woman named Ethel and a haircut that looked like a background Sims character. Not a good time. I did not get Valentines cards. Still angry about it.)

A great point is made in this testimony and one that I think is important for you to realise, and I hope is of some comfort. The most important things to access are not the most innovative, they are often the most simple.

We are seeing a vast range of initiatives ushered in that are often borne from technological developments. These include therapy and meditation apps, video chat group support, VR (Virtual Reality) for exposure therapy resources and online share platforms for keeping in touch with supporters but the crux of it is; these are just new ways of helping us access traditional, evidence-based forms of support.
Our schools and universities can spend as much money and time as they can on redesigning the wheel and we are definitely creating a great many new and interesting tools and resources for supporting mental wellness, but do remember that no matter where you are and the schools you are in, support is available. These initiatives can greatly increase access to this support and that is to be respected and applauded and I welcome these changes, but do not feel that you will always be left behind if your school is a bit more traditional. These examples are simply modern variations of traditional good practice.

At further education level we have a lot of ways of accessing help. I am yet to find a university that does not have some sort of (often free) counselling service available for students. There are student led services available at many institutions for those that may feel more comfortable speaking with a peer in the first instance and organisations like the Student Minds charity offer a range of workshops and courses that can provide support.

Look After Your Mate is a 2-3 hour interactive course led by the Student Minds Charity and is for those that are supporting someone with a mental health problem and/or those seeking advice for themselves on accessing university support and the different options available to you. They also run a Mental Health In Sport workshop that is specifically for teams (or individuals) participating in university sport. This is a great way of having a group discussion about mental health and if you are involved in Uni sport, definitely get in touch with them to see if they are able to offer guidance.

As with 'reasonable adjustments' in the workplace, students are able to access these in their learning and the way they access their education. This could include extra time and rest breaks in exams or extensions on deadlines. If you have a diagnosis officially or not, you may well have specific options available to you designed to remove barriers to study. There is also a Disabled Students Allowance (DSA) that is available to full and part time students, in addition to your student finance, that is there to cover extra study related costs that you may incur due to your mental health condition. This is not a loan and does not need to be repaid.

The University of Portsmouth has a 'What'sUp' phone app, where students can access wellbeing and emotional health support from their own Student Wellbeing Service, and the same school has an award winning 'Welcome Ambassadors' scheme in place for new students to connect with experienced students to help the transition into uni life for undergraduates.

Universities UK is 'the collective voice of 136 universities in England, Scotland, Wales and Northern Ireland'. They have developed a 'Whole University Approach' which exists to marry the approaches used to 'transform cultures and embed mental health initiatives beyond student services'.

Using a four part model of community (involving both students and staff in all aspects of improvement), learning (the way itself students learn), living (the way we exist in our social, physical and digital environments) and support (the services provided, their review and improvement and advice on other issues including finance/housing). This may not seem relevant to you but hopefully illustrates that educational establishments are definitely now thinking beyond just grades and how to get to grades. This shows the whole, rounded approaches to student wellbeing that will be an important part of modern day education going into the future.

As with my interview with Sherelle and the many other primary school staff I spoke with, it is now clear to pretty much everyone that what was once considered 'a senior school problem' (i.e mental health issues) is now understood to be something teachers and educational staff will be first responders to in earlier settings. Not so long ago even secondary school ages were thought of as being too young to really experience acute and chronic mental health problems and thankfully we are beyond that now.

The expanding approach I spoke of previously is the way that, although we may have more options available at university level than we do at primary school level to support mental health, as conditions often become more complex/those living with them become experienced enough to understand themselves better, the basics of how we support are actually fairly similar.

The way teaching staff and school staff can support you does not need to be groundbreaking. Consistency and quality counts for far more than innovation, but if initiative is what we are looking for then that is chiefly a concern for institutions, we need educators to focus on being open, transparent and informed.

The importance of supporting the whole person and not just 'the student' is a must if educators are going to make education safe, inclusive and even possible for all.

This chapter goes to show that although there are a diverse amount of initiatives available and many modern and exciting ranges of services coming into everyday student life that I hope has been interesting and helpful to you, the real and human relationships we can form with our teachers and support staff can be the catalyst for staying well in school.

I've put together some tips that I hope will help that is developed from speaking with teaching and support staff directly. Here are some of the most common things teachers tell me that they wish their students knew;

**'If I don't know how to help you myself, I'll know someone that does'** – Teachers have an immensely broad spectrum of responsibility and with the hours and workloads thrust upon them, I think they are real heroes. A common theme from my interviews was that teachers tried to make sure they knew their limits. With more pastoral support coming into schools in the 21st century, secondary and further education teaching staff told me often of how they may not be able to support further than 'just' listening – but it's highly likely they can signpost you to someone that can.

**'I'd like to know as much as you allow, to help me teach you'** – I heard from many that feel like they would benefit from knowing a little more. Not necessarily a full blown counselling session but enough to know when things are good or bad. I had suggestions from teachers to maybe even check in by a quick email to say the week is particularly bad or good so that they can adjust accordingly for this. Some teachers spoke of the times they had marked students down believing they were not working hard enough but the reality was that they were debilitated by mental health symptoms.

**'Students tend to do better when they help or lead the conversation on their own health'** – Obviously when you are struggling it can be so difficult to be motivated or able to discuss your needs, but the general consensus here was that if a meeting is arranged to discuss your schooling and any actions that may need to be taken to support you, having you involved is a big plus. Also, giving timely feedback on the changes, or the practices that are already good, can be a helpful note for assisting your support. If a change has come in to help you and isn't, but you know something that may, speak up. You are the expert on you.

**'Your first point of contact doesn't have to be me, in most cases you can choose'** – As I've discussed, positive and mutually beneficial relationships being fostered provides an excellent launch pad for guarding you and making sure the support you are receiving is good enough. If you and your tutor do not have this relationship but you do have it with another member of staff, speak with them and ask if it may be possible that they act as your point of contact for school support. Some teachers may feel comfortable leading this and being very hands on, and some may accept this but ask to be a messenger to those that can help further.

**'Don't underestimate the little things that can help'** – Secondary school teachers in particular advocated, quite rightly, the benefits of doing the basics right, when possible. For some people this can mean getting to class early to reduce anxiety, asking for coursework help early enough that something can be done to help, eating and drinking right at school, being prepared for every class of the day to reduce stress, sleeping earlier the night before a big school day. As with many tips people will give you on supporting your own mental health, these may seem small and insignificant but they do add up.

**'Peer support is a really successful way of keeping you mentally healthy in school'** – We know the importance of community and understanding and we know the downfalls of isolation so developing the right peer support can be a vital advantage in keeping you feeling well and healthy at school. People do lose people when they live with a mental illness so readdressing this can make a really strong outlet become available again. Teachers may be able to support this with access to clubs or community events that are of interest to you.

As is the case with mental health and life in general, no one has the same school story. Some people have periods they do well and excel academically and (more importantly) in their health, and periods when this is not the case.
It may be that you loved primary school but hate high school or it may be that school was never enjoyable for you but university is the best time of your life.

Do not judge your journey by anyone else's. If you are in a time in your life where you feel like you should be enjoying yourself more but you really are not, that is a totally valid position. The way you can be supported will change throughout your education but we are in a place now in the UK in 2019 where support is available everywhere. Some areas have underperforming or unavailable support services that would accelerate your positive wellbeing, but where there are people, there are supporters. I can guarantee you, no matter how much support you currently receive, be it none at all or an extensive network of support options – more can be done, more can be improved and your current position can develop into something more manageable for you. Just because it has not been good to date, or not as good as you would have liked, does not mean it will be this way forever.

# When Things Go Wrong In Public

If you're like me, this is probably one of your biggest fears of them all.

Also like me, you've probably had to experience it. If so, it's something we can agree isn't something you'd like to be repeated!
Having an anxiety attack or the feeling of potentially having one was one of the first big hurdles I had to overcome in order to establish normality back into my life. I think back to being 14 (this being the period in my life anxiety was most actively an issue for me) and how it all centred around entrapment.
By entrapment I mean the feeling or knowledge that I am unable to easily or immediately escape the current situation I am in should anything right now go wrong or I start to feel unwell. This can range from the obvious things like being in an exam, a job interview, being in a sports game or on stage etc., the sort of places you can't normally quickly leave – to a more all-round feeling of entrapment that may be along the lines of 'my room is my safe place but I am out now and I cannot be there for several hours now'. Both are feelings of entrapment. Being the age I was mine had a lot to do with being at school and feeling 'stuck'. I would hyperventilate worrying about hyperventilating in front of my school mates! It was constant and all-encompassing and one of the most difficult periods of my life.

Two things occurred to me during that period that changed the game for me. Firstly, my sheer panic about the potential of panicking resulted in; more panic. I soon realised that anxiety is a physiologically good thing for us – it's important to us as animals to experience anxiety so that we can appreciate where and when danger occurs. We feel worry in situations we know to be unsafe and that worry is what keeps us safe, a lot of the time. So really, anxiety is here as a protector. The difference with you and I and those that do not have issues with anxiety is that our anxiety levels progress beyond what we need to have to function, to what we do not need and that is where the issue becomes so and makes us unwell. I realised that I am not alone with this. Not by a long way. In fact, I realised this feeling is something that pretty much every person on earth can relate to in some way. So I stopped keeping it secret and I started being honest when I felt rough and the reaction was overwhelmingly positive. The reason for such a positive reaction was the basis of my second realisation – people are by nature, good.

No one likes being unwell or going through a difficult patch but one of the only positives of these things is that every single human on the planet can relate to that of the world crashing down around us. And that is very much what a bad panic attack can feel like. But, people want to help people. There are stories every day in the media of the bad side of people but the reason this is news is because it is so much rarer than acts of kindness, generosity and charity. Try to remember that if worst came to very worst and you did have a full blown anxiety attack in public (rarer than you think). If this happens, you'll see that people's reactions will be to either to ignore it or offer to help, that's it. That's all that will happen. So either you are left in peace or you are supported in a lovely way. Do not fear people's reactions to this situation. Imagine the shoe was on the other foot and someone fell and hurt themselves in front of you, I can bet with some certainty you would not walk on and ignore them, you'd simply offer a hand. Equally, if they fell, hurt themselves but were able to get up and go and sit somewhere comfortably, you'd possibly leave them to it as they are all OK. That's exactly what would happen in return to you, people would either give you your space or help if needed. So there is always a safety net in public – if anything, it's the place to be when you're not feeling great! So please, please do not let this fear ever stop you from going out, you'd be wrong to do so.

# Why You Should Do That Thing Right Now

Procrastination is something we can all identify with. We all have a little perma-list in our head of things we'd like to try or need to do but that has been sitting in our in tray for a long time. Often they'll be a goal of some kind. Maybe to write a book? (It's easy, just start!) Maybe it is to go and change banks for the better deal or maybe to arrange that mate date you've been putting off. Adult friendship is basically a series of bumping into old friends and saying 'we absolutely must do something soon!' for about 60 years until one of you dies.

Sometimes they'll be practical life admin procrastinations, to take the letter to be posted, grab the bin bags you need, take the book back to the library. That sort of thing. And sometimes it'll be 'book that appointment with the Doctor'.

One of mine is Gaelic football, of all things! As someone that grew up playing football and loving rugby, I've always taken an interest in the frantic sport loved by the Irish and thought 'I fancy that, I'll try that this year'. I think the first year I said that was around 2008. Still haven't. So I get it.

Everyone delays things. There are millions of excuses we tell ourselves as to why we haven't done it yet and they are mostly, let's be honest, rubbish. Even reading this I'm sure you're thinking of one of yours. It's just human nature. But it is also something we can shake off.

A big reason why we do not do something is that we know we won't like it or that it'll feel scary or nerve-wracking so we avoid it as we just know we're setting ourselves up for a fall. But again, this is rubbish. We have no idea how it'll feel.

One of the biggest life lessons I have learnt so far is that; nothing feels as you imagine it will. Nothing. We put into our heads how something is going to be and invariably it never is. It happens every day – people freak out about going to the dentist and leave afterwards thinking 'why did I wait so long?!' or worry endlessly about having to speak in public and afterwards recall feelings of enjoyment and pride, or maybe a phone call they've been worried about making and then after hanging up they realise it was nothing like they imagined. I'm certainly not saying some of these things will not feel negative or difficult, of course some will, but I guarantee if you're putting something off through fear – you've made it worse in your head than it ever will. Our creativity as humans knows no bounds when it comes to petrifying us beyond acting on things.

I think this is a really important point for you if you have just discovered or been diagnosed with a mental health problem, or if you've had one with little progression for a long time. As much as there are incredible people, charities and organisations in existence to help bridge these issues and make things easier for you the fact of the matter is some or a lot of what you need ultimately needs to be led by you.

I hear from people all the time that tell me they are planning on pushing their GP for more access to therapy. They'll tell me how they feel ready for it and how as soon as they get a free moment they'll be calling up to make an appointment. Well, that free moment is now. If they tell me this in person I always offer them my phone to call. There really is no time like the present. Right now reading this, if you are planning on calling your Doctor or scheduling an appointment with a therapist or emailing your teacher to discuss your mental health, do it right now. Put this book down and do yourself a favour you'll be thankful for in the future. I guarantee as soon as you put the phone down or click send you'll realise it felt nowhere near as hard as you thought or feels nothing at all as you imagined it would be. Take this advice (from yourself!) with you. Nothing feels like you expect it will, so do not let fear of the unknown stop you from doing the things you know you need to do.

I may not yet have tried Gaelic football, but I did make that appointment with my Doctor. And now you're reading my book about recovery.

# BE BETTER THAN EVERYONE ELSE

Capitals for effect, of course.

A peculiar side effect of the fast and furious nature of everyday life in the modern age is the almost reckless obsession with living better than other people. Chasing our own tails, bossing our lives, lapping ourselves in a race of progression. Social media and shortened attention spans have led to the viral sharing of quick videos by inspirational speakers aimed at giving you the shot in the arm you think you need that has the subtlety of a brick in the face.

The rise and rise of this 'top 1%' way of living will often show a shouty man on stage, mic dangling by his ear, foaming at the mouth as he tells you that you MUST. WORK. HARDER. You must be stronger. You must be better. It gets your blood pumping and your pupils dilating. You puff your chest out and get focused and you reap the rewards of nodding along to their message of extreme focus and sign on the dotted line to live your life this way from now on! Always. Forever. And then, y'know, we just carry on with our lives.

Motivation has to have substance and content beyond being simply good oratory skills to actually be productive. Imagine a computer game with great graphics but no story. You'll want to play it, but when you do the enjoyment is nothing more than what you see. It's a dead end.

A wonderful politician is one that goes out and achieves things, a famous one is one that stands up and shouts about achieving them. There's a difference between creating desire and creating actions. I don't mean for this chapter to be deemed to be aimed at the likes of Tony Robbins and Eric Thomas, speakers that have developed huge followings internationally for their words and wisdoms and absolutely no doubt helped many people. They have a place and for many of you they may provide some real positivity, but if so, this chapter isn't really for you.

My cautionary tale is to those of you that see these videos and posts being shared around the world and feel the obvious and often crushing pang of 'but I can't be like that'.

The tricky thing about cosmetic motivation of this type is that it is fleeting and exclusive over inclusive. It invites you in but tells you that if you don't subscribe to this methodology that you just do not want it enough. You're not committed enough to success or change. That's a negative outlook that I totally reject. Telling you that you do not want it enough is not the same as you actually not wanting it enough. We all want to improve, but our paces and methods greatly vary.

Sadly for human productivity motivation is a fleeting occurrence. It is a bright light that flashes in front of us and draws us in but ultimately it passes, so we need to gather as much good from its presence as we can in the short time we have it.

I'd take being methodical over being motivated every day of the week. Of course we need motivation to help us do and achieve a plan but the true rewards come from when we turn habit into lifestyle and that is achieved in a much calmer fashion than some of our modern day prophets would lead you to believe. It is when we approach our goal with a clear and concise mind that we create the lifestyle that results in our successes in achieving the lives we wish to have.

I'd love to be built like Mark Wahlberg. Obviously I would. He is basically godly. I'm pretty sure he was sculpted. But what would I rather, a personal trainer that can motivate me to achieve the one single greatest workout of my life? Or one that can motivate me to change my life to make my workouts count for more than just today? That's the message we need to remember. We need to try to be consistent to really go where we want to go. The 'get-rich-quick' level of incentive allows no manoeuvrability for human error or the days we fail (and we will), whereas the 'investment' level of inspiration, maybe less flashy and glamourous, is something more realistic that understands we will have highs and lows and how hard we work isn't necessarily the ultimate decider in how successful we are. It gives us something to turn into consistency which becomes habit which becomes lifestyle. If this sounds like buzzwords, please do go back over the point here. Those working in finance will tell you there's money to be made in quick turnaround investment, but they'll advise you the real money and the longevity derives from calculated long term investment.

A boxer may spend the hours leading up to a title bout listening to music to pump her up, she may be bouncing off the walls inside her changing room and she may well explode into the stadium as her ring music blares out and her arrival is signified by the brash and unforgiving chorus of fireworks surrounding her walk into battle. But before those hours, she was training for months. With purpose. With a plan. Do not be fooled into thinking a change of mindset and a big loud exclamation that 'I will achieve!' is all you need, it may be the first thing you need, but success comes from following that up.

If you're able to enjoy and gain from this inspirational content then as long as it is supporting something lasting and envelopes itself into something more substantial than just the fleeting high of motivation – great stuff. But for many people, these things can be a huge knock on confidence.

If you're living with depression, these widely shared examples of extreme passion can be a constant and popular reminder that you cannot currently live like this. Please do not take this feeling as a lack of dedication or let something aimed at building you up simply knock you down.

To need a calmer influence towards inspiration to take action is not weakness. Some people stand on the edge of the cliff and jump into the water after beating their chest for a few minutes and screaming into the ocean. Some people find the courage in allowing themselves to enjoy a few moments of calmness and serenity. Some need a mixture of both. None of these are the right way, they are all just a way.

Even in this book I write with a passion that I hope cajoles you into taking action, but I do so in the hope and aim that the actions you take are purposeful and with reason.

If you can relate to this and find these populist content creators anxiety inducing, remember, they are not talking to you or for you. You are not their audience and that is absolutely OK. There is no set way to achieve mental wellness and your inability or reluctance to sign up to their programmes is not evidence or a lack of commitment, it is simply a reminder that you are using or searching for your own programme.

# Dating With A Mental Illness

As a single man, never married, never engaged and someone that probably should start considering collecting an unreasonable amount of dogs – I think I'm qualified to bring you a chapter on dating.

In a book that openly and unashamedly discusses mental health I must confess that I think people that enjoy dating are by and large absolute nutters.

It's a minefield at the best of times. What to say? What to do? When do I tell her I watched Star Wars in the cinema 5 times? What if she likes Coldplay? The list of questions we have running through our brains can make us insecure and confused, but throw in a mix of a mental health condition and those questions start to become more anxiety inducing.

Let's get the facts out of the way. It is believed that 1 in 4 of us will experience mental illness in our lifetimes, therefore you've got a pretty good chance of dating someone that either has an intimate knowledge of mental illness personally, or secondary experience due to being around people close to them living with it. That's a good start.

Already this means that in 2019 our dinner table date conversations are able to be far more open and honest than our grandparent's generation enjoyed. Taboos and stigma are still unacceptably available in society, but the odds are now firmly stacked in our favour that the person we go to Nandos with will most likely not find the state of our mental health being imperfect a completely unfathomable thought. They may not fully get it, but they'll likely accept and respect it.

Because I've sought to use this book as a way of relating what you're going through to what I've been through it's only right that I give you a story from my illustrious dating career, but believe me –I'd much rather not share.

Anyway, I was in Finland and dating a really brilliant young lady who was one of life's real sweethearts. She was kind, funny, intelligent and understanding and pretty much the ideal

person to discuss this sort of thing with. Back then I was far more uncomfortable with myself than I am now and would avoid telling anyone I dated of my condition unless I absolutely had to so to this point she thought I was a little odd and quirky but didn't realise she was seeing the physical symptoms of my mental illness rather than displays of personality. I think she just thought I was a bit edgy. Or at least that's what I tell myself.
6 weeks or so into dating her I suggested we visit a local pub that was known for being quite classy and cool. I'd never been in but a few friends had and they said this was an ideal date venue so we got dressed up and headed to this little place just outside town.
It was a gorgeous midsummers evening and I was out with this beautiful girl and the whole evening ahead of us. We parked up and walked a little through the sea of trees and embraced the stereotypically stunning Scandinavian landscape, greeted the doorman who welcomed us warmly and made our way to the entrance.
Shit. Tiles. Fucking square tiles. 'Wow!' she said. 'It looks amazing in here tonight' as I stood, frozen, transfixed.

'Where shall we sit?' I ignored.
4-5-6-7-8. 'Anywhere', I pleaded. '5-6-7….8'.
'Ok, let's walk to the window'
'No, here' I demanded. '1, 2, 3'

Within a few minutes of this exchange and me physically saying those numbers as quietly as my voice would allow, we took our seat. I was sweating like Donald Trump at a feminist rally and my normally confident and assured voice now scratched and separated. My date shirt became a bad choice as it restricted my breathing and my heart thudded so loudly in my chest I made eye contact with everyone around me convinced they'd be hearing it. I was a complete mess.
At that time my OCD was transfixed on counting to the number 8 in different variables. My condition was unchallenged at the time as I wasn't engaged in therapy and I had discarded my mind's advice to seek help and was paying the price. If you do not know how OCD works, I didn't want to count this way. I felt I needed to, or something terrible

would happen. We'd crash the car. I'd get sick from the cutlery in the pub. I'd rape her. I'd kill someone. I'd become a terrorist. Obviously none of these thoughts were logical, but OCD is an illogical mistress and tends to pick on you with the things you would LEAST like to happen. I 'knew' I had to do the compulsions and count my steps in the way I did or one of these things would happen, however morally or logistically unlikely. The whole experience was messy. We left the venue after a very quiet, very sad evening and on the way home she pulled up facing a lake. We sat in silence for a moment before she asked me what on earth had happened and I broke down explaining. I had chosen my time to tell her all wrong. She completely understood, that was the worst part. I'd gone through all of that worried by what she'd think and she didn't even flinch. I could have had that evening and simply said I needed to leave for a moment and enjoyed her calm understanding, but I'd got it totally wrong here.

So what we've learned is, be honest right away and it avoids all embarrassment down the line, correct? Sadly, nope.

Let's talk about Sarah. We'll call her that because, well, that's her actual name.

She was a little different to the girls I'd been out with so far, she was a touch quieter and I found her super sweet and pretty and somehow convinced her to go out with me, so we arranged to go to an Irish pub near home. (Note; I do take dates to more places than just local pubs).

We had such a good evening and I felt like James Bond when we kissed on the first date. Admittedly, that last sentence could have made me sound cooler but it's too late now and it's already printed. We laughed all night, it was so easy talking to her and I remember feeling perfectly calm and relaxed around her. She was as sweet as I thought and it was one of the best first dates I've ever had. I suggested we drop by the café near the canal (see, not just pubs) and sit outside with a hot chocolate. The conversation flowed and we were already discussing a second date and ribbing each other a bit in that flirtatious tone we all know.

I vividly recall thinking to myself 'just tell her now, she's cool'. I really wanted to tell her about my mental health because she was so warm and genuine I knew she'd not be fazed. She brought up a celebrity that had that week been discussing their mental health on the

*Jonathan Ross* show and I saw the opportunity to let her now I could relate, 'because…'

And then I told her. I spent two minutes explaining how I felt and how my mental health is and she listened keenly and honestly. I felt much better and knew this was the right choice. I made some joke about how as I'd brought the tone down I ought to buy her another marshmallow hot chocolate to bring the fun feeling back and she laughed.

I went inside, ordered our drinks and made small talk with the cashier as I waited to pick up my overpriced but quite delicious round of drinks. I turned around and my heart sunk. She was gone.

Obviously, this was horrendously embarrassing and one of those moments in life you simply do not know what to do. I sat down, messed around on my phone for a minute and did a little fake call pretending I was on the phone to her for anyone that witnessed this and drunk up quickly and darted home.

On the way home I was triggered and anxious and looking for answers. She didn't text me or call me and I resisted the urge to contact her as I debriefed in my head why this had gone wrong.

It wasn't really until the next day and I was out of the adrenaline rush and excitement of a date and in sobering reality that I took in that what I'd put on her, 90 minutes into our first ever date, and the weight I'd unloaded all in one go.

As I say above, she was a really lovely lady and we really did have a really good time but I put her in a really uncomfortable situation that inevitably taught me a great deal in the long run.

My prediction that she was someone that would have been comfortable with my mental illness wasn't an incorrect one – it was a premature one.

If you think to the people in your life you love most and the big things they know about you that your everyday acquaintance does not, those closest to you know more about you simply because they have a longer lasting, stronger, experienced relationship with you. If I had timed it right, she would have asked me questions or simply told me she was grateful I was honest but I gave her an all or nothing, almost an ultimatum.

What my 'confession' essentially did was say to her 'this is me, take me as this or do not take me at all' and that is a completely courageous and correct stance to take with the people we choose to share our lives with. But that was unfair of me. Are we clear and truthful about everything about us early on in relationships? No. Do we discuss exes in detail with vulnerability? Not at all. Do we have serious conversations on when we want children and what their names will be over our first meal with a Tinder date? Probably not seriously. Do we cry and hold the person we are enjoying a first romantic outing with whilst we explain the bereavement of our childhood that set the tone of our formative years? Nah, we don't. We pick and choose what to say to present the version of ourselves we want them to see today, not the one we want them to see when we're 80.

My suggestion here is to take your time. Choose to invest your past with someone only when you feel like the present is already invested together. Think of it as going hand in hand with the status of the relationship and not in how you feel in the moment. If you're going on your first date, that's a fair time to tell the other person you're allergic to fish before a seafood restaurant meal, of course. If you're on your third date and you're planning to spend a year travelling in Australia, that's time to mention this may not be a long term thing. That's some information on the same level as the relationship is itself. If you've been going out for two years and your tenancy is up, that's possibly a fair time to discuss living together. If you're getting engaged soon, you can certainly talk about children together in the future. But if you mix them up, the pressure of the conversation isn't relevant to the situation.

Mix those up and see what I mean. Would you discuss moving in together on that fifth date for example? Probably not successfully. Would you only talk for the first time about possibly spending a year abroad on your own just before you become engaged? Not if you want the relationship to last. The conversation isn't the problem, the timing is.

It's obviously not an exact science but I think giving it at least five dates is about right. For some conditions that present themselves publicly or that are accompanied by triggers that will be obvious and regular, you may need or be forced to discuss it earlier. If that is the case, I think explaining the practicalities of what you need are more important at this point than what you feel or too much into the 'why'. Being open and honest about how we feel is paramount to recovery, vital even. But choosing when to be honest is a lot better than choosing to not be honest at all, and choosing to pick a time to be honest to be realistic to the situation you are in is not the same as being untruthful.

So be practical. If you've not yet discussed your mental health fully and food is an issue, tell them you want a more interactive date. If you shouldn't be around alcohol it is OK to suggest the cinema rather than the pub. It they want to see a film with themes you feel are going to find triggering, explain they may be triggering for you without needing to delve deeper is completely enough of an admission.

As with the Coming Out chapter, your story is your own and the way you telling it is for you to choose. You may lose the wrong people by your honesty, but you'll also keep the right ones with it.

# From Now On

These three little words have the potential to be the three biggest words in your vocabulary.

Together they become more than a statement. They become a commitment. A call to action. An agreement of change. An adoption of the necessary. A signal of intent. A line in the sand. The first steps in your marathon.

We, as humans, possess great personal and collective power to mould our worlds. We are able to design and create everything around us and we are free to make choices that affect the way we see all that surrounds us.

Look back at each stage of your life – no matter how old or young you are, and you can probably see some very clearly defined chapters.

Some of these chapters in our lives happen upon us. People leaving our lives, ageing, adversity to those around us. Circumstance or environment forces significant change in our lives and makes a period of our lives become defined in a certain way that wouldn't necessarily be our choosing but nonetheless has become so. This period right now may be your bad period. It may be your recovery period. It will probably look different when you look back to how it looks today.

The most exhilarating changes are the ones we choose to make and do so for ourselves. The times we make active choices and put the things in place to make these changes meaningful and when a thought becomes an action and an action becomes a change and one we can truly see and feel, it is one hell of a feeling. Think of a time you have done this and the domino effect from it. It probably began with a declaration of 'I'm going to try'. You may have one day thought; 'I have no GCSE's, but I want a degree so I can teach. I'm going to call the Open University'. That is making an active choice from a thought (going to university) and putting things in place (getting in contact with them) that will one day allow you meaningful change (a degree, a teaching job, accomplishment etc.).

This is a luxury in life and choosing to change the way we see things or the way we do things, be they in big ways or small ways, is something afforded to each of us. Sometimes we can change the way we do things, and for the things we cannot change, we can change the way we view them. That is an incredibly freeing thought to me.

I've always been comforted by the ability of personal reinvention. When I look back at the chapters of my own life I can quite clearly see several versions of myself, all based on the stage of life I was at the time.

Carefree infancy, getting unwell, sport, losing a sibling, anxiety taking hold, living abroad, first love, homelessness, therapy. They all seemed to fit, in hindsight, together. The real prize here though is knowing when to redefine it yourself.

There's a certain romance to starting over. We grow up on films and books where the key characters are undergoing some huge coming of age and changing, often with challenging experience, for the better.

Our own lives do not quite work like the movies, they are far more unpredictable and infinitely more magical than that. Practically speaking, having the understanding and confidence to allow yourself to accept 'from now on' as a powerful **choice** you can make whenever you need to offers you an immense amount of real, and practical, control.

I do not see this as just a way of thinking. As a way of thinking it is certainly lovely and airy and easy and calm and all that, but it's the actions that can come with it that have the true, meaningful effect on our lives.

When I was trying to become well, my biggest issue was being tied down by baggage and everything behind me. I couldn't see anything in front of me as all I was doing was focusing on everything from before. That which gets us to today is the process that made us who we are today and therefore has relevance, but it certainly does not need to be what makes our tomorrow.

It is about accepting that just because you WAS, does not mean that you ARE.
Just because you've 'never been one to talk', 'not the sort that opens up', 'not one for therapy' does not mean that you cannot stop and say 'well, from now on, I am'. You do not need to stop yourself, avoid potentially great choices and opportunities and live as you always have 'just because'. There is no need.

I do this with my attitude all the time. If I'm in a bit of a mood and feel myself being rude or dismissive or just generally negative I like to stop myself and say it is time to be positive, from now on. Then I judge myself from that moment onwards. I do not say 'well, I was negative earlier today, so I can't be positive now'. I accept I can change right away, so I do. I do not let what came before taint how I deal with what is coming.

Of course, just saying so isn't good enough either. We all know actions speak louder than words so living by the process of 'from now on' only works if you commit to what it actually means.
An example of this; in 2013 I used the words in a different way when I told those around me that I promised to seek help for addiction. Saying the words meant a lot to many people, but they only began to mean anything at all when I began to actually do what they meant. I said that 'from now on I will live healthier' and I stood by it. I said the words AND made the change. The words without the actions are simply talking.
Sometimes, as is particular with addiction, my words fell down and I relapsed. But that did not mean it was all over and that I couldn't once again stand up and say 'from now on'. Then, shortly after, my 'from now on' came true and to this day I have stood by that.

You can do this. And you can do this unashamedly. As the quote preaches, 'it's not about how many times you get hit. It's about how many times you get hit and keep on going'. You do not need to feel bad for having to start again with something. Nor if you start again twice. Or a hundred times. We all need to do this from time to time.
If you've been keeping a promise to yourself to eat right to be healthier and then have a day of eating rubbish, that doesn't mean everything is ruined and the good work from

before goes out the window. It just means you start again with it. You can say 'from now on'. It is not a case of shying away from accountability and pretending the past or mistakes we have made or people we once were no longer means anything, but it is a way of accepting that there is no bad time to start doing right by yourself.

If you're looking at your life now and thinking; 'therapy/health/trying/friends/careers would never work for me' – have the courage to know that maybe that has been true until today, but you can always choose to say that absolutely it can work for you from now on. As of now you are actively choosing to wish for better for yourself.

# The Media

It is believed that currently people are consuming around 10hours per day on average worth of media on various different platforms. From social media to news outlets via our smartphones, laptops and tablets we are taking in so much more information than we ever have before. We are taking in more information in this way than we are spending sleeping, on average.

The media plays a humungous role in the eradication or introduction of stigma towards mental illness and to those living with a condition. It is an industry that has an immense power to provide great influence towards the way the public views mental health.

Certain media outlets have made some wonderful programmes to raise awareness, which is absolutely fantastic. But some are so far wide of the mark it is almost painful viewing.

Every day, at least one of the major national newspapers or one of the leading television channels will have a large feature that is mental health based. This is a massive turnaround in the past decade and is very welcome towards finally securing those of us suffering with mental health conditions a platform to truly and forcefully have our opinions heard and our needs met. However, there is such a thing as bad publicity.

More often than I'd like I'll be sent an article that completely misrepresents an illness or a sufferer and wholly misses the point. Sadly, this is often done to dramatize the issue to sell more papers or promote a new TV show. Non-fiction is done better as this revolves around lived experiences and hearing from people who have genuine experience. Sadly, getting mental health 'right' in characters within fiction is proving quite the task in mainstream media.

We know that our own individual stories of recovery or illness are completely personal to us and totally unique. I think this is an important point to remember when we see or hear something in the media that upsets us.

Just because a TV show or newspaper report presents your illness as something foreign to the condition you know, does not mean you are doing anything wrong or that yours is 'worse' or 'better'. The problem with the influx of quick media and the start-to-finish-in-one-page stories that are populating what we see and read daily is that invariably it is impossible to tell the whole story.

When we did Extreme OCD Camp on BBC3 (it's on YouTube, check it out) it was impossible to show each of our stories to the fullest, and that makes complete sense. We are complete and broad people and so the way our illnesses co-existed with us would be more than just what you see for two hours of television. My condition was shown a certain way that told only half of the story and that was not the fault of the production company and director, both of whom did an incredible job, but they had to tell a time-concise story that would be easy to follow. Showing the full package may have been more factually accurate but would have been totally confusing and possibly lost an audience that ultimately ended up learning from us.

I feel that right now we are in a position that requires us to hold our breath a little. We are getting much more space on TV, radio and print but with that increase in good depiction we also gain an increase in poor depiction.

One such issue is when a show introduces mental health issues in a long standing character purely to fast track towards them doing something negative, almost as if showing their illness as the answer to their criminal motivations. It's just very lazy and makes the takeaway for the viewer 'mental illness = dangerous'. Thankfully we do see a lot less of this now but we do still have to police productions to think a little more of their responsibilities.

Sometimes we'll see characters living with a physical disability and the character has their whole personality based around their wheelchair and it's all quite fucking ridiculous. If you're a production company reading this, stop doing that. Disabled people do drugs and sex and fight and run companies and countries and do everything your other characters do. We are shown that they are brave and inspiring and it just becomes a weird inspiration porn dressed up as representation and that is a backwards step.

We need to show fictional characters as living with a mental illness and not just characters that are there because of their mental illness. And show it long term.

Coronation Street nailed it last year when they ran a storyline of the character Craig

Tinker suffering from Obsessive Compulsive Disorder. OCD Action, the national charity, had been consulted on the storyline alongside a great campaigner named Richard Taylor and it showed. They didn't all of a sudden have him doing stereotypical things, they built it up slowly and methodically and showed his symptoms developing. I noticed things myself that pointed towards the condition but that were not explained further but became a jigsaw piece in hindsight when the story reached it's 'conclusion'. The important thing though is that this is not a conclusion, it is a process. I think Corrie will get it right and continue to show the way Craig's diagnosis affects him long term and that is how it should be.

If you are finding yourself being affected by the way mental illness is portrayed in the media, I completely empathise with you. It's a horrible thing to see when something is shown so wrong when you know exactly how it feels. Equally, it can feel frightening and depressing to see a condition that has played a big part of your life shown in the right way! If it is shown for how bad it can be, that can be petrifying too. My advice would be, from someone that has been there, to remember that the media have to show us things as big as they can - because they have such a small window of attention span from us to make their point. Try to take into account that they are either showing worst case scenarios or are showing things to entertain. This does not mean your own story is less valid or true than what is being shown. If you know people living with your condition or even attend a support group/social group for those living with similar diagnosis, definitely bring it up and you'll see others feel the same and understand your frustrations.

I feel a great deal of enthusiasm for the next decade and the way the media will be forced to approach mental illness and I think we are on the verge of a really concentrated effort to reduce stigma, increase representation and promote the feeling of inclusion and understanding. We're not there yet but we are getting there.

Curating our social media timelines to be positive and calming to us can be a good way to reduce the harmful consumption you endure. I have a rule with social media that if I'm not interested, learning or benefitting from the person I follow – I stop following them.

If your Instagram is full of people that make you feel bad about yourself, or you follow pages on Facebook that have comments sections that display ignorance (I'm looking at YOU local newspapers!) then opt out. Make your online experience calmer and healthier and take back a little control over exactly what goes into those 10 hours a day.

# Being A Carer And Being Unwell

I've only ever prayed once by choice. I was 14. Sitting alone in our bathroom I locked the door and sat down and drowned out the sounds of the sirens of the ambulance for just about long enough to say out loud 'if you don't let him die today, I'll be a better person, please'.

I was pleading to a God I didn't actually even believe in out of sheer desperation as I sought any means of control over a situation that was spiralling out of my control. Dad had been ill for about 6 years and it had always been serious but this was his second heart attack. The first had involved resuscitation and him being 'dead' for several minutes. Things had got worse for him physically and mentally and I didn't think his chances were good. The man I had absolutely idolised as a boy was in a very bad way and the look on the faces of the paramedics when they arrived told a story I didn't want to know.

Earlier that summer I'd refreshed by First Aid course, something I had done regularly since he and my brother had become so ill. I didn't really think about it and it wasn't really a decision it was just something I did because the reality was I was likely to have to use it. Every time I'd do it and have to perform CPR on the little Annie doll they use for practice I would freak out and ask the rest of the students, normally all adults, if I'd be strong enough to save my big and burly Dad if I needed to? What if I wasn't strong enough? Would he die and it be my fault? The pressure felt relentless.

So now I was downstairs looking at Dad slipping in and out of consciousness and just waiting in case I'd have to jump into action. It must have been no more than 5 minutes before the ambulance arrived but each second felt like he was slipping away and I was stunned with fear.

When they got to him they didn't mess about. Paramedics are truly wonderful people and these two were no different. Dad looked bad now, really bad. There was no colour to him whatsoever and I remember telling myself as he was wheeled out to not cry because I didn't want his last image to be of me being scared so I stood and smiled, as strange as that may seem.

As he was about to go down the ramp he shouted 'stop' with every single part of him, as sick as he was he did so with his usual velocity to startle the medics into observing his request. 'Jack?' he enquired, searching around the room for me (all but five feet away but in his condition he was mostly out of it) and then did an action I'll never ever forget and always be beyond grateful for. He gave me a thumbs up.

Now Dad was always a strong man. Probably too much so. The victim of a truly horrendous upbringing that centred around his Mum's death, his Dad's outward disgust in him and abuse and neglect sadly not uncommon in the 50's and 60's. He was a true Cockney and what would be seen as a 'manly' bloke. He was tough and sometimes scary but loving and warm and he had just used every single ounce of strength he had in him to make sure I saw him as 'OK'. It was probably the greatest show of human strength I've ever personally witnessed.

As they began wheeling he lost consciousness and they ran him into the back of the Ambulance as we arranged to follow on before the petrifying realisation the ambulance hadn't even started moving yet, making us aware something wasn't right. It wasn't, he had gone into cardiac arrest and both paramedics were working on him.

Thankfully this story had a happy ending and years later he is still with us. Still a very unwell man but still here.

In the UK there are around a quarter of a million young carers, Of these 250,000 children and young people providing physical, mental, emotional and personal support for a loved one and often a parent, nearly half of them have special educational needs or a mental health problem. Not only is that the case but these young people are sacrificing many prospects by choice or not, due to circumstance. This means significantly lower GCSE attainment levels and a lower than the national average chance of being in education, employment or training. More often than not, as was the case with me, these young people will come from lower income families by quite a notable way.

For those of you reading this that are in that situation or have been in that situation, firstly, you are absolutely beyond incredible. I know you do not expect thanks or gratitude as this is just how your life is (right now) but you deserve it and as with most young people I meet, you fill me with immense pride. I have been there. I was a carer for my brother and my Dad growing up and alongside my own mental health issues the enormity of responsibility can be absolutely crushing. Then on top of that you've got to fit into your life; growing up! It's already such a difficult period to navigate (much harder now than many adults give you credit for) without the added pressures of caring.

It is absolutely vital that the love, care and compassion you show the person you care for extends to yourself. Empathy is limitless and so is your opportunity to self-care. Not only is a healthier and happier you a practical advantage as obviously this makes your ability to care and support others easier, it also provides a valuable reminder that the most important person in your life, the person who most needs your support, the human that will be with you the longest and the one you need to most cherish, respect and help is; yourself.

By the fact you are reading this book it means you probably already know that, or it means someone else knows it enough to think you need reminding of it by giving you this book to read.

To be a carer you most probably possess a better than average level of organisation. Use this skill for you, too. I'm sure you're used to GP appointments or social worker meetings and if so, speak to them about you. As we know from our own conditions, illness affects more than just the person that is unwell and these healthcare professionals are there to be a general support so find the services right for you, as there are hundreds of good ones. These can range from helping you out logistically, finding alternative care for your loved one and assisting with the paperwork that comes with that, arranging for you to attend support days with other young carers (I highly recommend this) and also simply offers you a place to chat.

This chapter is also relevant to those caring for another that may not be in the 'young' (sorry!) category anymore, the lesson still stands at any age. If you are a friend of a young person and reading this book as a supporter with a desire to learn more on how to better support a friend, you may not feel you class as a carer but the same words apply to you. It blows my mind the lengths people will go to in their support of others and it is an incredibly beautiful thing, but do look after yourself and do ensure your own needs are not neglected. For the young people caring full time at home, one day life is going to open up for you like a treasure chest. Just like it did for me. And you will be so ready.

# Time To Write Your Chapter

Recently I was walking over London Bridge on my way to a meeting, looking both ways as I always do to enjoy the city's outstanding beauty and as I slowly walked and savoured the sights and sounds, the bustle and business of the capital, I reminded myself of the most important fact in my life today.

I notice the bad days.

Once upon a time, and not so long ago, that was the complete opposite. A good day would stand out for me as it was so rare. Maybe once every other month I'd go to bed thinking 'today was good', now bad days are so rare that I notice them. And I love that. Noticing them means things have moved on so much that they are the exception to the rule.

This didn't just change on its own. It was a series of big and little changes that benefited from good timing and consistency. Some changes were so difficult I've struggled to eloquently describe them to you in this book and some were so small at the time I didn't even realise their impact but I had a lifestyle that was dictated by mental illness that soon become a lifestyle dedicated to combating mental illness.

I worked hard and I worked smart and I listened to myself and others. I was diligent, aiming long term, honest, positive and in some capacity lucky.

This is a direct message to you reading this now. You can do this. You are everything you saw yourself being when you were little and if you are not, you have all the capability to become it.

People including yourself have taken the time to label or dismiss you and I have no doubt you are probably as guilty of this as anyone. Stop and stop today. Work out who you want to be and how you want to become so and work every single day towards being that best version of yourself. Be bold and brave and take the decisions you know are right. Do not let your decision making be led by illness, let it be led by recovery.

Believe people when they tell you the world is beautiful and remember that people are overwhelmingly good. Don't forget we are all in this together and we all want the same things and that there are not just a few people out there that want to see you succeed. We all do. Know that your talents, personality, ambition, emotion and view of the world have been masked but not removed. Those of you that danced before you became unwell? You are a dancer. Those that have always wanted to sing but let anxiety stop their attempts, you are a singer. To the artists, sportspeople, politicians, Doctors, lawyers, mechanics and authors – you are whatever you want to be or you can become whoever you should have become. Those of you that haven't finished school and want to, you can. Maybe not today but you can. Illness often foggies our vision and makes us only see to the end of our nose, but see through it. To the many that 'chose' to not attend university, when really illness chose for them, you can become scholars. People's opinions of you are their property, not your baggage. Some people just won't like you and that's absolutely fine. Do something everyday that reminds you that you are lucky because you very probably are, and once you work out what makes you lucky use it as positive fuel only – do not use it to make yourself feel bad for not feeling happy or for feeling unwell. You can and should be selfish with positivity, do not find something you are happy about in your life and use it as a stick to beat yourself with. If you have a great job, loving family, physical health, wealth, prospects or things 'better than others' – this does not mean you cannot feel unwell and does not mean you must apologize for this.

If you are young and struggling with mental illness remember angst and illness are two different things. Yes you can be suffering from the things that come with being young (and they are all valid!) but you may be unwell too. Do not let people put you in a box as 'in a phase'.

Choose to make time for yourself. Be adventurous or find calm ways to have free time, however you prefer. If you want to go to a concert and get knocked out in a mosh pit, do it. If you want to sit under a tree and read a book, do it. Accept and enjoy the fact that living a good life has no manual and your way of doing so may be different to the next person, and that is absolutely fine. Be yourself as everyone else is taken and learn to like yourself and then learn to love yourself.

Rid yourself of the shackles of time based achievement. This is not a real thing. Harland Sanders of KFC (yep, Col. Sanders) didn't franchise his first KFC until he was 62, Charles Darwin didn't publish anything of note until he was 50 and Samuel L Jackson's first role's came in his 40's. Beethoven was a child superstar and Facebook's Mark Zuckerberg became a self-made billionaire at 23. The thing Darwin, Sanders, Jackson, Beethoven and Zuckerberg have in common is that they are not you. Your story is your own. You write it. Some chapters may be written for you but the details are your own. There's a very strong chance illness has stopped a few plans in their tracks, that is a postponement not an abandonment. Life isn't a paint by numbers, it is far too interesting for that. You do not need to have met the love of your life at 18, you do not need to be in your career by 25 and your dream home doesn't need to be bought by 30. Things are not different for you because you've unfortunately had to deal with mental illness, things are different for everyone. Set realistic plans and goals and put times on them by all means, but not having them does not indicate failure, it indicates you need to reassess the goal or reassess the time. Achievement can be at any time and can start at any time. You can put this book down now and choose to start doing something good for you now, that's the beginning of achievement. There is no finish line you run through to attain it and no medals given by yourself for achieving. It is a process. Start it today.

Listen to yourself and your body and if it feels like you may not be being totally honest – you're not.

There are 168 hours per week. If you can't find 7 of those hours to dedicate to doing something just for you then you need to drastically change things. You can do a hell of a lot as a human and more than you think you can, but some things will have to wait. Some things will have to be done differently and some things you may not be able to do at all. This lack of control is not a bad thing, it's just the way life is and you can control your reactions to it.

Be patient with those around you. They will get frustrated and they will get angry. This isn't at you, this is at your illness. They are scared and unsure how to react, that's all. It's ignorance, not arrogance. Forgive them and work with them.

Distinguish the difference between you and between your illness and do not let them merge. One of them is you and one of them is a part of you, currently.

Accept mistakes are human and do not let them be your reason for not doing something. Mistakes are merely road bumps. You'll do them every day and you can't completely eradicate them so certainly do not fear them.

Never roll your eyes at those of us that preach that things will get better, they will. Reread my last sentence again now and be open minded to it. I would have read that sentence 5 years ago and stopped reading. I didn't believe it until it happened. There are mentally healthy success stories all around you and they are repeated and championed because they are important and every person that tells their story of recovery has another story of once disbelieving their own recovery was possible. If you can't believe it'll get better, at least believe you could be wrong. That's the first step.

When we eat our bodies take the nutrients we need, and dispose of what we do not – do this with your days. Be choosy with what you take from your day, if it was a good day – celebrate. If it was a bad day – let it go. A bad day doesn't equal a bad life and it is true that a setback is a setup for a comeback. If you have 3 great days and 1 terrible day, you've not gone backwards. You've just not gone forwards, learn from it and move on. Do not let its weight drag you down. Do not automatically assume a bad day or moment will 'undo' all of the good work. It's rarely that case.

Compliment excellent therapy with whole health decisions. Sleep well, eat well, exercise well and things will seem easier.

Consistency is key. Natural talent is mythical. Some people will start ahead of others but it is consistency, hard work and smart work that make us good at something. If you're climbing a mountain and it gets difficult you do not start walking down the mountain as you get your breath back, you stop. Pause if necessary, then keep moving. You've come this far, make it count now.

Life really is a beautiful challenge. I'm so sorry if it's only been a challenge so far but I promise you there is no big secret or club you aren't invited to. All the opportunities, experiences, people and places you want or need to feel happy and healthy are out there. All of the options of treatment to improve your life already exist. They are already out there. You've just got to mix the right ones at the right times to get the right results. If you just keep going – you'll find the right mix.

All of the grey can become colour and all of the missed opportunities can become invaluable experiences.

Purely by reading this and seeking answers you are showing your bravery and willingness to improve things for yourself. By giving the other side of this book to family and friends, you are showing a desire to share your own story or to have your own conversation on you and your mental illness and that action may be the first step on the way to recovery or it may be the 500th, but it's a step forward.

I hope you've found my own story of recovery helpful and I've been as honest as I could have been. Your own story will be different but it's time to pick up the pen. I look forward to reading yours.

battles in their head is a life skill. We learn first aid and appreciate how knowing how to give CPR, dress a wound or support a broken bone may be exceptionally useful one day – so learning how to perform emergency mental health support, dress an emotional wound and support a broken person has just as much, if not more opportunity to pay off one day. I hope you feel more confident in this pursuit having read this book.

And of course, to those of you switching roles, living with a mental health problem and reading the other person's book. If you have read the other side of this book and are now finishing this side to see how your own supporters can best support you, I hope this book has given you some practical tips and some great ideas on how you may help them to help you. You've got this. I believe in you completely.

I've not broken any ground in the chapters I've put together for this book, but you have by reading it.

Mental wellness and supporting it is not generally achieved by humungous acts or one, great gesture. It is a series of consistent realistic actions, realistic persistence and realistic goals. And that is why I so strongly believe finding our own version of recovery is achievable to us all. As long as we bridge the steps to be manageable, we can all find a way across the bridge.

I'm going to give the final words of this book to Fred Rogers, the legendary American children's TV hero. Mr Rogers taught a young audience about many things, including the kindness within people and the human desire to help others. It helps me often. Always look for the helpers, and you'll see yourself. Good luck.

*'When I was a boy and I would see scary things in the news, my mother would say to me; 'Look for the helpers, you'll always find people who are helping'.*

# LIFE ON THE OTHER SIDE

A personal story of how to support a loved one living with a mental health problem. You might be a parent, partner, friend, teacher or colleague. This book is for you.

This book gives honest, realistic and easy to read examples and stories of living with a mental illness by someone that knows. You will learn how to support someone at school, work, accessing medical support and much more with a series of chapters devoted to giving you a clear understanding of your role. This is not a medical book.

# Life On The Other Side

**By Jack Pridmore**

A Personal Guide Of How To Support Anyone Living With A Mental Health Condition.

# How To Read This Book

This is book one of two and is aimed at you, the reader supporting a loved one living with a mental health condition. If you care about helping someone in your life that lives with a mental health problem – this book is for you.

There is a second book included in this book, aimed at the person you are supporting.

Ideally you will read your side and then pass this book to them to read their side. Once they are done, read their side too and you'll get to the issues that matter to people living with a mental illness.
After this is done, let them read your side. When you've both read both sides, I'd love for you to have a conversation on how to make life easier for you both.

Chapters are not in a fixed order so pick this up and put it down as you please.

If you've got to this point and realised this book isn't for you but the other side may suit someone, that's great. Please pass the advice in the book on and please get talking and doing. Good luck.

# Contents

# About The Author

Born in East London in 1990, Jack Pridmore has spoken extensively on mental health in print, radio and TV and continues to campaign for change for those living with a mental health condition.

Following on from featuring on BBC3's Extreme OCD Camp in 2013 and beginning his own recovery journey - the author has spoken with many young people, parents, teachers, employers, doctors and the general public on mental health to try to promote understanding of how to better support those living with a condition and the things we can all do to make the lives of those that need it better, healthier and more prosperous.

There are many answers and thoughts based on these questions and how we can create genuine change and enough of them to fill an entire book or two.

This is that book.

@jackjpridmore

# Today Is A Good Day

Today is a very good day indeed.

There's a very strong chance that you've just read that sentence and immediately thought 'yeah, not quite mate!' and that may well be because you, or someone very close to you, is in desperate need and at the end of their tether. Maybe they are your son or daughter or friend and they've just handed you this book for you to read to better understand how they feel inside. Maybe they've never told you and maybe these words are your first time hearing something is wrong. Maybe you are absolutely petrified by what all this means and confused, scared and anxious.

Maybe they've not said anything but you know anyway – and you've picked this up to try and see if you can gleam any sort of information that would shine some sort of light into the darkness. You may even have your own mental illness and have read the other side to this book so have decided to try and see if you can try and get in the mindset of a supporter.

If it's any of these things or, really, any other reason at all, it doesn't matter. What matters is that you've picked up this book. Not because it's the greatest book ever written or the golden ticket to recovery (I mean, I've tried, but that's a lot of pressure!) but simply what matters is that you have. The first step is taking any step forward at all.

Before we go anywhere I want to explain two things; the layout of this book, and what a supporter is.

This book is aimed at facilitating conversation between someone personally living with a mental illness and those around them. This can be a parent, partner, friend, colleague, boss, teacher or anyone else they so wish. The book is split into two books, this one, aimed at the supporter who is around the loved one and then if you flip this over there is a whole other book for the person living with a mental health condition. My ideal aim is that you'll read your section here and then flip it over and read the section from the point of view of those going through the stages of the condition. Hopefully this will provide some answers for you both but the aim really is for it to unlock some questions for you both to get the conversation started together.

I originally planned for this book to be a positive look at a negative situation and wrote the entire thing as so. As soon as I'd finished I realised that doing so would be doing a disservice to you and patronising those you are supporting. Thankfully it has now morphed into an honest look at a negative situation and in the spirit of this I must warn you it will not be pretty or glamorous - but it will be truthful. It is a story of recovery, but it will not be easy going. But you knew that already.

The process of supporting someone living with a mental health diagnosis (or in the process of getting one) can feel nearly as frustrating as living through the condition itself. It is not something you have asked for nor wished for and it is one most of us are certainly not prepared for.

As the world develops I hope this will be something that is a thing of the past. Schools, employers and governments are being forced to recognize the utmost importance of their positions as frontline first responders in the battle against mental illness and the stigma and misunderstanding around it. But for anyone reading this book, you probably grew up in a far less enlightened world than the one we live in today. So the way you viewed mental health growing up may be very different from today's reality, but progression is occurring at unprecedented levels so this is the best time in history to educate yourself on the subject.

At school I learnt the periodic table, Pythagoras theorem and of course, how to put a condom on a banana. Which was, in hindsight, quite the misleading ambition for pre-pubescent 11 year old me. One thing I did not learn how to take care of in health class was my own mental health, and nor did I learn where to go if I did want to seek help. In fact, minus unofficially receiving support from teachers that understood personally, I have zero recollection of it ever being brought up.

That's not an indictment of my schooling necessarily as that's how things simply were, but it's not acceptable in 2019 and it highlights my point that unless you've been through the system of accessing support yourself you are probably feeling completely underprepared for this.

I think it is important to learn right away that you cannot play god with this. No matter how much you love this person, or how dedicated to them and their recovery you are, you are not here to cure anyone. You are here to support, champion, console, enthuse, respect, illuminate and applaud but you can't, won't and shouldn't shoulder the responsibility of being their door out of the bad times. You can however be the sign pointing to the door.

# What Is A Supporter?

Anyone can be a supporter to someone living with a mental health condition.

The roles and responsibilities that are thrust upon you or volunteered by you can be incredibly wide ranging and sometimes pretty much all encompassing. Much like anything to do with mental health, it's never black and white and the type of support you may provide will be entirely unique to you and the person you are supporting.

I think one of the most confusing aspects of supporting someone living with a mental illness is knowing how involved you should be. It's not an easy science and there aren't any hard and fast rules but I think there are some things that are true for everyone.

Growing up I helped support my parents, one of whom is schizophrenic and living with a brain injury and the other who has bipolar. Both are aggressive and serious conditions that can be debilitating and are certainly life changing. As a teenager with my own mental health issues this was a challenging balance to get right to say the least, and it seemed like day-to-day the person most needing support would change, including myself.

First and foremost, to all types of supporters; you are not the most important person in this. They are. What you do can certainly have a profoundly positive affect in your loved ones life but your role is not to stop your life to kick start theirs. It is absolutely vital that you appreciate this fact or your emotional investment in being a supporter to them will potentially become a pressure and burden to you both of you that actually happens to cause more unnecessary stress.

The best types of supporters are those that can keep us calm when we cannot, or those that can keep themselves calm when around us is chaos. Think of any high pressure situation and we all look and listen to the person that is purposeful and confident in their actions but calm and collected in the way they go about them. The best managers and leaders are those that can keep their calm in times of need. Kipling wasn't wrong when he reminded us that 'if you can keep your head when those around you have lost theirs, you'll be a man my son'. I vividly remember during my darkest hours my emotions completely betraying me and my body and mind feeling like they were a whirlwind of uncontrolled mess. I felt like I was spinning and the butterfly effect of one bad thought or a bad day or a bad hour would spiral to something much more unmanageable. Sometimes when this would happen, in their desperation those around me would those their cool too and all that did was validate to my mind that I was in trouble and it would become a vicious cycle.

Your role here is to be versatile. Sometimes you need to be completely open and accessible when we need to talk, if you can. This doesn't mean your job is to be on edge all day every day that some huge heart to heart is going to happen, but it does mean that we know that when we do need to make that phone call or have that sit down, the person we are speaking to is one that listens first and wholly. It's very true that we have two ears and one mouth for a reason.

That person needs to also understand that today we may want to tell you every single detail of us. Our hopes, fears, dreams, nightmares, the lot. We may want to elaborate into intimidate and excessive detail and we may well be the open book you wish us to be, but then that person also needs to be acutely aware that this can and will change depending on many factors.

The day after the most honest and frank discussion you'll ever have with us that felt like a great unburdening and a new dawn may be followed by a day of isolation, silence and frustration. During both periods your role does not hugely differ – just be accessible. Half of everyone I know would refer to me as the most honest and open man they've ever met, the other half will think of me as a completely closed book and someone difficult to read or hard to decipher. The truth is I'm both and that's not uncommon for someone in my shoes. It's not uncommon for anyone, really. But when mental illness is playing a starring role in your life your emotions can be so intense and blinding that the days themselves break up into a series of mini versions of a day, some good and some bad. Some open, some closed.

One thing I want to talk about here that I talk about on the other side of this book is making sure we know who is in charge of disclosures about someone's mental health. It's a very simple thing to work out – if it's your mental health we are talking about, it's you. If it's not your mental health we are talking about, it's not you.

You'd be surprised how common it is for this to be an issue. It is almost unbelievable the amount of times I'll hear someone spoken over or spoken for by a well-meaning loved one when trying to help an awkward or delicate situation along that involves someone else's mental health.

For me, this would always happen at restaurants. I've always been a fussy eater by personality (personality and condition = two separate things!) so sometimes I'll have trouble in certain restaurants due to this and sometimes it'll be due to OCD. A few years ago I was in a restaurant in Manchester with a couple of colleagues. As it was Jamie Oliver's restaurant I was sat with my non-sugar Coke substitute (not that bad, give it a go) as we began to order our meals. I fancied the chicken and some pasta but wanted plain chicken and plain pasta, a probably unusual but nonetheless simple culinary request.

The waiter, meticulous and attentive that he was, took my order with a little apprehension and began a mini version of the Spanish inquisition with me to quiz me on my odd choice. Sensing my growing impatience at the exchange, my colleague, who always did his very best to understand my condition jumped in to let the waiter know 'Its allergies. He wants it plain due to allergies'. A simple but effective lie that I've actually also used myself. This day however, not so simple.

The waiter now began quizzing me on these allergies to find out exactly what the allergy may be; 'is it the chilli powder?!' 'Is it wheat?!' 'Do you need Gluten Free?' and every question I batted away with 'Nope, not that' and desperately hoped for the barrage of questions to finish.

Sadly, this guy wanted to know more than I wanted to tell him so he just kept on and on and was now, without meaning to, quite loudly questioning me on my non-existent food allergies and the medical ramifications of the chef accidentally contaminating me. Feeling rather embarrassed by this point I firmly but politely told him 'Listen mate, I'm just not going to tell you here in front of everyone. So either I'll have them plain if the chef will trust me on this or I'll just eat elsewhere'. I assured him the 'allergy' wasn't in anyway life threatening and that at worst I'd feel a bit bloated after so don't worry about liability, I'll not be suing him for my untimely demise.

Mercifully he relented and skipped off to tell the Chef that the strange man at table 6 has the advanced level taste buds of a picky 4 year old boy.

The above story shows the kind-hearted approach some people may take that can turn a bit messy. My friend had done the decent gesture of helping the situation to ease my embarrassment but it had inadvertently become worse than if he'd have left me to explain it. These scenarios can occur on a daily basis and show the absolute importance of not only communication, but mutual understanding between yourself and the person you are supporting – and the reason this book exists. If before we had entered the restaurant I'd have turned round to him and said 'Do me a favour, I don't want to explain this today, can you order for me?' we'd have been fine.

It's good to help but it's important to not stifle natural conversation and mistakenly patronise. It's so easy to almost baby someone with a mental illness and obviously other than not exactly being great for self-esteem, it can also become enabling quicker than you'd expect. There is a chapter on enabling in this book. The critical importance of letting someone stand on their own two feet when they can is paramount.

When we learn to swim we start off by just dipping our toe in the shallow end. Then we graduate towards swimming with armbands at a slow and comfortable pace with someone alongside us to keep us safe. Maybe next we learn in deeper waters, or at a faster pace. We are then ready to learn how to swim alone, supported only by armbands and not with a person swimming next to us, and finally we can learn to swim unassisted. It is a process.

Yet as soon as we do learn, we aren't immediately put in the deepest part of the pool - instead we find our comfort and consistency in the shallow end and often recovery can be very much like this.

It is a case of building slowly but one of the greatest risks to our confidence and trajectory isn't in swimming unassisted, we've learnt that already. It's in being told that despite having worked so hard to learn to swim without armbands, we must now always keep them on.

I'm very conscious to make sure the above analogy does not accidentally profess that recovery is linear and about moving forwards only. Of course it is not and of course sometimes we'll fail. However, if we must fail it cannot be because we are blocked from moving ourselves. To overuse the aquatic analogy a little more, someone may be a world class swimmer now, shooting around the deep end of the pool like a dolphin – but they may also choose or need to go back to the shallow end and get their armbands back on, but it would be their choice. We can support the pace at which people aim to find recovery, but we are not qualified to set the pace.

Knowing how to recognise how fast or slow you should be moving to benefit recovery is a skill that someone living with a mental illness learns over time, experience and trial and error.

The reason the above relates to a supporter is that regardless of the direction we take, your role is to support and encourage, not dictate. If someone feels comfortable making some huge strides, as long as they are not obviously unsafe, then your role isn't to sceptically buffer, it is to optimistically and realistically enthuse and then support, be it good outcome or bad.

Should the direction be a little more negative, your role is of course to simply support and encourage still. The process of seeking recovery is not in anyway a straight line, sometimes we'll take five steps forward and one step back, and sometimes it'll be vice versa.

It is important to not become jaded yourself by this process and it is important to recognise that things will sometimes seem like they are heading positive and then turn negative fairly quickly, and vice versa. As you can imagine this dynamic nature of mental illness can be very disorientating and chaotic so a calm and moderate presence will always be a helpful thing.

I think if we look back on our lives at the people we most felt warmth and safety with, they tend to be those that were simply present. Those that were there with you without any strings attached and who were easy to be around. Be the person you would want supporting you.

# What Signs And Symptoms Should I Be Looking For?

There are many common signs and symptoms of a developing or worsening condition and these are often used by primary care (GP's, nurses, schools) as an indicator of a potential illness or that an already diagnosed illness may be getting worse.
I'm often asked by parents of young people recently diagnosed or seeking diagnosis to give examples of what may be signs their child is potentially going downhill. It's a tricky one. Firstly, I'm not a doctor, despite my handwriting – and secondly, if I was, it would still be a very individual thing.

Some people have very clear and very obvious signposts that they may be heading towards a mental health crisis, diagnosis or difficult period. I know people that will go out and shop recklessly, spending a month's wage in a day as a way to try and give some sort of positivity injection to their mood. I know some that just stop talking. People that would normally verbally interact as most do/talk even more than average that withdraw verbal communication during a poor period of mental health. They may still be very present and turning up but not actually contributing and that is their sure fire sign that things are not as healthy as they should be.

For me personally, my symptoms actually take me by surprise. It'll normally be a case of one day realising 'I'm not being very polite to people right now, maybe I'm not feeling myself' or 'I'm feeling bored. I never feel bored. Maybe I need to keep an eye on myself'. This is my way of spotting an issue. An often subtle, often slowly progressive change in myself. It's important to note sometimes I am just a little rude to people, or sometimes

I'm bored temporarily. It doesn't necessarily mean anything is truly wrong, unless I notice it consistently.

Rarely, I will have a day where I am off and free and rather than use it to do something I want to do I'll just stay in bed all day. Not in an I've-had-a-long-week-lets-spend-a-day-in-my-pants-eating-sweets kinda day, but an I-don't-wanna-be-a-part-of-the-world kinda day. That one is more obvious and hurts more, but being so obviously there can actually be easier to address and certainly easier to spot.

Here is a small list of common signs and symptoms the person you are supporting may be dealing with a difficult period or is struggling to progress as they would like;

**Apathy** – avoidance of commitments and of being social, a lack of desire to do the things they normally do or to do things at all.

**Poor coping mechanisms** – a use or increase of drinking, drugs, gambling, unhealthy pursuits or hobbies.

**Expressing feelings of sadness** – maybe a seemingly more obvious one but increased feelings of loss or unhappiness, maybe even hopelessness. Language can be important here because we are sometimes dismissive if the words aren't more formal. 'I feel sad today' may make us take note whereas 'I feel a bit shitty today' may go under the radar. They are one and the same.

**Withdrawal** – maybe wanting isolation or choosing options that isolate them, maybe offering to do things that would isolate them e.g. 'No, you guys go ahead, I'll stay and look after the dogs'. Maybe innocuous but potentially a withdrawal/avoidance tactic.

**Poor hygiene** – This is more common than you may think. If they are the sort to shower twice a day in the morning and at night and begin only doing so every two days, every three days even – it may be a sign of detachment or an early symptom of a bigger issue. See also; not bothering to do makeup when they normally would, or going out with messy hair when this is out of character, not brushing their teeth, allowing themselves to get or seem dirtier than they normally would. This can show a lack of care in themselves.

**Expressing harm thoughts** – some people will openly express either outright words of harm 'I want to hurt myself' or others 'I want to knock him out' and some may do so with more subtlety or in a more roundabout way, maybe with a qualification they won't; 'I feel like cutting myself sometimes to release some pressure, I won't though'.

**Lack of esteem** – this can be before and leading to mental illness or as a symptom of it. A lack of self-esteem can mean a negative and overly critical view of one's self. Maybe the person you are supporting has a constantly negative commentary of their own life. They may pick and choose the opinions they believe to favour the opinions that are negative about them. They may go beyond self-deprecation to presenting themselves as 'bad', 'wrong', 'incorrect' or 'not right'.

**Over the top reactions** – another potential sign that things may be deteriorating for the person you are supporting is a potential for 'bigger' reactions than the situation dictates. This could include; anger over minor issues, despair over small inconveniences, an over excitement for something they would normally be reserved about, a general 'bigger than necessary' reaction to the scenario.

**Sleep patterns** – if a person is sleeping much more than usual, or much less than usual, this may be a sign that their mental health needs to improve. Disrupted sleep, poor sleep or a slow falling to sleep can also be indicators.

**Inability to meet expectations** – if the person you are supporting finds themselves struggling to keep up with their usual day to day expectations, or other relevant and realistic non day to day expectations this may point towards the possibility that their life and their health is overwhelming them. This is particularly true if you notice the type of jobs they tend to find easy or non-strenuous are becoming difficult. Some people may see them as 'flakey'.

As you can see here normally the things we notice are the changes. There will most likely be parts of them that have 'always been that way' but are actually, in hindsight, the signs of mental illness – however the signs you are more likely to notice come with the process of change.

*What are their differences in the way they are between a bad period and a good period?*
*How would I describe them now? How would I describe them at their best or their worst?*
*If I am noticing a change in them, why might that be?*

The easiest way to know – as always, is to ask. It really is that simple.

Those that have been living with poor mental health for a period of time are likely to know some of their own signs and symptoms (they may refer to them as 'triggers', but that's not how I would) even if they do not really immediately see them as signs. They may think 'well, I'm particularly tired because I've got a lot on at work' and then realise in time that actually work is much the same as usual but it is they that is somewhat different.

The questions to ask can be simple and open; 'How do I know when things are difficult for you, is there anything that you do differently?' or 'when you feel unwell, what changes do you see in yourself?' or if you would like, ask them direct questions using this chapter. 'Do you feel you sleep worse when things are not good for you? Do you drink more?'

This is good for three reasons. Either a) they realise their symptoms and arm you with vital information to spot the issues or b) they do not spot the symptoms but have a chance to have a think on what those signs may be or c) they do not know the symptoms, do not know how to notice them but do get to talk openly with someone actively seeking to help. It's a win win win.

I am a big fan of keeping notes and diarising. I recommend it often to people as it is healthy analytics and it often shows patterns we did not expect to see. Therefore a good practical tip is for both you and the person you are supporting to keep a diary to record changes that you can discuss as and when, or at a regular time slot (when you are both clear and free to talk openly) or with their medical professionals.
A vital part of that process though is asking for permission to do so. Just ask. No one wants to feel like they are being judged and having their behaviours questioned, and if they are in a negative position currently they are likely going to feel like doing so is against them, and not for them. Having a discussion that explains that you want to help and be an effective support is important – it cannot be seen as you waiting for them to make a mistake, or act unreasonably to record it against them. Anything like that and you can risk the person you are supporting purposefully shutting down and keeping things from you. If they are happy for you to do so and see the benefit and you are in an appropriate position to (parent, partner, close friend, sibling etc.) then this could be a positive step for you both.

# First Steps

When I truly began the process of getting better I would often hear something like; 'well, the first step to recovery is…', and would recoil at this seemingly blasé attitude to my previous endeavours, as it felt utterly belittling of everything I had been through before. It felt like people were saying I hadn't even started yet and this would frustrate me. As if everything I'd tried so far counted for absolutely nothing just because I wasn't living in my recovery. Plus, there felt like so many different options where this first step could apply to and ultimately I felt confused by it all.

However, as fantastically broad as everyone's recovery story is – they nearly all begin with making a plan.

I've always looked at recovery as being a lock and key scenario. For some people, there may be 100 locks they need to unlock to get in and truly experience life as they wish, for others it may be 3 or 4. In some cases you have each key yourself and it's about the combination and in many cases you do not yet have the keys yourself. Sometimes you are going to need to find these keys in other ways, be they a certain therapy, a specific medication, a new lifestyle change, an improvement in a current relationship or simply (but not easily attained), experience. For some people it may be one lock and key to get where they need to be, maybe their first therapy provides this key to unlocking recovery. For many that is not the case, but for all - collecting the right keys is a possibility.

I look at making a recovery plan as a team game. I knew what I wanted but I didn't know exactly how to get it so making a plan to get better alone would mean I'd possibly fall short, I needed good people around me in the right places to make a plan that made sense. This more often than not should begin with a trip to your GP who is medically speaking your most likely 'first responder'.

Having a good GP on board can be an essential component in recovery and if the person you are supporting does not have that – certainly look at alternatives.

If the person you are supporting is in a position of having a good GP that ideally they know and trust - that's already a good start.

Booking appointments is something many find stressful and awkward that aren't even suffering mentally, so there's a chance you may be making the booking on their behalf. Bear in mind if this is the first time they've ever spoken about this with a medical professional it is likely to be a longer affair, therefore definitely ask the receptionists to book a longer appointment and do take care in the time you pick. If you are taking someone straight from school, or meeting them from work as examples – try to not book it for so close after finishing that they'll be overcharged and overanxious anyway. Although it's 'good' for a Doctor to see that natural anxiety, if it prevents conversation happening it's not going to help. I would suggest arriving locally with great time to spare or maybe grabbing a coffee nearby first, something that makes the appointment seem purposeful and not rushed. I personally prefer appointments first thing in the morning so I do not have much anxiety beforehand and can get it out the way.

Also, it would be wise to have a chat beforehand on your involvement in the appointment. Are you in the waiting room or the Doctor's office? Are you there simply to be there? Or are you an active participant? The person you are supporting may wish for you to speak first, or speak up, or they may only want you involved at certain points. Arranging this role pre-appointment makes for a much smoother visit.

As someone that has seen more medical professionals than a Holby City casting call, I have an almost superhuman ability to forget everything I wish to say as soon as I am sat on that plastic seat. Immediately, everything I have been completely passionate about for the days leading up to the appointment betrays my memory and leaves me sitting there making minor points and missing a good opportunity to discuss something important. One good habit I have got into is making a list leading up to the appointment to take in with me. I highly recommend this becomes routine for you and the person you are supporting. I'm a very open man and I often know the medical terms and treatment options being discussed with my doctors, but when in there I just go completely blank.

So for those of you starting out it's absolutely imperative you make a checklist of things to speak about.

One thing I try to consider from any visit to a doctor is the 'why' and the 'what'. If I'm there with a stomach ache I want to know 'why' (diagnosis) but ultimately that's redundant without getting rid of the 'what' (what I'm feeling, the symptoms) so although both of you being armed with knowledge and your own thoughts on what a potential diagnosis may be ('I think the symptoms are those of Asperges Syndrome, Doctor') do not neglect the 'what' and how it actually feels.

When I was 14 I realised that the diagnostic criteria I had been researching (fun childhood) was evidencing my potential to have Generalized Anxiety Disorder and Obsessive Compulsive Disorder. Ultimately proved right, I made an appointment the next day and discussed in quite some depth with my Doctor how I met the criteria for diagnosis and this was now something we could move forward on.

I described symptoms both physical and mental and assured her the tick boxes were ticked with the vigorous panful enthusiasm of a first year teacher, but I never once described how those symptoms made me feel. I gave details of what they were but never what that meant for me.

When preparing for the appointment it can be helpful to find some resources that will be illustrative of the medical complaint. As above, that may well be something like a summary on a certain condition and then a tick box next to each showing exactly which does and does not affect the person you are supporting – something you may need to assist with, for honesty purposes (you may see something in them that they do not yet).

Do exercise caution when researching via some medical sites. Often these are built for professionals and are rarely written with the soft approach of a calming Blue Peter presenter lovingly teaching us about life and death when one of the pets die.

If you've ever had the misfortune of winding up on one of those sites after an innocuous google search to 'just put my mind at rest' you'll know full well that your minor rash caused by a washing detergent will very soon become the bubonic plague, smallpox or rickets to even the most uncreative mind. As is the world today, it's very likely your loved one has spent time researching how they feel via these platforms so it's important to speak with a doctor in person as soon as possible rather than relying on these online resources for validation or confirmation as their sterile approach will leave them feeling dejected, frustrated and quite likely scared. Doctors offer the 'however' option.

These websites, often for disclaimer purposes, will give a wide ranging potential diagnosis list for symptoms. If you say you're having headaches regularly this can absolutely be a sign of anxiety, but the websites will also helpfully let you know it may also be a brain tumour. With a potentially already fragile mindset on their health, it's wise to speak to professionals in person or whoever you are supporting may go off on a tangent that will not be helpful.

GP's will of course check for more than just one thing, as they will with a physical complaint. They will be able to offer the 'however' option described above though, so when they are presented with all symptoms they'll be able to give you a far more informed choice and ultimately, treatment options.

As I've discussed on the other side of this book, once you are in the room with a professional everyone there owes it to themselves to be honest. This isn't the time for half-truths or saving face. One of the devastating parts of living with a mental health condition can be the way it strips your self-esteem and embarrasses you in ways those not suffering may not be able to fully empathise. To give an example, as a 22 year old man (and at my lowest point) I had to have my Mum make my food for me – under my very specific instruction. I would also, on days I was utterly unable to leave bed, have to pee in water bottles as I couldn't face getting out of bed and into the bathroom which she would ultimately have to throw away for me. At this stage in my life my mates were finishing Uni, due to my football background half of them were professional footballers and some had marriages, kids and mortgages. I was pissing in bottles and having my porridge made for me every day. It made me feel less of a man. Less of a human even. It robbed my independence and made me feel so, so small. It was a symptom of the condition and a nasty one that people didn't see.

So when I was with Doctors, I wouldn't bring myself to say any of this. They knew my

OCD was severe and encompassing my life, but they didn't see just how much because I never gave them the information. That was naïve. As soon as I started being 100% honest about everything – I started getting better.

Hopefully, as we've discussed above, you and the person you are supporting have made a game plan before you've arrived at the appointment and one of the questions you should agree on with your loved one is; 'if I feel you aren't being totally honest, should I speak up?'. Hopefully they'll say yes, and hopefully you'll speak up.

The final major thing to remember from this first appointment (or first appointment in a while) is to have an idea of what your end goal from the meeting should be. Assuming you want some action here it'll probably go a few ways and if they currently aren't receiving any sort of therapy, beginning the process to attain that is probably a great goal for a long term improvement. My first goals were simple; 'I want something to make today better and I want something to make tomorrow better'.

Going into this appointment with the goal of accessing therapy is brilliant and I applaud that, but the person you are sitting next to is probably/possibly about to hear that their appointment will not be next week. Maybe not even next month, and sad to say in some cases, maybe not even next year. So we have to be prepared to make their expectations of waiting times a little more realistic. But more on this later.

So you've agreed you are going there today to begin the process of receiving therapy, or begin the process of formally receiving a diagnosis. That's for the 'tomorrow' of this process, but the person sitting next to you, having maybe spent years getting to this point has just heard that after all this they have to wait. This can be terrifying, demotivating and actually incredibly disorientating ('I'm doing all the right things, why am I not getting the help now?!') This means you should ask about the 'today' of this process. You've been told you'll be referred to your local CAMHS (Child and Adolescent Mental Health Services) or CMHT (Community Mental Health Team) so that's the moves you need to make but you're sitting with someone riddled with anxiety and your fear is that they won't be well enough to access the therapy when it comes, which is a common worry and reality.

Explaining to the GP that you'd like to discuss options for stabilising things right now may have what feels like a slightly ambiguous response that sometimes amounts to 'let's wait and see after your first appointment via CHMT'.

If they've been seen before it is likely the Doctor may offer the option of a lighter dose of medication for now to keep things stable, or bring them back to being stable. This option may well come up if they've never seen the GP before but it is less likely as the Doctor will want to offer other forms of light therapy first like a good exercise programme, ecotherapy (gardening, outdoor), mindfulness, art therapy and so on. I see merit in each of these treatment options and know that alongside a good talking therapy they can contribute effectively in a person's recovery. But in all honesty if before being offered medication and a talking therapy I was offered alternative treatments as a stopgap, I would have genuinely stormed out of the Doctors office. It would have just felt like I wasn't being taken seriously. Now, much further down the line, I know why this is the case and the myriad of reasons for some delay in treatment and the offer of simpler, easier to attain alternatives in the meantime - but I would be ready to find the person you are supporting upset at any similar potential offer.

Should a medication be offered it is likely to be one of the four main forms of psychiatric medication; Antidepressants, Antipsychotics, mood stabilisers or tranquilisers/sleeping pills.

# Medications

Depression and anxiety is now statistically the most common mental health condition in the UK, with around 7% of the country meeting diagnostic criteria. This makes antidepressants one of the most prescribed form of medication. The 'depress' part of the name does not mean it is a medication available only for depression, it is also commonly written up for those suffering with anxiety conditions amongst other mental health and physical health conditions.

As a disclaimer here, I'm writing here entirely through lived experience. I'm giving you some facts and stats that may be helpful (please see the glossary for more) but I'm certainly not a medical professional.

I will give a very light (!) introduction to antidepressants, which aim to essentially boost and alter the brain chemicals like serotonin that you may well have heard about. SSRI's (Selective Serotonin Reuptake Inhibitors) are the most commonly prescribed antidepressant in Britain and include drugs like citalopram, fluoxetine and sertraline. These names are something you'll probably come across in this process and although the amount of medication information can be overawing it does give enough info for the people you are supporting to make a decision based on a lot of good evidence based research.

This research does not cater for individual experiences of antidepressants or any medication for that matter. Although some medications have harsher side effects/withdrawal symptoms, these are really on a case by case basis.

One thing people starting out the process maybe do not expect to encounter is that there is a small delay at the beginning of the prescription before any noticeable change occurs.

The very nature of being given the medication means those taking it are probably at the stage of a serious need for change, so this time between beginning the course and noticing change can and will be frustrating and disappointing. However, it is very important that at this stage perseverance is sought and that a fully compliant attitude towards taking them is employed or it will just be a longer process. This is a vital time for those supporting to do their best to be an encouraging and positive ally, be it reminders to physically take the medication or emotional support that this is a positive step. Of course for some, medication isn't the answer and for some it will sadly have no particularly positive affect. But I am a big believer in there being a full and broad menu of options for recovery so if medication is a route they go down, doing so to the fullest and most medically recommended way is the only true way to know if meds is or is not going to be a benefit. Half committing to it and then not being impressed with the results is no position to disregard this important potential springboard to health.

Having asked for it for several years, aged 18 I was finally given my first dose of psychiatric medication in the form of the SSRI, Fluoxetine. As an OCD sufferer, this particular drug had the confidence of my GP, psychiatrist and counsellor as being relevant to my condition and keen for any sort of progress I was very happy to give it a go.

At the time I had a particular hatred for taking pills (more on that elsewhere!) so opted to have a liquid version of the drug. This is something the person you are supporting can definitely look at themselves if pills are an issue. I wouldn't recommend the taste, which is a bit like when you were at school and chewing on your pen and accidentally broke the plastic so the ink flooded your mouth (true story), but a non-tablet format was ideal for me.

My first real feeling was a proud form of elation. I hadn't really expected that but having made the decision to give this a go I felt like I was moving in the right direction so felt a real sense of pride. I did note I was a little more anxious than I had been, something completely normal and expected and after a week felt the occasional feeling of desperation. Not so much a suicidal feeling but certainly a chorus of 'wouldn't things be easier if I was dead' in my mind. Thankfully the anxiety subsided and the deathly feelings evaporated completely.

Within two weeks I started to feel different and at first I wasn't convinced it was a good different. I felt sluggish but also really quite apathetic. Quite the animated man (dramatic, basically), I was calmer but equally less up when things felt good. I just felt a little boxed really – like I was in a state of suspension I suppose. Nothing ever felt too bad but nothing ever felt too good either.

Physically I felt quite bloated, would sweat more than usual, had a dry mouth and for the first few days had a bit of an upset stomach. I had also developed the non-existent sex drive of a nun and my erections now went down quicker than the Titanic. All of these are common side effects of starting medication.

Writing this I appreciate the above paragraphs probably sounds quite negative, particularly if you've not experienced mental illness or psychiatric medication yourself but I can assure you this change was something I considered very positive. It allowed me breathing space. It slowed my world down and that was exactly what I needed.

I stayed on Fluoxetine for about a year. Halfway through that period I began a form of Cognitive Behavioural Therapy and I decided that it was time to come away from medication as I was curious to see how things would develop by just talk therapy in the form of CBT.

For those taking antidepressants (which is what Fluoxetine is) there can be almost a feeling of shame in some people, it can hit your self-esteem or make you feel like by altering these chemicals you're sort of cheating, a bit like you aren't truly living life naturally. I've spoken with thousands of sufferers of mental illness and this seems to be one of the top reasons people come off of meds. I didn't feel shame at all really, but I did feel like I wanted to try and continue getting better 'naturally'.

Withdrawal symptoms are something people really do worry about before starting a dose of medication, particularly if it's their first prescription for any form of mental illness and I can attest that in parts, withdrawal symptoms can be unpleasant. I didn't ever experience it particularly badly myself but I did take the time to meet my psychiatrist and

GP before I began the process and followed their advice of slowly weaning myself off. Many make the decision to come off of meds and simply stop and they seem to be the ones most affected by harsh withdrawals. Also, for clarity, some people stop completely and feel no negative impacts at all but if medication has been tried successfully or unsuccessfully I urge you to assist the person you are supporting by agreeing a withdrawal plan with their medical team.

In regards to how long they may stay on their medication for, this is purely down to the individual, their circumstances, condition and the drug itself. In some cases it may well be a few months to get things back on track up to a period of two years. In some cases it may be decided that an indefinite prescription will be a benefit. Their psychiatrist is there to support this process so they should be encouraged to ask questions and not be afraid to ask how long this process may take.

It's common for the dosage to change. Psychiatric medication is not a definite science and despite the masses of fantastic research worldwide used to guide the decision making of medical professionals, it will vary person to person.

Quite quickly into my own course of medication it was decided (mutually, this is very important) that we'd up my dosage as although the changes were occurring I felt that period in my life was ideal for me to commit fully to medication. My psychiatrist agreed and we slowly increased the dosage to the point it felt beneficial and manageable and stuck to that for the remainder of the course.

For those of you that haven't experienced or been around antidepressants or psychiatric medications, a few words on language here.

Medication for mental health conditions are not 'happy pills'. They never have been and never will be. They are not there to make your loved one happy. They are there to make them well. Far too many times I have been with a parent who has suggested their child could do with some medication to 'make them a little happier' and that is not what these do. They could very well play a major role in their wellness, which in turn is a major component of their happiness but please be both realistic and understanding of their functions. I have written a chapter on the flip side of this book called 'The Medication

Myth' that I hope you read. As I state in there – there has become a societal narrative that we 'give out' too many pills to conquer mental illness and that's not only incorrect but highly dangerous, and if you're expressing views like this in front of a loved one going through mental illness, highly detrimental. We are certainly prescribing much more medication to treat mental illness than we ever have historically but that tells you something about the gravity of the battle of becoming mentally healthy rather than the happy handed pen of the medical professional prescribing. I am a huge advocate of medication plus therapy so would happily concede medication alone is, for most people, not the answer – but please do not express a negative outlook on a system and process that you're not fully aware of. Even then, the biggest sceptics for medication must agree that for some – it is life changing. Not finding out if that is the case for your loved one due to a misguided fear that is perpetuated by a gutter press is a move no one should be in a position to make. I would also agree some people are prescribed medication that they should maybe not be, much like a Doctor giving someone antibiotics when it may not be the right course of action, but this does not point to over prescription on a general scale. Medication is a considered and potentially effective treatment for mental illness and in many cases can well be the catalyst to health. From a supporting point of view, this is a great time to encourage your loved one to implement a self-care routine as they begin courses of medication, as the process will often feel like a very big step, so it is important they take care of themselves in a more rounded way.

# Self-Care And Why It Matters

Over the past few years 'self-care' has propelled itself into being considered a big part of any treatment plan from nearly all medical professionals.

Of course, the medical profession has always appreciated and championed the benefits of a holistic approach to recovery and extending treatment beyond what is learned in medical school. However, the general public's understanding of why this often forgotten form of therapy is so highly thought of within psychiatry circles is often due to a misunderstanding of why it can be so effective.

For those of you that are supporting someone who is awaiting their first treatment, appointment or therapy, this chapter is certainly for you. This is a therapy that can begin today, be tailored by you and by them to their individual needs and unlike conventional therapies has less scope for negative connotation.

Defining what it actually is can be a little subjective – but essentially self-care is the deliberate, regular and personal actions (or attitudes) that positively influence or enhance our physical, mental, emotional, social or spiritual well-being.

That gloriously wordy sentence encapsulates the aims and ethos of self-care. For me personally, I gain from sensory self-care. When I allocate some time to this (normally around 10 minutes in the morning) I'll try and take care of my sensory needs. I'll lay on my back in front of my fireplace with candles on, knees up and hands by my side, I'll then breathe deeply, listening to the sounds around me and then begin by gently ruffling my hair in the form of a head massage. Normally I'll play the ludicrously relaxing music of the classical pianist Ludovico Einaudi and for those 10 minutes it's all just about me. Nothing can get in the way in those minutes as I schedule the time and therefore I plan it to be free.

Self-care has to become a habit for it to truly benefit long term. It must become something ingrained that the person you are supporting can understand is a coping mechanism they can employ during stressful periods but equally a double threat of being something that can actually progress their recovery too.

Other examples could be; watching a movie (with no other distractions), creating artwork/crafts, walking the dogs, going photograph hunting, meditating, dance, napping, yoga, singing, going to the cinema with a friend or alone, learning to play an instrument, learning a language and many other things. Basically, anything soothing, fun, physical, relaxing or enjoyably challenging. It can be nearly anything.

Your role here can be hugely beneficial. If you live with this person, agreeing a 'house time' to engage in self-care can be wonderfully rewarding. If they are aware that between 7 and 7.30 each evening you and they will be doing things for yourselves, it makes the process so much easier to stick to. We all know how much benefit we can have from having a gym buddy to will us on, so think of this as being their care buddy. But maybe don't name it something as patronising as that!

This can mean, on their choosing, maybe you both take part in the same activity and walk the dog together, or maybe it can mean whilst they meditate they know you are nearby and calm as you are upstairs lying in bed reading a book. It can take the awkwardness away for those unwilling to try self-care, or unsure how to, and can normalise this very normal behaviour. Also, we all like knowing our loved ones are doing well so if they know you are doing something nice for you it adds another element of enjoyment and another emotional need met whilst adding reason to engage in it for themselves.

If you are able and willing, making the social or outdoor aspects of self-care easier by supporting them with lifts or encouragement to participate will really go a long way. Should they not live with you, being their social option or team mate can be incredibly supportive and appreciated. Making yourself free for their selected times to grab some lunch, take a class together or just go for a walk is an optimum means of support.

A word of reality here too – self-care won't always work, and will sometimes slip. Read the suggested activities listed above, how often do you do any of them? How often do you sit down and take the time to do something just for you that's sole profitability is improving one of the needs above? Not often I'd guess, and that's just how life is. It's a busy world getting busier.

Look to the world's most successful people and you'll struggle to find me one of them that doesn't take at least a small period of their day to themselves to nourish one of these needs. Success is normally the by-product of purposeful actions. A businessperson doesn't often achieve acclaim by accident, it is normally something they have strived for and worked on. And benefitted from luck too. What greater commodity to work on than ourselves? Along the way many of these people recognize the importance of taking care of the bigger picture and that includes themselves and I think this is a great lesson to all. Unfortunately though, as those dynamic individuals will attest to, life gets in the way sometimes. Some days we simply do not have enough hours – this is not the end of the world, it is just realism.

Therefore before creating any self-care plan, your support to acknowledge that some days this will fail and that is absolutely OK is recommended. Encouraging a programme that is committed to, but also under the understanding that failure or inability to keep to it during certain periods is no reason to feel any sense of negativity or counterproductively or stress, is important. It is just an opportunity to enjoy the routine more during the next opportunity. It is a therapy that is all bonus. If you can help create an attitude that helps your loved one feel excitement and pleasure when an opportunity to keep to a self-care routine arises, AND a calm and reasoned approach to when it cannot - you will be providing a wonderful service.

Those purposeful actions create a barrier where to stop self-care turning into self-neglect. Allocating time to practice it is favourable as otherwise it can sort of lose its shine. If someone chooses to watch a film during their specified time (a time which can change, as above) and this soon becomes 20 films and a whole weekend in bed every single weekend – maybe it's stopped being positive. It could be argued that if they are doing that it's because they simply need to, but exercising common sense here would be good.

Another benefit that I think can be forgotten about is the premium self-care routines put onto personal responsibility of one's own care for your loved one.

By forming a programme of self-care, they are taking complete ownership of a means of treatment and progress. Think of how incredibly liberating that can be but also how endlessly positive it can be towards understanding the rounded approach to seeking recovery. It is literally learning to initiate regular boosts to yourself and accepting the precariousness of their success. Just like conventional therapy. It shows that some things will work for you over the long term and be a routine source of benefit, and some won't. Just like conventional therapy. Some will need to be tried again in a different way (for example exercising at night may be great, but in the morning a disaster) and the utter importance of input. Just like conventional therapy. They have a huge say on what does and doesn't work for them, and grow to appreciate the reasons behind why they'll feel the obvious benefit in holding the majority stakeholding in leading their own recovery.

Developing a programme will help in the short term and long term and between therapies but as you can read above I think quite potentially the strongest benefit with embracing a self-care routine is its ability to promote the process of other conventional therapies. This is not to be underestimated. Understanding that personal responsibility in your own care is not only a vital stage of the process but also one that I think can be quite comforting as it allows an element of good control. If the person you are supporting is struggling with the lack of control they are feeling in their own treatments, please do take the time to encourage self-care and reiterate what self-care teaches, rather than just what it does.

When therapists would try to persuade me to form my own programme I initially reacted with scepticism and negativity. I saw it as a bit of a cop out while I waited for CBT and at first did not embrace it. I thought it was an easy way of keeping me quiet. Once I realised that not only was there a benefit to it in the short term and long term but that it could also teach me good practice with attitudes to other therapies that I deemed more important and I became more responsive.

It's a good idea to put a programme together of allotted self-care and specific times to practice it and then also to have an 'as and when' programme ready. Some things like a cinema trip may be brilliant on regular days but on certain days when things are particularly tough it is wise to have a plan for when something is needed for right now. More often than not this will be something like meditation, listening to music in a dimly lit room, exercise at home etc. Things that can just be picked up there and then when needed. Encouraging both of these also allows the person you are supporting the opportunity to better understand their triggers and gives them the chance to practice taking care of themselves. Learning to negotiate the times when you feel like things are getting bad teaches us/them the importance of listening to yourself and understanding where their own invisible line is. A self-care plan in place to implement when things are starting to get out of control promotes this honesty and forces us to recognise our emotional responses, which is a brilliant thing to learn.

A note to those supporting younger people, or people living at home. Do not remove self-care activities as punishment! I was talking with a parent fairly recently at a talk I did at a school and she said to me that they have a programme in place and one of the things that her son gained a lot from was painting. He received a poor report from school for his disruptive conduct in class (not at all uncommon in children living with mental illness) and so lost his rights to paint. Not wishing to tell anyone how to parent but that is exactly the same as telling your child that they cannot go and see their counsellor this week as they were a bit naughty. It's counterproductive, puts a negative connotation on the next time they attempt to use that outlet (no one can enjoy an activity fully knowing it may be taken from us at any moment) and is simply not the way to go. It's about looking at the bigger picture.

When I was about 10 or 11 I began attending an art therapy group run by a charity named 'Headway', based in Essex. Headway supports those that have an acquired brain injury and the people around them. This particular group was for the young carers of brain injury survivors which included me as my Dad has a brain injury.

At this point I'd already had quite a large amount of experience with counsellors and therapists in various guises and had never ever felt the benefit of any of them. I protested a little about going to the art therapy anyway but I went along (there was a promise of McDonalds, I believe) and absolutely loved it. It was calm, easy and freeing. We did speak about the pressures of being a young carer at times but never in a formal setting. It was more of a social club of kids that knew each other's backgrounds but didn't need to always talk about it. We already faced the constant reality at home so this was more respite doing something relaxing and enjoyable than forced talking. Something just for us. Art therapy is much its own thing but there's some similar ethos there. I was spending one hour per week in a safe and secure place where my sole responsibility was doing something that nourished me for no other reason than my own mental wellbeing. That can be incredibly fulfilling and was probably a huge reason why I persevered with other therapies in the future.

Supporting someone during a self-care plan is the most straightforward assistance you can provide. Encourage it for those not yet willing to try and simply ask those that are keen to try; 'what can I do to make this easier? What can I do to make the time more worthwhile to you?' This will provide the understanding needed to make the most of one of the most underappreciated roads to recovery.

# It's Not You, It's Me

If it's not already happened, you will be scolded for your support at some stage.
As we all know, the sharpest tongues seem to be possessed by those we love the most, and in reading this book it's safe to assume you are close with the person you are a supporter of. That makes you a fairly likely target at some stages for a torrent of abuse you might not expect to receive, but believe me; it will happen.
They say we hurt the ones we love most and I can see some logic in that from my own experiences. From my teenage years up to my early twenties I was a walking rage machine. (Walking Rage Machine should probably be the name of a punk band, if you're in one, that's a freebie)
I spent more time than I wish to admit seeking out my next opportunity to vent the frustration and omnipresent anger I had burning up inside. It was not uncommon for me to specifically choose train times at weekends that I knew would be full of drunk revellers so the promised theatre of some sort of row would be potent. I'd walk through the dodgy parts of the city during the night just hoping someone would pick on me or make me have to defend myself. Arriving home unscathed was the ultimate disappointment. I wasn't a thug or out to commit crimes, I just had so much festering anger eating me up inside I had to do anything at all to expel it. I was probably an extreme case in this instance, but mental illness can often rob its victims of calmness and serenity and I was no different. People around me would do absolutely anything they could to try and make my situation better and although the vast majority of the time they would be greeted with gratitude and some embarrassment, there were times when I would throw it back in their face. Those around me would walk on eggshells at my mood swings and felt like they couldn't do right for doing wrong, I knew I was being offensive or unfair but I just couldn't stop it. I just lashed out verbally because my patience had worn out. I felt like I

was always just a few seconds from losing control of myself and my mind and that is the sort of feeling I wouldn't wish on anyone, it's completely unsettling. If I was in this way and someone entered my space with anything – be it an offer of a drink, a quick reminder they are there if needed or even the simplest of questions I would feel like I'd stepped over the edge and snap at them. Even whilst this was happening I appreciated I was in the wrong but I comforted myself with a reassuring reminder that I'm going through a tough time so I'm sure they'll understand? I allowed myself. And they did, most people do, but it certainly didn't make my manner correct.

The reason why I can write about this now is that thankfully for me, and those around me, this time has now passed. I have progressed enough to have a much firmer grasp on my emotions and this allows me to react appropriately a hell of a lot better than I ever could before. I do not go seeking the unhealthy ways of ridding myself of anger I did previously and now deal with it in a much more appropriate way. But, the person you are supporting may not be there yet so I am going to tell you something on their behalf.

Please understand we are not seeking to be absolved of blame for any harsh words or actions we do when we are not feeling our best selves. That is not what we need and not what we should want. In fact, being completely OK with us reacting in an unhealthy or unreasonable manner isn't actually helping us at all. It's normalising behaviour we need to be able to work on controlling.

What we do ask is that you understand that this is not in any way about you, not really, but completely about us.

One of the absolutely frustrating parts of living with a mental illness is finding the words when words just will not come. Hopefully, that's what this book can help achieve and I can find some on behalf of the person you are supporting.

When we react in these ways we are reacting out of an immense and unmanageable level of frustration that is emitted entirely from the symptoms of our mental illness and is not something we wish to aim at you, even when it seems we may be.

Of course, being a person living with a diagnosis does not make you any different to everyone else. We are still people and as people we get wound up by our peers and loved ones on a regular basis just like everyone else, but before reacting to our words or actions please assess whether this is during a particularly tough period and caused by this or if it's around an issue we may find triggering.

To give an example, I used to be an absolute nightmare around any sort of eating times. In the way OCD was affecting me at the time, I couldn't handle meals. The whole process was completely draining to me and inevitably someone would try and help me out by cooking for me, setting a table, passing me cutlery or making me a drink and I would fly off the handle. It sounds ridiculous (and it is) but it's very true. I'd be rude, unreasonable and unkind and I just felt like I couldn't control this feeling so acted out. Obviously this isn't a nice thing to witness and be on the receiving end of but that's sadly part of the harsh reality of living with a mental illness.

One thing I wished those around me knew was that I was truly sorry for reacting this way, but in the heat of the moment I couldn't say that. Sometimes I would apologise but if time had passed I'd feel silly bringing it up, even to say sorry, so I'd just move on. It made for a very frosty house growing up.

I'm not suggesting your loved one should be apologising for what is essentially a symptom of illness, but I do think taking responsibility for reacting unreasonably is a positive way of regaining control of your life in the search for recovery. If you're looking for an apology, from some of us it just will not come, even if they wish they could as much as you wish they would. Take it from me, in that situation, they are completely filled with regret for talking to you in this way and want you to know that their frustration is at an illness they cannot talk to, not to a person they love and respect and that is trying to help. This is an example of the mental illness talking, and not its victim. Please bear this in mind the next time you think we are angry at you rather than angry at our own condition. You are appreciated.

# Genetics Vs Environment

Negotiating the countless perplexing facets of mental illness from your position as a supporter leads to many confusing and big questions, and one that seems to lead the way, particularly for parents of those living with a diagnosis is; 'Does genetics or environment play the largest role in my child's illness?' Or, to blunt it up a bit, 'Is my own mental illness the key factor behind my child's illness?'

Some years ago I was present at a support group for parents of children that have been hospitalized due to mental illness. Firstly, it was absolutely one of the most inclusive and lovely environments I have ever been a part of. It was completely supportive, wholly open and everyone was there because they wanted to better understand how to support their kids, or themselves (which in turn supports their children).

There were a few medical professionals present including a psychiatrist and a psychologist and a closing Q&A for the parents, which was irretrievably eye opening to me and something I think of often. One of the repeated questions, asked very similarly each time was 'am I to blame for my child being unwell?'

It was asked in different ways throughout as it was obviously so preciously important to each parent there and I want to talk about it here as I think it's something that as a supporter, particularly if you are a parent, you'll need to put to bed early on to be as effective as you can be.

The factors that cause/increase mental illness can mostly be categorized into three areas; environmental, biological and psychological.

To briefly summarise, environmental factors can include the likes of parental divorce, changing jobs or schools and societal factors including unemployment and poverty that affect our everyday life, the world we live in.

Biological factors do of course include genetics (hereditary), substance abuse or brain injury/illness amongst other things and psychological elements include neglect, childhood trauma (including sexual and emotional abuse) and the effect of bereavement.

As promised, that's a very brief introduction to each factor but you'll probably relate that some of these things can possibly be key causes in the mental illness the person you are supporting has experienced. In some cases it may not be as simple as knowing one of these things is a chief contributor to their mental health and that can be tricky but for now I want to focus on the biological factor and the worry about hereditary conditions.

Genetically we all inherit behavioural and physical characteristics that we can all recognise. Eye colour, height, blood type, hair colour and unfortunately susceptibility to certain illnesses like cancers, heart disease and dementia.

When it comes down to our mental health, yes, there is potential for a genetic input towards us being unwell. This can be really difficult for parents to get their heads around as it can be incredibly easy to become self-critical and put the onus onto yourselves rather than the myriad of other reasons an illness can occur. Doing so is self-defeating and can cause a vicious cycle.

Firstly, it adds a pressure on the person you are supporting. Living with a diagnosis is difficult enough but knowing that the family that you love more than anything in the world see you at your lowest and then blame themselves can be devastating. It can also mean that to avoid the guilt on both sides, the young person may just stop talking about their illness to stop their parents feeling upset. No one likes hurting the people they love so if discussing your mental health hurts your loved ones it can be easy to stop, and that can be fatal to recovery. If you were discussing your mental health openly and then immediately the person you confide in begins to tell you it's all their fault, be it parent or partner, you'll straight away be inclined to reassure it's not their fault and probably not really readdress a possibly important conversation in the interests of saving everyone awkwardness. That exact level of not talking is where the big issues begin so if you are a parent reading this and are beating yourself up thinking your child's mental illness is down to you genetically, that's not a conversation you need to have with them. And I rarely say 'that's not a chat to have!', but in this case it really isn't. But, it is something you need to approach mentally yourselves and possibly professionally too or by the many great peer support groups available to parents.

On the other side of this book I write about how we naturally choose to undersell our abilities or how it's so easy for humans to automatically side with the negative aspect and many parents I have spoken to do exactly this when asking themselves the questions they asked that evening at the support group.

One thing to consider here that I find helpful and illustrative is remembering how height is determined. If your Mum and Dad are both 6ft plus, there's a chance you are going to be tall. But if you are malnourished or suffering from certain illnesses, you may not hit that height as the environmental factors versus your genes makes your height what it is. I'm about 6ft1 but spent the best part of my teenage years eating terribly or not at all and ruining my health with a painkiller addiction and poor all round health, whereas if I'd been healthy throughout my adolescence I'd most likely be taller now. Therefore, it's not simply about genes, it's also hugely about environment and psychological factors.

This translates an important message about the role genetics plays in mental illness. Of course it has to be accepted that there is a higher chance that if you suffer with a condition yourself, your offspring are more likely to personally experience that condition than a child whose parents do not have that condition. But, it has to be understood that the reasons and causes behind mental illnesses are so incredibly complex that it would be both a little insulting and even naïve to simplify its existence in your loved one as just based upon whom their parent is.

In my favourite film, 1997's 'Good Will Hunting', the title character is discussing a date with Minnie Driver's character 'Skylar'. Skylar suggests going for coffee. Will surprises her by retorting 'Maybe we can get together and eat a bunch of caramels. When you think about it, it's as arbitrary as drinking coffee' and that scene is something I always think back to when I get too caught up in the reasons behind my mental illness. The sheer amount of factors behind it points to the randomness and complexities of luck in life, therefore why become obsessed by the part of it that is predetermined before you've even met the person they shall become? Who we are is such a colossally vast mix of a galaxy of ingredients we couldn't attribute it to one reason even if we wanted to. As Will eloquently shows when describing their date, the 'how' of the date itself isn't as important as why they even wish to date in the first place. The picture is far bigger. The reasons why we are ill are not as important as the reasons why we strive to get better. Why is that one issue such a prevalent issue to parents? And is it even worthy of their worry?

Genetically, we can learn lots from our DNA and genes. We can see a trend of heart disease and realise our obesity may cause us an issue down the line. We can see the beard our Dad can grow and realise maybe the clean shaven look is the way forward. We can appreciate the breast cancer dangers in our family and be extra vigilant to lumps. The key in these examples is not the 'why', but the 'what next'.

Do we blast our parents for supposedly faulty genes? Of course not. It's far too complicated to be simplified as 'you'll definitely become ill because your parent did', it doesn't work like that for physical illness so we shouldn't find reason to fault ourselves due to mental illness. Nothing is gained from it and there is only potential for losses. What we can do is, and stick with me, is use this familial knowledge to understand and notice the warning signs in ourselves and in those we love and use this information as purely positive. We need to completely transform the way we see and use this information, like all data – it is only relevant to the point we are trying to make. If the point we are trying to make is 'it's my fault', you'll find many reasons to support you and make you feel awful, but no one will get better from it. I have OCD, like some of you reading this I do sometimes have moments of being petrified that my child will have OCD too. Is this more likely? Yes, possibly so. But what better chance does a child have of conquering their mental illnesses than being born to parents that absolutely understand through lived experience what to look for?

If that does happen and I can use this information and experience as a positive by appreciating it's potential to be useful if they did, then I would be doing my children a wonderful service. I would just have to apologise to them for the eyebrows, no one deserves that.

The genetic factors behind mental illness are important but they are to be used to understand, not used to validate a self-sabotaging attitude. If you are a parent of a child attending an assessment with a psychologist, one of the first questions they shall ask your child or have asked their GP is 'is there any family history of mental illness?' Immediately this information gives the medical professional something to consider, rule out or diagnose. It's an important tool.

If you're not with me on this and agreeing that yes, while your own mental health may play a role in determining the factors behind your loved one's mental health, you still feel responsible for its presence then I urge you to discuss this with your own Doctor/s. Letting this thought become too strong can seriously hamper your perception of their own battle and ultimately be damaging long term all the while making your child or loved one feel guilty for having spoken about it. You are the supporting cast in this movie, not the lead. It is vital you work through this in my opinion to be better placed to be the most effective supporter you can be.

Being a parent is, I am sure, an overpowering smorgasbord of emotions and insecurities and I have little doubt that in your quest to make everything OK you'll make mistakes and believe things you probably shouldn't and I can assure you now – this is one of them.

# Supporting A Crisis

When we think about supporting someone with a mental illness we tend to think of the most dramatic versions of support, namely crisis and maybe even suicide attempts.
This makes sense. We learn first aid to know how to do CPR and not so much how to treat a broken finger. But naturally, we will be far less likely to be supporting a crisis than we will be supporting someone negotiate the day to day aspects of their life with a mental illness.
This is worth mentioning first, as I think 'supporting someone with a mental illness' can often conjure up some difficult images that, although possible and true, are not the majority of the support you will offer. More often than not you'll be supporting in a much more subtle and controlled way. This is important as this significant image often puts people off providing a support as they feel they are unqualified to do so. I do not believe that. I do not believe that anyone is unqualified to help another human being steer themselves through difficult times in at least some capacity. It is true that we are unqualified for some aspects and absolutely should not overstep our boundaries, experience and knowledge - but there is always something we can do.

This chapter is about crisis though and to clarify what 'crisis' means in this context, I am defining it as; when the person you are supporting is in a position where their mental health is having a serious and current impact on their quality of life to their version of breaking point and they require immediate support and help.
I'm not specifically writing about a crisis where they may be a danger to themselves or others, but will discuss this at the end of the chapter, although much of the options to support them below remain exactly the same.

***Do not wait to see a diagnosis!***

People in crisis need good support as quickly as they can, it really is as simple as that. For that reason if you have any fear that a person is in a crisis, do not hesitate or wait to support. Sometimes well-meaning people and supporters will believe a person is not in crisis as they've 'never been in one before'. This is not a valid reason to rule out a crisis. If they tell you it is a crisis, certainly proceed as if it is, if you believe it is a crisis or not. They may have been in a condition recently that would make you feel they were not likely to reach a breaking point but remember that mental illness can personally affect us all, and so can reaching crisis point.

This person may also be someone that has never actually been diagnosed with or spoken about having a mental health condition, but as sure as we are that people are feeling more and more comfortable coming forward and discussing their mental health nowadays – there will always be people that reach mental health crisis without anyone knowing, and sometimes without even realising it themselves. Therefore, ignore diagnosis or previous thoughts. If you suspect crisis, or they suspect crisis, act as it is a crisis.

It is also worth noting that people may show signs of an acute mental health condition and crisis in non-mental health circumstances. For example, a drug overdose or even an infection may cause hallucinations or delusions. This is still an emergency but shows why we cannot think we know better than the symptoms.

***What changes do you see?***

Can you identify differences between the person you are supporting now, in crisis, and not so? Is their behaviour different? Is their speech different? Are they saying things they wouldn't normally say?

It can be helpful to use this as an indicator of how the crisis affects them and will be useful to a medical professional when they access help.

Changes may be things like the way they talk about themselves becoming darker or less hopeful. It may be that they no longer eat meals and just pick at food. They may no longer care about things they would normally care about i.e. appearance, work, social responsibilities.

A way you can support this is to provide non-judgemental encouragement towards the healthier option. So rather than 'You're not eating. That's wrong. You must eat' it would be better to say 'I think eating will make a difference in feeling better. It does for me. Can I make you something?'

Sometimes they may not see the changes themselves so there is a potential that what you say is different about them is actually a shock to them to hear. Be prepared for that.

***If so, have I seen these changes before?***

If you are witnessing a change in the person, it may well be that this is something you have seen before from them. Potentially during a previous crisis. It may not be every change you have seen before (every crisis is different) but there may be similarities. If these are logistical changes, like not taking care of themselves with eating, sleeping, hygiene, commitments etc. try to remind yourself, or ask them, how to best support bringing those changes back towards something healthier. This may involve cooking for them, offering them a place to stay for a day or two to relax out of their normal routine, offering to help clean up their room with them to create a more comfortable place to rest, a lift to any appointments or making phone calls on their behalf to either keep up commitments or put alternative plans in place (maybe with work or school).

***Ask them what they find helpful.***

Particularly for those that have experienced crisis before, many people will have a few

things they are able to explain that helps them during such a difficult time.
Often this will be things like not being left alone, being distracted, just staying with them, supporting daily tasks like cooking or paperwork, calling a professional on their behalf, supporting breathing exercises or helping them write a plan for what to do next.

***Sometimes talking may take some time.***

It's not uncommon for those in crisis to know they want to talk, but to also know that they do not wish to talk *yet*.
Some may need a little time before they can be eloquent enough to explain how they feel or what they need or to even talk at all. For me personally, during a crisis I probably talk much more than I normally would. I want to talk right away and often, whereas some will want to talk eventually, and seldom. Don't rush it. Do let them know if and when they are ready to talk, you are ready to listen.

***How they speak to you may be different to how they speak to someone else.***

When they are communicating, it is worth bearing in mind the conversation you have together is unique to you. Do not be upset or confused by the fact they may speak to someone else more openly, more honestly or more often. It may well be that you are very close to the person and they shut off to you but talk freely with someone not as close to them, that makes perfect sense. Some people feel much more comfortable conversing with someone 'out of the situation' than someone so close to it and them. Equally, someone may only wish to talk to someone in their immediate family or a partner – so if you're an acquaintance or even a best friend, do not be shocked or show them that you are disappointed if they choose to talk to someone else.
This is particularly true I think for parents. If your child talks to your co-parent about a crisis but not you, that isn't a reflection on you as a parent or your relationship but purely their preference in that one instance. It can be helpful to let them know others are

available to speak if they so wish and that you won't be offended if they'd like you to get the other person.

***Create realistic talking opportunities.***

Make sure you make the person you are supporting aware they have your full attention and concentration. I've been in situations myself where I have been in crisis and needing support but know the person I'm with has a train to catch or a meal to get to so I've preferred to not speak.

If at all possible, make time to speak to each other with undivided attention if you can. Bear in mind your surroundings and environment. Is this an appropriate and safe place for them to talk openly? If they are in crisis outside of home, are you able to safely get them home rather than offer support where you are? If they flatshare, are at a uni house or live with someone they aren't particularly close to, is home and the people around appropriate for this?

If the person you are supporting lives with friends and may have a medical professional visiting them, they may wish to be elsewhere. Are you able to offer a free space, support finding one or take them to one of their choosing?

***You are not their doctor, know your limits.***

It is of importance that the person you are supporting through a crisis accesses the appropriate medical support as soon as possible and getting to this goal is a priority. You may know the person intimately and may have even supported many other crises with them or others over the years, but it is unwise to assume you are the person to lead the next step. Although we DO want to get them through the most difficult period, we do not want to just get them through temporarily without a next step. That's a bit like running a marathon and then not planning on how to get home, if we do not, we'll just need to find a way back anyway. Medical professionals are absolutely the people to lead this.

***If they are suicidal.***

It may sound obvious, but many people assume A&E's in the UK are specifically for physical health conditions and that is absolutely not so. If the person you are supporting feels suicidal, feels they are unable to keep themselves safe or you feel either of those is a possibility; that is a medical emergency. Seek immediate help, get to A&E in person if you/they can or feel free to call 999 on their behalf – or suggest they do so.
Should they already be under a CRHT team (crisis team), contact them immediately for support. If they are unwilling or unable to go to an A&E, or if it is deemed a better/quicker solution, contact your local GP practice for an emergency appointment. A little note here too, if you are not registered with a GP, they will still see someone in an emergency.
As is well known, the Samaritans offer a free 365 days a year, 7 day a week, 24hr a day service by calling 116 123 from any phone. They can also be emailed, visited or written to in the post. So if you live in the UK, you know, without doubt – there is always someone that you can talk to.

***Tips for keeping calm.***

Obviously this might seem like an impossibility during a crisis. Some of us find it difficult to keep calm in day to day life so remaining/finding calm in crisis is no mean feat. Some tips I and others find helpful would include;

- Create a 'nest' space. Blankets, comforting drinks/food, pillows, calm music, comfortable clothing and a space they can sit or lay down.
- Talk about getting over this immediate feeling, first and foremost. Sometimes even discussing the great things in life to come can be overwhelming in crisis. 'You have Uni

to look forward to next year!' may actually elicit anxiety, not reduce it. The feeling post-panic/crisis will be tiring, but can be almost euphoric as you 'escape' the feeling of crisis. Focusing on finding this is more realistic than finding 'feeling fine', at least in the short term.

- Regulate breathing or use breathing exercises. I like to use deep and consistent breaths in and out, counting from 1 to 5. i.e breathe in….1….2….3….4….5, breathe out….1….2….3….4….5.
- I find music or films that I know really well help me to have on in the background. A film I could recite or a band I can sing along to. Even in crisis I can find myself 'joining in'. I wouldn't try and sit and watch the film or listen to the music completely as they'll be too much 'noise' from the panic, but it can provide a reassuring backdrop and calming focus.
- In the other book I mention how I use a 'Remember Box' for when I feel in crisis. It is to keep things in it that remind me of the good side of life or are simple, little pleasures. Maybe not necessarily photos or anything that may evoke bad memories, but including a favourite children's book (The Cat In The Hat is in mine and I'm nearly 30!), keepsake from a special day, a favourite food etc. can be a big help. Basically a box of things they would want to open during a crisis, put together by them when they feel well enough to.
- Writing down some questions they would like to ask their medical team when they see them is a great way to use this time. They are already feeling horrible, it would be no loss to record that feeling so they may be able to provide accurate descriptions to their team. Also, writing down questions they want to ask about how they feel, how they want to proceed, things they want to try or simply asking 'what do we do next to make me feel better?' may make the time feel more productive than just feeling in crisis. If you can promote that doing so may make a good long term outcome from a bad short term situation may add some wonderful perspective to this.
- Keep yourself calm. Displaying and 'modelling' calmness can help those around you get onto the same level

Finally, when this is over it is absolutely worth having a debrief with yourself, those around you and your own GP to ensure you feel OK about witnessing or being a part of a mental health crisis.

If you already suffer with your own mental health then this can be a particularly traumatic or triggering experience but even if you do not, witnessing anyone in pain is distressing, but someone you love and care about can be terrifying.

You can use this opportunity to ask your Doctor if there is anything else they feel may have been worthwhile doing in this instance, which can be good feedback, and beyond this it is worth keeping a note of your own thoughts and feelings to ensure you stay healthy post-supporting crisis. Your own reactions to the crisis and how it makes you feel may be delayed, broad or varying in severity in time so listen to yourself and seek help whenever you need it.

# What Is Enabling?

A word often thrown around in mental health (and particularly addiction) circles is 'enabling'. Usually this is in the context of describing loved ones heartfelt and good intentioned actions that are actually causing more harm than help.

Difficultly, this does feel paradoxical and normally those that do the most enabling are those that are trying the hardest to help. The closer you are to the person; you more likely you are to be, at times, enabling them. It is one of the many unfair parts of living with a mental health condition or supporting someone that is. But here is an idea on how to approach it.

Firstly, it is worth realising that the person you are enabling may not actually even realise it is occurring, and neither may you.

This is one of the more delicate issues to write about as I have written extensively on the importance of being a supporter, a cheerleader, an asset and a teammate to those around you living with a mental health condition, but the thing to remember is, you are not enabling the person (good thing), you are enabling the mental illness (bad thing!).

Enabling them to have a day of self-care or to be in a safe and comfortable enough position to seek help is wonderful. Enabling their illness to take precedent over healthier or more realistic options is obviously not.

The way I would define enabling is the taking of responsibility away from the person for either tasks they need to do themselves to maintain a sense of normality, or allowing behaviours that are unacceptable due to a misguided thought of your own that this poor behaviour is absolutely fine due to their condition.

This will not be a newsflash to you, nor anyone that has known me for any amount of time, but I can confirm with great confidence that people living with mental health conditions can be arseholes. Yep. We really can.

So can people without mental health conditions, obviously. We all are from time to time. I tend to be a bit of an arsehole at least five times before breakfast.

A great rule of thumb to use when deciding whether to challenge behaviour is; would I accept this behaviour from someone without a mental illness?

If the answer is 'no', you should appropriately call it out. Maybe not immediately, but you should absolutely make it clear that they are acting or behaving out of turn.

This is a kind thing to do. Sometimes, when you are in the deep waters of mental illness, you will lose sight of what is normal negative behaviour/emotions and what is mental illness, and being reminded appropriately of the truth is a healthy thing for a supporter to do.

To give an example, in my bad days, I would have a very fierce and very unforgiving tongue. I would routinely shout and scream at family members for innocuous reasons and could get very unpleasant to be around. I would be in my twenties and kicking off at someone for trivial things. But Jack! You seem so incredibly well rounded mate? This cannot be true. You're such a gentleman I'm thinking of naming all of my children after you. Well, dear reader, even I can be a bit of a tit. Here is an example
I can recall.

A friend of mine had come over and ended up spilling a drink on an easily wiped kitchen floor that resulted in me giving them an almighty dressing down that would have made an Army Sergeant blush. It was about more than just the spilled drink. It made me anxious and stressed during an already difficult day so in my head I had a valid complaint.

In reality, I did not. It was an accident. It was easily rectified. It was one of those things. I was being rude.

There were two ways forward for my mate in that situation. a) Apologise profusely at their sheer incompetence and top level bastardry and promise to never make such a heinous mistake in my presence again or b) Remind me that, in fact, I'm being quite rude and that my words and actions are not on and unwarranted.

I wanted a), but instead I got b). And with it, a fantastic lesson.

If this person had 'let me off' my behaviour, it would be very easy for me to stay within that behaviour and it would have validated it. It would have normalised it. And my reaction was definitely not normal.

After that incident I could well have gone to work and behaved the same way, deeming it an acceptable response and ended up losing my job. I could have done it in a restaurant and made a staff member feel absolutely horrible. Most importantly though, by not calling it out I would have moved further away from healthy interactions with people and more controlled by my reactions to my illness, rather than more in control.

I was still angry, and a little bit embarrassed - but it made me snap out of the feeling and gave me a little perspective. This was a great example of empowering and not enabling a person.

It allowed me the autonomy to face up to the situation, the feelings and the symptoms of my mental illness in a safe and appropriate way. Such a simple moment that chipped away a little at the hold my health had upon me.

In a task sense, enabling can occur by taking away the opportunity to improve by removing the responsibility. This varies person to person but a good example would be, if the person you are supporting is having an off day and does not want to partake in a regular or expected activity (going to work or school, taking an exam, meeting a friend, doing a chore), enabling them may occur by allowing them an 'easy out'. Calling on their behalf and making excuses to work or school or friend maybe, or doing the chore for them. Making it easier for them to make the easy choice, even if it isn't the best one. Of course as with everything discretion is important here as if they are having a crisis or if going to school or work is an unhealthy option that day, forcing them into it would not be empowering.

During my GCSE year I had become incredibly unwell. The walk to school alone was nightmarish. A well-meaning Head of Year decided to offer me the 'out' of working from the library only and not partaking in any lessons. They thought they were helping and in an immediate sense they were, they removed me from the anxiety producing activity but in reality they were enabling my illness, not empowering me personally. There was not an encouragement to try, or an agreement to go to a lesson and then if things became uncontrollable to retreat to the library. It was simply agreed I'd work from there and that was that. I took hardly any of my GCSE's. I found new anxieties in the library and I lost a great opportunity to challenge the illness. This teacher was well meaning, kind and thoughtful. They were just a little uneducated about mental illness and my own mental illness and did not understand that this was an imperfect solution.

This book is about being realistic, positively. It is not about being positive without caution and as with everything there is a real trial and error at play here but this is one with a potentially really effective reward for the person you are supporting and for yourself. It takes an incredible amount of discipline to not take an easy option, marry that with a mental illness and it can seem impossible, so most people are not going to hand over information that you are enabling them, if they are aware you are. During a panic or a difficult period or an all-out crisis it is unrealistic to expect a sufferer to stop and say 'Hey! Thanks for trying to help, but you're actually enabling me!' It is more likely they will be lost in the moment so broaching the subject about how to stop longer term potential enabling is best done at a calm time, when you can discuss why you wish to police yourself in enabling their mental illness. Hopefully, this conversation can be collaborative and allow you to ask the person you are supporting if they have examples of when you may be enabling, or potential scenarios forthcoming or previous that present opportunity to do so. This will hopefully also help them gain a better understanding of their behaviour and of their mental illness itself.

# Being A Carer And Being Unwell

I've only ever prayed once by choice. I was 14. Sitting alone in our bathroom I locked the door and sat down and drowned out the sounds of the sirens of the ambulance for just about long enough to say out loud 'if you don't let him die today, I'll be a better person, please'.

I was pleading to a God I didn't actually even believe in out of sheer desperation as I sought any means of control over a situation that was spiralling out of my control. Dad had been ill for about 6 years and it had always been serious but this was his second heart attack. The first had involved resuscitation and him being 'dead' for several minutes. Things had got worse for him physically and mentally and I didn't think his chances were good. The man I had absolutely idolised as a boy was in a very bad way and the look on the faces of the paramedics when they arrived told a story I didn't want to know.

Earlier that summer I'd refreshed by First Aid course, something I had done regularly since he and my brother had become so ill. I didn't really think about it and it wasn't really a decision it was just something I did because the reality was I was likely to have to use it. Every time I'd do it and have to perform CPR on the little Annie doll they use for practice I would freak out and ask the rest of the students, normally all adults, if I'd be strong enough to save my big and burly Dad if I needed to? What if I wasn't strong enough? Would he die and it be my fault? The pressure felt relentless.

So now I was downstairs looking at Dad slipping in and out of consciousness and just waiting in case I'd have to jump into action. It must have been no more than 5 minutes before the ambulance arrived but each second felt like he was slipping away and I was stunned with fear.

When they got to him they didn't mess about. Paramedics are truly wonderful people and these two were no different. Dad looked bad now, really bad. There was no colour to him whatsoever and I remember telling myself as he was wheeled out to not cry because I didn't want his last image to be of me being scared so I stood and smiled, as strange as that may seem.

As he was about to go down the ramp he shouted 'stop' with every single part of him, as sick as he was he did so with his usual velocity to startle the medics into observing his request. 'Jack?' he enquired, searching around the room for me (all but five feet away but in his condition he was mostly out of it) and then did an action I'll never ever forget and always be beyond grateful for. He gave me a thumbs up.

Now Dad was always a strong man. Probably too much so. The victim of a truly horrendous upbringing that centred around his Mum's death, his Dad's outward disgust in him and abuse and neglect sadly not uncommon in the 50's and 60's. He was a true Cockney and what would be seen as a 'manly' bloke. He was tough and sometimes scary but loving and warm and he had just used every single ounce of strength he had in him to make sure I saw him as 'OK'. It was probably the greatest show of human strength I've ever personally witnessed.

As they began wheeling he lost consciousness and they ran him into the back of the Ambulance as we arranged to follow on before the petrifying realisation the ambulance hadn't even started moving yet, making us aware something wasn't right. It wasn't, he had gone into cardiac arrest and both paramedics were working on him.

Thankfully this story had a happy ending and years later he is still with us. Still a very unwell man but still here.

In the UK there are around a quarter of a million young carers, Of these 250,000 children and young people providing physical, mental, emotional and personal support for a loved one and often a parent, nearly half of them have special educational needs or a mental health problem. Not only is that the case but these young people are sacrificing many prospects by choice or not, due to circumstance. This means significantly lower GCSE attainment levels and a lower than the national average chance of being in education, employment or training. More often than not, as was the case with me, these young people will come from lower income families by quite a notable way.

For those of you reading this that are in that situation or have been in that situation, firstly, you are absolutely beyond incredible. I know you do not expect thanks or gratitude as this is just how your life is (right now) but you deserve it and as with most young people I meet, you fill me with immense pride. I have been there. I was a carer for my brother and my Dad growing up and alongside my own mental health issues the enormity of responsibility can be absolutely crushing. Then on top of that you've got to fit into your life; growing up! It's already such a difficult period to navigate (much harder now than many adults give you credit for) without the added pressures of caring.

It is absolutely vital that the love, care and compassion you show the person you care for extends to yourself. Empathy is limitless and so is your opportunity to self-care. Not only is a healthier and happier you a practical advantage as obviously this makes your ability to care and support others easier, it also provides a valuable reminder that the most important person in your life, the person who most needs your support, the human that will be with you the longest and the one you need to most cherish, respect and help is; yourself.

By the fact you are reading this book it means you probably already know that, or it means someone else knows it enough to think you need reminding of it by giving you this book to read.

To be a carer you most probably possess a better than average level of organisation. Use this skill for you, too. I'm sure you're used to GP appointments or social worker meetings and if so, speak to them about you. As we know from our own conditions, illness affects more than just the person that is unwell and these healthcare professionals are there to be a general support so find the services right for you, as there are hundreds of good ones. These can range from helping you out logistically, finding alternative care for your loved one and assisting with the paperwork that comes with that, arranging for you to attend support days with other young carers (I highly recommend this) and also simply offers you a place to chat.

This chapter is also relevant to those caring for another that may not be in the 'young' (sorry!) category anymore, the lesson still stands at any age. If you are a friend of a young person and reading this book as a supporter with a desire to learn more on how to better support a friend, you may not feel you class as a carer but the same words apply to you. It blows my mind the lengths people will go to in their support of others and it is an incredibly beautiful thing, but do look after yourself and do ensure your own needs are not neglected. For the young people caring full time at home, one day life is going to open up for you like a treasure chest. Just like it did for me. And you will be so ready.

# The State Of The Union

'It's time to talk'.

Abraham Lincoln is credited with abolishing slavery and was believed to suffer with depression, Winston Churchill led Great Britain through the deadliest conflict in human history whilst apparently having the black dog of bipolar on his back and Edvard Munch painted one of the greatest masterpieces of all time whilst debilitated by crippling panic attacks, so it is believed.

All of these potential diagnoses are purely speculative as society at the time hadn't got to the position we are in now so each case is retrospectively diagnosed.

This isn't something we'll ever have to do again for the future historical figures of today.

We now accept and acknowledge the awesome importance of our mental health and are far removed from the limited understanding and perceptions of yesteryear where anyone ill was simply 'mad' and cast aside.

Now, in this country at least, you can talk and be heard. You can show symptom and be understood and you can seek those openly willing to discuss the diagnosis you both share and in general find them with relative ease.

This has led, particularly in the past decade, to a huge number of shared lived experiences and this is, of course, absolutely powerful. This kinship is one of the chief ingredients to understanding being achieved and stigma being buried forever.

One quote I'll often read and hear is that it is 'time to talk'. And I could not disagree more.

50 years ago it was time to talk, 100 years ago even. Thankfully somewhere along the line, and sadly not too long ago, we began talking. We began really, truly listening to ourselves and questioning our attitudes around mental health and finally processing the inescapable

fact that mental illness is not a popular fad or passing challenge but one of the most significant parts of life.

Things have evolved rapidly, relatively speaking. The way the general public sees mental health in 2019 is far removed from how we saw it in 1989. I can even see massive differences now than in 2009. This is one of the most encouraging truths I can think of. But, despite all of this mammoth progress it is certainly not fucking 'time to talk'. My word, no.

It's now 'time to act'.

We know many of the things that are needed now and lots of things we are still learning, but there's a worldwide acceptance of some core principles of what needs to happen to make the world a mentally healthier place.

Now I don't want to politicise a mental health self-help book. But I'm bored of hearing about when is the 'right time' to make a point political. After every depressingly common school shooting in the US, those in the gun control camp will come out and talk legislation and action and they'll be dismissed by those in the 2nd amendment camp as being vulgar and war profiteering from tragedy and heartache. They'll be told that yes, big questions need to be asked. But, that no, these questions are not for today. If they aren't for today, when on earth are they for?

Here in the UK we are at a critical point in our development as a nation when it comes down to mental health.

We realised it was time to talk and we did. Mental health discussion is no longer just the talk of professionals and the sensitive but something discussed by those previously deemed too 'strong' to bring it up. CEO's, sportspeople, teachers, politicians, actors, police officers. Everyone acknowledges it is good to talk and that the discussion we are having is important but every discussion is supposed to have a point and ultimately ours has to be to make changes to facilitate this commonly held understanding of the importance of mental health.

Then if this is the case, as it undoubtedly is, why are we in the position where, with mental health services nationwide reporting an unprecedented engagement from service users, we constantly have reported analysis demonising the chronic lack of funding of these vital services?

90% of psychiatrists work within these trusts, according to the Royal College of Psychiatrists. Yet, in 2016/2017, 62% of these trusts reported lower income than they did at the end of 2011/2012.

Within that time certain services have changed governance from NHS to local government and a proportion of this funding goes towards sexual health clinics, community services and other medical services and this is an important point, but it highlights the sheer lack of clarity and concise invigilation of a vital component of government spending. Matt Hancock, the embattled Health Secretary, will argue that spending is at record highs and aspects of his claim are true. I will definitely say we have increased funding since the last available statistics. I'm not certain that is what the facts will say when released, but I'm pretty sure. Obviously I welcome this. But whilst we have been talking, we have not been acting and it is this inaction that has led us to the crisis we find ourselves in.

Reliable funding information has become so scarce that major players in mental health development have to 'agree to disagree' on the numbers. If the Royal College of Psychiatrists and NHS England can disagree on how much money is being spent and where it is going, how can the person on the street be sure? How can the public be given reliable information to make informed choices when the authorities on the matter cannot even agree due to a lack of proper scrutiny towards where the money ends up? Obviously all statistics can be presented in a way to prove a point, but we aren't simply talking agreed facts being kicked around to mould a point – we are talking actual numbers being disputed from both sides. They aren't arguing where the number is going, they aren't even at that stage.

This means we simply do not know exactly where critical funds are being directed. We do

know how much is needed, but we do not know if it is reaching those areas.
Although the NHS (and the medical profession in general) can always benefit from greater funding opportunity, the real issue is making sure it reaches the frontline. Spending and economy are only relevant when taken into context of inflation and using treasury analysis, the RCP raises serious concerns of the £105million (in real terms) of underinvestment in the 2016/17 period that was seen in 2011/12, but with more people seeking and needing treatment now than there was since the first or second dates.
This means, simply put, people now realise the importance of seeking help, but when they get there, are they being failed?

When researching this book I appealed to parents with experience of supporting a loved one through treatment with CAMHS (Child and Adolescent Mental Health Services) and interviewed many on the subject. An appalling amount of them began correspondence with me by saying 'this is going to be quite negative, is that OK?'
For balance, I realise that most people are more likely to feel inclined to go online and give a bad review than a good one. Regardless, the feedback received was overwhelmingly negative, sadly.
I want to jump in here with something really important for those of you reading this feeling deflated by my words, or reviews you've read, and give an opinion that is personal to me but also widely shared.
Yes, CAMHS and the CMHT (Community Mental Health Team, adult services) are beyond dangerously failing. They have gone past breaking point in many areas and are crippled by what is needed of them versus what they can currently achieve but as negative as this is – this is NOT a reflection on the wonderful, world class care that can (and is) achieved within its systems.
There exists a fallacy that when you step through the doors of a building of a mental health trust in the UK you'll be failed from start to finish and that is not true. There are many internationally renowned medical professionals and support staff operating within that have the ability and desire to make outstanding contributions towards the fields of

mental health research and treatment.

The issue is not within their ability as mental health professionals, in fact, we are considered a world leader in this field – but rooted in their physical capabilities of being able to help as effectively as they can due to the many constraints they are under. We all know our medical professionals are overworked and underpaid but this issue transcends beyond salary and working hours. They are not being given the resources and tools to be anywhere near as effective as they can be.

It's near unanimously understood the NHS needs more but is an incredible asset to our country and CAMHS/CMHT should be viewed much the same. It is very much a part of it.

I can write tributes to many working within the system and that is because phenomenal professionals exist within every trust in this country so despite the rightly worrying statistics emerging daily on their working conditions, this should not mean you do not engage or support someone in engaging in what they do offer.

The issue of apathy is a present one. It's impossible to (honestly) write this chapter without confessing we are in a delicate state of affairs and in many aspects must do better and acknowledge the overwhelming challenges prevalent. But, apathy is a first class ticket to plateauing in your treatment.

The politics behind the issue couldn't be ignored if we tried, as those decisions and decision makers play a role that those of us experiencing the system will encounter in some way or another as their choices emanate much farther than Westminster. Some fatally so. However, we must also prevent ourselves using this fact to become detached from the system itself. It is broken, certainly. But even the ever imperfect system could provide the treatment that supports you or your loved one towards being mentally healthy.

As with the 'TripAdvisor' analogy from before, you will hear far less testimony from those that have used the system to the point of recovery or life changing improvements than those that have been failed.

I believe wholeheartedly that the most efficient way to change something is to be a part of it and with the CAMHS/CMHT system in the UK, most of us need to be a part of it. The horror stories are there, but the triumphant successful examples of treatment are there too. And that might just be your story, or that of those you love. It must be given a chance and the negatives you've heard although all valid and important does not necessarily represent the course your own recovery may take.

We have a 'first response' issue in the UK with mental health. In a primary care sense this means your GP but like the funding issue above being spread out, those we can and probably should consider as 'first responders' can now be a broad group.

A specific budget nationally, regionally, locally and school by school towards improving the mental health welfare of its students is an absolute must for every educational establishment in the country. No student, child or otherwise, should be neglected as a whole person. No school in 2019 wants to enjoy the learning career of a young person with Oxford University potential if they'll never achieve what they could due to poor mental health. Seeing our young people for who they are as people rather than just what they do and do not achieve as students is the only way to get the best from entire cohorts rather than the select, healthy, few.

For teachers reading this, I know this is how you view this issue already and I know as educators you go above and beyond just grades and for that you're unsung national heroes. But as you'll also agree, currently, the training and tools needed to be truly great first responders to young people suffering with their mental health have not yet been bestowed upon you.

Equally, workplaces must develop a culture where mental health is treated within the same category and urgency as physical health. This cannot be simply a case of small businesses leading the way as the personal and human factor of their employee/employer relationship is more intimate, or conversely lead by the big guys, because they have the budget and resources to make something more of their support – it needs to be universal.

Mostly, this can be achieved without great cost. Wherever you work, I'm sure your health and safety officer, manager, directors or MD have been on their first aid courses. It's a necessity and expected professional basic so why is this not extended to mental health first aid? There are many great accredited courses and conferences available to choose from. If you run a business, get yourself or an appointed person on one. Do it yearly. Keep up to date and invest in people.

Elsewhere in this book I've written of the fact that most people are out to help and this allows anyone the opportunity to find someone to open up to within their personal, educational or professional lives to assist in setting up what is needed to make your time within each of these as beneficial and healthy as they can be. But currently, this is being done by relying on the natural good nature of people and not without the professionalization and modernisation this pursuit could and should have.

According to 2017 statistics by the FSB (Federation of Small Businesses) 99.3% of all businesses were 'small' within the private sector. This means the vast majority work for a company where you can probably find and speak to a specific contact trained to offer support and guidance towards attainting mental health treatment easily within the day. In most cases, they'll be within the same building as you.

It not being deemed an absolute professional requirement to have at least one member of staff specifically trained in this manner is a scandal.

I'm not advocating giving Dave from HR a Doctorate in Medicine and allowing him to start giving professional advice way above his experience (and possibly desire). But I am supporting every single person, be they at work or school, being able to have an everyday point of contact that they know can pass on the information or processes needed to access treatment.

I think it unwise and dangerous to put people underqualified in a position of offering medical guidance, obviously, but offering procedural advice and simply having the knowledge and qualification to say 'sorry to hear that, you can contact these people for help and this is what happens next' would be a significant step forwards for us. It would develop a healthy culture of understanding and would also provide a good support system per workplace to not only do the right thing as humans in supporting each other, but also make the everyday challenges those living with a diagnosis will know to be challenging something that employer and employee can work together on to become manageable. Rather than one side (employer or employee) dictating how things need to be, it can be mutually agreed so that everyone is on board with how mental health is supported within the workplace. It's about the whole person. You can't expect a staff member to perform at the level required and above if personally they are unable to function, or when they are functioning it is with great difficulty, or when they are functioning with great difficulty they are in turn losing a part of themselves doing so. They may be pushing to achieve for you as a business, but their life outside is failing due to it. Neither indicates success.

There needs to be a greater collective ownership from the establishments that we dedicate our time to on supporting each other. It is absolutely in our interests as a group to do this.

For those of us in employment, school, uni, college or any other structured day to day environment, you're probably giving 40 hours plus of your week, every single week, towards that cause. That's a very substantial amount of time. Why can that not be a time that is mental health progressive for you? If it can't be that, it can at least be safe and non-detrimental.

Thankfully, as with the attitudes to mental health, this progression towards understanding from schools and workplaces is accelerating in a way we've not seen before. Schools in particular have done some sterling work towards creating safe places for young people to learn in appropriate and personally beneficial ways. This will all just continue, I am sure of it.

Intervention times are very important and this is what makes first responders proficiency vital.

For me personally, I believe I was failed in this aspect. I had been attending my GP surgery for years for my mental health and between 6 and 14 no one mentioned OCD, not even once. It was me, a child, that brought it up. Looking back at my behaviours and what I'd spoken about it was absolutely obvious what I was going through. My GP seemed to have a particularly 'no mental health diagnosis for kids!' policy it seemed, so it took many years to be taken seriously.

Within that time I deteriorated rapidly. The environmental factors of my mental illness symptoms (bereavement, serious illness) were maybe masking my health being understood as chronic rather than consequential and ultimately I really suffered because of this.

Whenever I discuss that time with someone I describe that as being my 'reins' period. I felt that I was spiralling out of control but if between that formative period someone had 'grabbed the reins', I could have been stopped from ever progressing to the serious and critical levels I did. The life changing illness I have experience may have been something addressed and recovered from far earlier than actuality if that had been the case. But as I've repeatedly said, times were different then and the understanding of child and adolescent psychiatry we have now is far more advanced, as is the first response.

In spite of all of this insurmountable evidence that mental illness is the issue of our time, children's mental health services funding has been cut all over for years. This is the time we can often 'grab the reins' with mental illness.

Research by the Mental Health Foundation found 1 in 10 children are diagnosable with a mental health condition. That's 3 members of each school class, at least.

Facts are telling us that currently around 70% of children that need treatment are not receiving it. Just think about that for a moment. If you had a school hall of 100 children needing mental health support, in one of the most developed nations on the planet, only 30 of those will be getting it. That's absolutely beyond failing.

Of those children, some will be displaying symptoms of a mental health condition that will be a lifetime condition. 50% of people are experiencing symptoms of their lifetime mental illness by age 14, yet, only 30% are getting the help they need. This, obviously, has a devastating effect on quality of life, opportunity and complications from other mental and physical illnesses.

The politicians that history shall be kind to will be those that take the lead in understanding not just what needs to be said and understood about mental illness, but take the lead in what can be done about it.

There are some wonderful people in politics (no, really!) that dedicate a large part of their professional and personal lives toward creating better services for those living with a mental health diagnosis. The Prime Minister or President that enters office and uses their maiden speeches and first actions to truly and irreversibly use the crushing weight of their office to set out and make substantial and sustainable change will go down as the politician of our time. I truly believe that. The greatest leader of this century will be the one that makes the most significant difference towards the lives of those living with mental illness. Imagine that, the President coming into office and immediately doubling the efforts towards maintaining and improving mental health services nationwide. A 4 year term would change the course of history. It can be done and one day it will be done. Right now too many people are arguing over its cost. Arguing as if 'cost' is measured on a balance sheet, sadly it's measured in so much more than that.

As a 29 year old man, the thing on the planet most likely to kill me is me. Myself. My own hand is more likely to be what ends my life rather than cancer, heart disease, accident or anything else. In fact, any male reading this under 50 is in the same boat. It's THE leading cause of death amongst young people.

Once upon a time, those that understood mental illness would say 'if mental health killed in the way cancer does, people would soon take it seriously'. Well, here we are. It does. Are we taking it as seriously as we thought we would? I think not. We see it as seriously as we should, but I think our actions are demonstrably slower than they should be.

It is paramount that we expect more from ourselves and our establishments in order to make a true success of our approach to mental illness and our determination to achieve mental health.

If you are reading this and involved in society in any way whatsoever (ie all of you!) then you can contribute towards this. If you own a business, a mental health charter and agreement for staff and company will directly benefit however many employees you have. Agree this amongst yourselves and put into place appropriate-to-you policy on dealing with mental illness at work. Those of you that run businesses of any size, you WILL have staff taking days off due to their mental health that ring up and lie and say they have a migraine. Why should they lie about their health? Obviously, this is often due to embarrassment – that is why when we take days off due to a 'dodgy stomach', we really mean 'I don't remember what it's like to not be shitting water'.

You know the truth, they are being honest and in turn this creates a better environment. You then know if a staff member is taking many 'personal' illness days, you may need to discuss with them ways to manage this illness at work, with their help. Or raise concern personally. It's a little thing that goes a long way.

Parents can lobby their school to use appropriate lesson/assembly time to promote mental wellness and an understanding of mental illness. You saw above that 50% of those that live with a lifelong mental health condition are showing symptoms by 14, make it that your child and their classmates know what those symptoms look like! Uni's, colleges, schools – each of these can not only create their own mental health commitments, but they can team up and share information, routines and policy that has been successful with each other. We do this with so many other things, why not mental health? It does happen, but not enough.

Respecting the young people involved is the first step. That generation has is tough. Firstly, they are plagued by ignorance of those older than them referring to the privilege they apparently possess en masse. I would say that being a young person now is much harder than it was 30-40 years ago. Take away the whole 'but they have iPhones!' argument, and in reality they have it beyond difficult.

The internet has provided a non-concealable platform for those awkward years, gone are the days when your poor choices could be forgotten by adulthood. Instead, now, they remain. That's difficult. Online personas and the 'insta-fame' game highlighting people living their best lives (even when it's often not true) gives a celebrity level aspiration of what life should be, when it mostly is not. It's an incredibly tough age to be.

In this book I've ensured I've written in a similar way for the supporter pages as I have the young person. Young people are far more intelligent than the world sometimes gives them credit for, talk with them, not at them. Certainly not down to them, and I certainly hope I have not.

I promised you honesty in this book and this chapter may be providing the sort of blunt truth subtlety of a brick in the face but I don't think that should be scary.

We have some serious work to do here. There are challenges far grander than our own individual journeys to health facing us and I am not over dramatizing the issue when I say now is the time that those of us that can must absolutely stand up and demand and force the changes we need to move forward so that the issues we face today are addressed today. The worst thing a society can do is allow its follow on generation to inherit the problems it can fix itself. We've started talking and we've seriously changed perceptions but the wheels of legitimate change are turning slower than our own attitudes towards mental illness and whilst that is the case we will not provide the resources our services need to accommodate the growing nature of people's enlightenment meaning they wish to access these services.

The worst thing we can do, and sadly it is a position we are currently in, is becoming so ill equipped to deal with the influx of service users that the national discussion on mental health has finally created that we turn the discussion from 'it's time to talk and seek help' to 'it's time to seek help but that help won't be there'. We have urged people for decades to come forward and address their mental health problems but once they are there – they must be effectively treated within an appropriate period of time.

A very recent history a government issued Care Quality Commission report into CAMHS (Child and Adolescent Mental Health Services) highlighted that some young people were waiting up to 18 months for treatment and that many parts of the UK were not accessing the potentially quality evidence based treatment they should within an acceptable timeframe. The NHS constitution has an 18 week goal for treatment, not 18 months. 18 weeks in itself is too long, of course. 18 months can be personally catastrophic.

This delay has various obvious consequences that are needless. Deterioration of condition goes without saying, but not only can the delay in treatment courses be at a critical time for those needing treatment and result in their mental illness symptoms increasing, it can also lose reluctant patients before they even begin. Making someone that is pushing for help go backwards due to a large wait is one terrible thing, making someone who has finally and reluctantly agreed to get treatment give up on receiving any as the motivation has now gone, is a tragedy.

It is easy to see why more and more people (are having to) turn to private care and sacrifice major parts of their lives to be able to afford to be treated when they can ill afford to. It is a scandal.

From a supporter point of view, this can have a direct effect on you. The strain on marriages and relationships, particularly for co-parents when supporting a loved one, can sometimes be so strong that their/your own personal relationships suffer. Unfortunately the effects of living with a diagnosis are not limited to one person.

This, in turn, obviously causes a guilt factor in those already suffering. They can feel a burden and go from wanting treatment to wanting to be left alone as they feel their illness is causing all of this stress. It's a really tough place to be.

Dropout rates from work or school are not uncommon. Many people that have to leave a course or job some months into dealing with their mental illness would not need to make such dramatic 'decisions' should they be seen quicker. This, as above, has a ripple effect that earlier intervention could put a stop to.

The wait period is a vital time and means some of the things I've spoken of in this chapter i.e good first responders (GP's, teachers, colleagues, employers etc) and excellent primary (GP) care become vital to plug the gap. They should be bonus outlets in supporting an expedient and efficient treatment programme – not providing the actual support treatment itself should be providing. We should be aiming for great first responses/primary care as a good platform to great therapy and treatment and not relying on it to be the main support for people for long periods of time, which is sadly the case currently as we negotiate significant wait periods.

There's also a great natural progression for those of us with lived experience of mental illness, those of us with experience of the systems and those of us that have shared our stories before. We are in a position of personal understanding of what is happening and what is needed and therefore I urge those of us that have told our stories and had our conversations to use this knowledge for societal progression. We are the people that can turn words into actions. It is time, and it is important, that we mobilise ourselves and speak up for those who are not yet strong enough to do so for themselves.

We can influence so many factors that are critical towards becoming a nation that doesn't just acknowledge mental illness, the greatest health challenge of our time, but actually deals with it.

If you are in a position to do so, there is an endless amount of things you can participate in. I've given examples for businesses and schools, but personally you have the agency to make a genuine change and that in 2019 now involves something more than just talking. Setting up peer support groups, mentoring, working with advocacy services within charities, lobbying your local MP and councillors towards improving local services or offering support on their own campaigning, volunteering in schools or colleges to help teach educators of your own experiences of the systems, writing on the subject, holding your workplace to account and basically keeping yourself educated on exactly what is happening with the state of mental health treatments in the UK. No one needs to become aware to a professionally qualified level, but knowing where we are and fighting to be where we should be is something we can all do. If the information is difficult to find, request it. Don't let organisations and establishments settle into ambiguity and allow them to give snippets of info when they could release it all. Find out your local wait times, ask your surgery how they treat mental illness and how quickly they do it and if you're unhappy with the responses, question them further. Write to your local politicians, ask the NHS for its numbers and be open minded to it all. If enough of us are active enough in this, change will come.

We are in a precarious position right now in that we are a nation that can and does provides world leading mental health care, just simply not enough or quickly enough. This statement is not a directed in anyway at the abilities of our mental health professionals. Of course we have every right to question that, particularly if our treatment isn't going as we think it should, but that statement is an indication of the state of our health services currently, not of those working within them.

Therefore I believe that treatment is worth fighting for. Of course it is. It has to be. The way things are can lead to apathy and disengagement and that is potentially stopping you, or the person you support, from receiving the care that may well lead to mental health recovery.

The best way to change something is to be a part of it. Absolutely campaign to change the system and do all you feel able to achieve this, but do not look at the state we are in and think that this brittle system condemns you or those you support to a reality without quality treatment or attainable progression, as you would be very wrong.

*Current statistics are unavailable in full due to financial reporting methods but those here are correct at their time of publishing and publicly available in each instance.

# How Charities Can Be A Support

This book is written with a special Charity in mind, OCD Action. Every penny of profit from the sales of this book goes to the charity to assist their continued and sizeable support of those affected by Obsessive Compulsive Disorder. Unfortunately seeing as it is possibly just you and my Mum that have bought a copy, that donation may be modest. So do not be afraid to make one yourself!

An overlooked but important point is that this charity exists to provide guidance and be an outlet for everyone affected by the condition, not just those diagnosed with it.
As we well know, mental illness is not an isolated health concern but one that certainly affects those on the periphery. The Charity helps to illuminate those without personal experience that are seeking to educate themselves further, be that the condition itself or the stages of recovery, and provide wonderful examples of how we may support those that require it. Collaborations and confirmations to ensure a more accurate portrayal to an increasingly inquisitive media have resulted in a very wide and much safer level of journalism existing than would have without guidance. And of course to facilitate an awareness platform for the general public, whose understanding of the condition will always be a stepping stone towards forcing adequate provision of funds and resources to be allocated to ensure everyone that needs it is able to find treatment and support in a timely and appropriate fashion. It does far more than most may realise.

I think when people imagine the work charities do they'll maybe have a slightly outdated view of their work. I certainly did. Until around 5/6 years ago my understanding of this was far too limited. I only really took into account the things I could see – the fundraising drives, the campaigns for understanding, maybe the odd representative talking on TV about their subject and I didn't really delve much further into the less appreciated but often more lasting affects their work may have. Although the public facing side of the role is hugely important to draw any attention to their missions, the unseen assistance they may offer can be something you as a supporter or the person you are supporting can access for a lot of good, be that via this charity or your own relevant charity.

Charities are often able to provide representation for those living with a condition. They will proactively survey and build a general consensus of those with personal experience to ensure their direction and efforts are focused towards the needs of the community. Approaching politicians and organisations to demand better conditions for those living with a mental illness is a big ask for an individual, no matter how passionate and knowledgeable they may be – but having a national charity behind you, taking your beliefs and needs and presenting them to decision makers to create a safer and more inclusive world for you is a core part of what these charities do. It certainly is what OCD Action does.

I spoke with Collette Byrne, the National Advocacy Manager at OCD Action that has worked tirelessly for the Charity since 2012. Much like the rest of the team at the London office that I have met, Collette makes an enormous difference to the lives of people living with the condition in the UK and she has taken the time to explain a little further on the services available within the Charity.
It is worth noting that even if this condition does not affect you or the person you are supporting, some of these methods of support are available with other specific charities too, so certainly ask your chosen charity if something similar exists with them.

To summarise the core work of the Charity, Collette tells me; '*OCD Action is a national charity that provides support and information to people affected by Obsessive Compulsive Disorder (OCD), Body Dysmorphic Disorder (BDD), related disorders (Hoarding, Trichotillomania and*

*Compulsive Skin Picking) and their friends, family and health professionals. As well as providing support and information services, we work to raise awareness of OCD and related disorders in the media and with frontline health workers'*

We discussed the specific ways the Charity supports those that get in touch and Collette begins by telling me about one of their most vital and applauded services. *'One of the ways we help people try to feel less alone and better supported, is through our helpline. Living with a mental health condition can be incredibly isolating. We have two fantastic members of staff working on the helpline as well as a small (but brilliant!) team of passionate and understanding volunteers, many who have OCD themselves'* This is a great point. Many charities dedicated to mental health will often actively encourage volunteers with personal experience of the condition to become a part of the team. This is not the case for every member of staff, but you can often be assured you'll be speaking with an expert or an expert by experience. *'They take calls from people who have or think they may have OCD or a related condition and their loved ones, often chatting to people who have never spoken about their difficulties before calling us, sometimes after years of living with the condition.'* I have found anecdotally and then whilst researching this book that this is not an uncommon theme. In this day and age the first thing we tend to do is search online for information as a very first step. It is less daunting for some than going directly to a medical professionals or talking to someone already in our 'real life', so having a helpline, or any other form of communication available with trained staff and volunteers able to signpost appropriate information can be a magnificent outlet.

As discussed throughout these books, it is unlikely in most cases that treatment will start immediately after you attend your first appointment with a Doctor, but when it does, many will not know the process of therapy itself and how it feels, so the Charity have devised a unique and utterly brilliant means of support. *'For those who are about to start their treatment (Cognitive Behavioural Therapy - CBT), we also offer a unique service called 'Next Steps'. Treatment for OCD can be really tough and requires a lot of homework and challenges in between therapy sessions. 'Next Steps' aims to fill the gap in-between sessions. A volunteer will be paired up with an individual, and will provide weekly calls during their therapy to help motivate and support them to get the most out of their treatment'* Collette explained.

For those that are finding it difficult to get the treatment they need promptly, many charities will offer an advocacy service that can provide guidance over a range of professional, educational and personal needs. *'Some of the most challenging calls we receive are from people who are struggling to access, or in some cases even being refused, quality treatment for OCD.*

*On top of these difficulties, there is still a huge amount of people facing stigma and discrimination because of their condition, often affecting their employment, education, housing situations and so on. If people are facing a specific issue because of their OCD, our Advocacy Service can step in and help and individual take action to get what they need'* This is one of the key reasons this chapter is important for you as a supporter. If the person you are supporting would like to access some reasonable adjustments at work due to their health (maybe including flexible working or changing an hour lunch break to three twenty minute breaks) this is exactly the sort of thing we may know we need to support, but simply do not know how. The person we support may feel awkward going directly to the employer to say 'Can I have this adjustment?' outright. We may wish to arm ourselves with knowledge beforehand to be able to approach the more delicate aspects of seeking support first. This Charity, and others, can talk this through with you.

I'm a big advocate of peer support and support groups and I credit that system with being one of the biggest vehicles of my own recovery. Collette told me of the way their Charity helps facilitate this option. '*As well as the Helpline and Advocacy services, we support a network of independent local support groups across the country. Support groups can be a vital tool for people living with a mental health condition and their families and friends. Whatever stage people are at with their battle against a mental health condition, speaking to others with similar difficulties can be a life-line and support groups provide just that'.* If you search for these groups and are struggling to find something within a reasonable distance to travel, thankfully modern technology can play a role in an alternative. *'We recognise that not everyone can access a local group, so we also provide Skype/phone groups which people can access from their home. Using audio only (no video), the groups 'meet' over Skype and chat as they would if they were in the same room together, with a trained facilitator overseeing the session. We run various different groups, including habit disorders, parents groups, partners groups, groups for people with co-morbid diagnoses like autism and depression, and groups for younger people with OCD and BDD. We have seen so many friendships grow from the groups, with the support continuing well outside the call. It demonstrates that there is a need to bring together like-minded people who are facing similar difficulties'*

The Charity also recognises that younger people may find a greater benefit in being co-supported by people of similar age and have the incredible OCD Youth wing of the Charity. Run by young people with OCD, for other young people with OCD, they offer activity days (some of which I have volunteered at and my word these young people are brilliant), an e-helpline, online forums, peer support via social media and blogs and information specifically for young people under 25 with OCD or a related condition. As the Charity quite rightly points out; *'Talking to people your own age who just 'get it' is invaluable'.* Although this may not be for everyone, having this option can be a really positive 'way in' to support for any young person. It can be an easy, friendly, open and welcoming introduction to your chosen charity and being involved in this world and talking to others with similar or different experiences may provide encouragement to seek further medical support, or may 'simply' offer a place of solace.

As you can see, finding a reputable and supportive charity that can either directly support, or guide you to the right organisations for support, is an often underappreciated and unknown part of your supporters recovery armoury.

# What You Can Do As A Boss Or Colleague

According to a poll conducted* in 2018, the average British worker will spend 3507 days of their lives at work. That is around 9 years and 7 months of our lives being spent at work.

These polls are sometimes a little abstract, as although we can appreciate that is a long time it does just feel a little like trying to imagine how big space is. It maybe doesn't feel relevant to us. If we think of it on a week by week basis, the average person in the UK working full time will work 42.5 hours per week. To put that into context if you spent that time learning a language, you'd probably be at a basic fluency level in French in around 3 months. Vous comprenez? You could take those hours and spend them learning to drive and be ready to pass in a week. You could run a 100 mile ultra-marathon. It's endless. You get the picture. We are there a lot, so why do we put up with our conditions being uncomfortable, depressing or genuinely detrimental?

Often, we do this because the environment of our job or the procedures put in place to support us are not of a favourable enough quality so we have, for many years, decided to just put up with our lot and accept that that's just how it is. Well, it doesn't need to be. Why should it?

We are living in the midst of a mental health revolution when it comes down to awareness. The whole world is beginning to wake from its long, ignorant slumber and we are talking about the way we feel and the significant part of our wellbeing that is comprised of our mental health. Much like the examples of work being a big part of our time, the mental side of our health is also a large proportion of keeping us well.

So I'm going to tell you it honestly and bluntly and I hope either the truth is one you agree with – or should you disagree, I hope you spend some time investing in understanding why I know I am right.

It is now universally agreed that talking and communicating is a good thing, so if you are a leader and your environment is not conducive of open communication then that is your failure.

For the employers reading this and saying 'Listen Commie! My company needs to make money. Profit isn't a dirty word!' You know what? I totally agree with you. You do need to. Small businesses make up 99.3% of the private sector in the UK, defined by employing between 0-49 employees and your success and contribution to the economy is vital to us as a collective. But I'm trying to save you some money.

According to the Department of Work and Pensions' own report, poor mental health costs the UK economy up to £99billion a year. With £33billion to £42billion of this number being a cost to employers, with 300,000 people with a long term mental health problem losing their jobs every year.

Just in case an amateur Scrooge McDuck or a Poundshop Mr Burns is reading this and coming to the conclusion that 'Well, just employ mentally well people then! Problem solved!' Firstly, no, dickhead. Secondly, £225billion is contributed to the economy every year by people living with a mental health condition. 12.1% of the GDP. So get back in your bin.

This shows three things conclusively. 1) We are not doing enough to support workplace mental health 2) It is of our benefit, as employers, to promote mental wellbeing and good conditions for staff and 3) People living with a mental health condition play a significant role in the UK economy.

My belief, as with everything to do with ignorance towards mental health is not that those that are not doing enough are doing so because they simply do not wish to help, but because they do not know how to. Some are, obviously, being exploitative and not doing what they should because they just do not care enough, but I think that's rarer than those that are just unaware. Ignorance isn't really a negative, it's just a current position. Wilful ignorance, however, is a terrible thing.

So if you are an employer or a colleague of someone that is seeking or needing support with their mental health – and that's pretty much relevant to all of us, then this chapter is for you. Here are some suggestions.

**Panoramic Management** - Managers and leaders are spending vast sums of money and time on the learning and development of their employees, with 32% citing an increase in budget last year in the UK according to one report**. But this training, particularly internal, is commercially focused and not person-centred enough. A way to support, either as a boss or workmate is to actively seek this education that may be being missed. This book is a great example. As is reading up via charities like MIND and the Mental Health Foundation, both of whom provide guides on supporting in the workplace.

A generally more compassionate management style can also go a long way. As can your role as a team mate. Ask yourself; am I the sort of person that someone with a mental health complaint may feel comfortable coming to and discussing their needs? Am I making myself accessible enough? Am I taking into account the links between unmanageable stress levels and ill health? Am I more interested in what they can do for me in place of what I can do for them? If a colleague comes to me and is asking for support, do I know where to go or how to help? Answering these questions honestly and being ruthlessly self-critical in your approach can be a really incredible transitional experience for you and not only make you a better leader or colleague but make those that need the support feel like they can get it.

**Understanding Poor Performance –** People feel rightly cautious about treating someone differently due to their health and of course in a discriminatory sense this makes a valid point. However, we know all people are unique and we know everyone's mental health is unique. We put reasonable adjustments in place for many reasons with the practical side of working, but having a mindful approach to poor performance can be a wise move. When someone is at work and has a migraine, we appreciate their symptoms may disrupt their ability to perform at their optimum level. When someone is at work and coping with the symptoms of their mental illness, the same understanding should be extended. I don't think people should be excused for bad behaviour or even bad performance at times, but if a normally competent employee has seen a dip in their performance at work, would it be best if we reprimanded or disciplined them, or if we tried to understand and mutually agree a way of improving things for them?

**Breaktimes –** One easy way to begin changing the culture around your work environment is to take a healthier and more sensible approach to break times. i.e. make people take them! In too many places we are encouraged to eat at our desks and to not take the time to eat, rest, calm down and do whatever we need to do to feel better and be better. I think a big part of this stems from poor management and developing a way of working that means people feel they need to work through their breaks to show they care. Or that they are doing the absolute most they can. This is ridiculous, and illegal and just stupid. No one benefits from this. If you are a leader, encourage your staff to take their break times and strictly enforce they do. It is easy for staff to begin trying to outdo each other and makes everyone feel they need to do this to keep up. If you are a colleague and you see a workmate that is about to go on a break or is struggling to find time to do so, remind them they must and if possible alleviate their load a little to make doing so easier.

**Reasonable Adjustments –** As part of the Mental Health Act 2010, employers are legally bound to support those living with a mental health condition, including providing reasonable adjustments to ensure they are able to complete their job. Now, if you're a boss and reading this, I really hope you already know what I am talking about! For colleagues; this is a commitment to take steps, specific to the employee, that are designed to support them at work.

The most obvious example of this would be installing a wheelchair on premises as an adjustment for an employee. But, there can be adjustments made for mental health too. These can include; flexible working hours, reallocating specific duties to another employee, enabling them to attend therapy sessions without losing holidays, allowing personal phone calls during work hours if necessary, adjusting their lunch break from an hour to three x twenty minute breaks throughout the day, allowing a different uniform to be worn, creating a quieter space to work for them, offering a weekly or monthly meeting to discuss how things are progressing, giving them a different way to call in sick if a phone call is an impossibility. Which leads us on to the next suggestion.

**Calling In Sick –** No one has yet given me a good reason for forcing people to call rather than text or email an absence. What a weird and pointless little ego trip that is. Don't be THAT boss or colleague. If you prefer a call because you want to check they are genuinely sick, can you tell me how you assess over the phone if they're having a bad mental health day? Nope. So put a better system in place. My suggestion would be to have an email account that is NOT on all computers and only available to the boss and the HR manager and that can be used as a discreet way of emailing in a sickness.

The closest I can get to understanding wanting a call rather than a text or email is that you want to check on them and make sure they are OK. If that is the case, arrange a time at their convenience to discuss how they are that is led by 'how can I/we help?' rather than 'When do you think you are back?'

Colleagues are able to discuss with their boss/manager how to best make sure their first day back is comfortable. If you notice someone is off and know this may be due to a mental health issue (or any issue, really), offering to take some of their workload within reason to give them a clear return and a calmer 'in tray' can be a really kind piece of support.

**Preparing Returns To Work –** It's a statistical fact that the longer the colleague is off work the more likely they are to not return at all. I believe a big part of this can be due to the way returning to work is handled. Firstly, prevention (of the problem of returning to work) is better than cure so if your process has been explained to all staff members first, you are going to be more likely to have staff comfortable with the return process. This is yet another reason to be proactive with mental health in the workplace. However, if it is not there are ways we can prepare more efficiently, safely and to mutual benefit.

One of these ways is to install a staggered return to work. This is particularly helpful for those that have been off of work for a period of time. Rather than arrange a single date for return to their regular hours, arranging a few days of slowly returning to full hours can be a much safer and much more likely to stick routine. This could be potentially a return date that is for a meeting only, purely to discuss their return. Next maybe a full morning into work, then a longer day and an early finish and then a full day before returning to a regular week. It may make sense to do a week of just half days, maybe a week of every other day in full. It is worth discussing the potential options with the specific employee to find the option that works best for you both. But believe me, finding what works best for them will in turn be what works best for you, in the long run.

**Regular Check Ins –** This works brilliantly if you are a boss or a colleague. If you're a boss, offering a one-to-one monthly check in that is purely a wellbeing catch up and in no way performance related can be a great way to see where your employee is at and to have a conversation on things that have and have not been good over the month PURELY to do with their wellbeing. Questions that are relevant here may be; 'Did the adjustments we have put in place have a positive impact? If not, are we able to help there more?' or simply 'is there anything else you need from us?' This falls down completely if you ask 'Your work could maybe improve in this area, how can we adjust for you?' Although this may seem like it is seeking to support, and it probably will be, it is performance related and can seem like a critique. If these meetings feel too much like critiques it is easy for the person you are supporting to disengage.

For colleagues; simply checking in with a similar 'how can I help?' or 'Do you need anything?' is perfect. Not all the time obviously as this can feel patronising and like we are being singled out, but a regular check in is a good thing. This doesn't need to be just for your workmates that are living with a mental health condition either, obviously.

**Check Your Language –** Alright so if you can hear that absolutely deafening klaxon you have just heard the thought police arriving just in time to deliver you a healthy dose of political correctness and to let you know that you can have fun at work, you can have banter and enjoy being around your colleagues without resorting to making anything about mental health! See? I told you this book would be fun!

This is a difficult one to manage (only at the beginning) because normally workplaces have a wide array of different ages, backgrounds and sensibilities. So what is deemed acceptable to one will not be to another, much like most language really. If you are a boss that thinks this may be a step too far or a colleague that doesn't quite see the point here, have a think on if you would use a racial slur for banter or misogynistic language around your colleagues? If the answer is no (and I hope it is!) then extending this to jokes about someone's mental health, or their capabilities due to illness or stereotyping due to something you've seen on TV is a no-no. It may seem like harmless banter, especially if the colleague you are supporting likes to have a laugh and a joke, but it simply pushes normalisation a little further away. It creates environments where sincere talks on mental health become improbable and that causes significant issues. A training day or morning, led by a professional or in house can go a long way to be a line in the sand. I've seen companies using office wide memos to 'remind people of correct language' and it tends to get swept up in the day and ignored. Actually gathering people together for the sole purpose of addressing this is much more likely to reap reward. Colleagues may act as an ally and politely remind people that use incorrect language that they are overstepping the line if they feel so confident. Leaving the calling out to always be initiated by the people living with a mental illness can be a draining experience.

**A Job, Not A Business** – We've spoken about the socioeconomic factors involved in mental health and their link, but this applies to the workplace too. Far too often I will go into a business and hear from staff how they pay for more than they should. Too many employers or managers are putting too much responsibility on employees to go out of pocket for the company. Expecting an employee to 'put it on their card' when they go to a hotel, or travel/food expenses, paying for office essentials and so on is a favour from the employee. One you shouldn't really be asking for. But, of course, realistically sometimes you will. If you do, pay them back timely. By timely, I mean within 24hrs timely. So many people in the UK (and around the world) live their lives paycheque to paycheque and making them wait a week to get £60 back, or even £3 back, may tip them over the edge financially. We appreciate the link with financial factors and health, so this is a really simple way to support someone in the workplace.

**Create Wellbeing Action Plans For All** – In 1997, Mary Ellen Copeland developed the Wellness Recovery Action Plan®, a 'self-designed prevention and wellness process' that has since been adopted and adapted by many, including the mental health charity, MIND. The crux of this initiative is to create a workplace plan for every member of staff to promote mental wellbeing. This should be done proactively for all and not specifically for those with a mental health condition. If you are a leader at work, do not suggest this is just for those that have been open about a diagnosis but for every staff member.

The plan is an opportunity for staff to alert management and HR to things that contribute to their poor mental wellbeing or poor mental health.

This plan is open to interpretation but allows staff the opportunity to explain how to prevent any problems and improve any existing issues together. Questions (and potential answers in brackets) that may be asked can include;

- *What can support you stay mentally healthy at work?* (clear daily objectives, taking all breaks, leaving on time, open communication, a line manager to speak with whenever needed)

- *How can poor mental health or stress impact your work?* (It can make me take longer to complete tasks or focus on them, it makes me dread meetings, I find phone calls difficult in this period)

- *How may we (manager/boss/HR) support you to be mentally healthy?* (Regular feedback, more/less management, an opportunity to socialise or team build with colleagues)

- *Can you describe things that may contribute to poor mental health for you?* (Unresolved conflict at work, a poor atmosphere in the office, when mistakes are reprimanded publicly)

- *How may we tell you are struggling with your mental wellbeing at work?* (I become reserved, I clash with people, I find it difficult to focus or hold conversation, I am not forthcoming with ideas)

- *If we notice the above warning signs at work, how should we proceed?* (Contact my wife about it, email me about it privately so I do not need to discuss it face to face, talk to me discreetly at work, reduce my hours with notice)

- *In what ways will you try to support your own mental wellbeing at work?* (I will inform a designated colleague/HR that I'm not feeling well enough, I'll go for a walk or take an extended break, I will make sure I eat properly and take my lunch breaks)

These are just some examples and you can create your own. Using Copeland or MIND's template may also be a help. Please note that this is a voluntary exercise and is not a legal requirement for you as a boss or colleague and is not binding as so.

The great thing about creating these plans, other than the obvious benefits, is that it naturally develops an open and honest culture amongst colleagues. If mental health has never been formally spoken about in your company or workplace, these plans can be a very real and practical way of showing that you have a genuine interest in providing a support and doing more than just enough.

**Encouragement And Positive Reinforcement** – It's a failure in management to be quick to offer 'constructive criticism' but to be slow to praise when work is done well or even to praise effort itself. This is not a suggestion to constantly fawn over your staff, pen them loving sonnets and offer to name a star after them – but simple, positive, specific positive reinforcement can go a long way towards self-esteem and with an eye on people's mental well-being. Ambiguity in our position (the job itself) and our role (how we fit in and why) can lead to confusion and frustration.

**Confidentiality** – I'd hope that any HR managers and work leaders will already appreciate the paramount importance of confidentiality in the workplace, particularly if you do use wellbeing plans, but a gentle reminder to all colleagues that as easy as it is to 'redistribute information' (i.e. gossip) this can lead to people feeling outcast or betrayed. A complete no-no. If someone confides in you that they are struggling with their mental health at work and you believe the safest option is to inform your manager that they may require support, this is an understandable (and kind at its core) thing to do. However, broadcasting a private conversation you have had with someone that has confessed an issue to you to your general colleagues is obviously completely wrong.

**Be Honest About Your Environment –** It can take confidence to be willing and open enough to audit an environment you have worked incredibly hard to cultivate, so as leaders it can be easy for us to just search for where we are going right. Hopefully this chapter has given you, and colleagues reading this, some practical insight into how to improve your workplace. You spend your time there though, and you know it as well as you do so being proactive and creating a self-developmental (not self-critical, we aren't out to criticise, we are out to positively change) audit of how things currently are will allow you to prevent further issues and celebrate and cement the things you do right. Ask yourself; are we an open and inclusive workplace? Would I be proud for people living with a mental health problem to visit here, knowing they would feel accepted? Have we/I done enough to promote mental wellbeing? Do we as a senior staff have a great enough understanding of what we need to do to promote a mentally healthy work life? These questions are all valid and important and will not only improve the lives and health of your staff and colleagues but genuinely positively impact the company. If you re-read my opening paragraphs in this chapter you'll see why it is not only compassionately vital, but also commercially.

**Know Your Limits** – This is a common theme in these books! Assuming that you are not a highly trained psychiatrist with an occupational expertise, you need to be aware of your limits. Your role, as discussed in this chapter, is to be an outlet and a positive, proactive and kind supporter. You do not need to provide amateur therapy, nor should you. You are here to assist in ensuring your workplace is as mental health positive as it can possibly be and to be open-minded and keen to learn how to always improve this. If you do not feel confident supporting or feel out of your depth supporting mental health in the workplace there are many training providers and charities willing to offer information and practical assistance. If the person you are supporting is in the UK and needs urgent (but not life saving) help, you are able to call 111 should you be in any doubt and require quick and reliable advice, or encourage them to speak to the Samaritans. Should they be in an active-emergency and a danger to themselves or others then it is absolutely appropriate to call 999.

To summarise, I believe mental health in the workplace needs an immediate, innovative and long overdue revolution of the way we talk about, think about, and act on mental health support at work. Although we do require innovation and evidence-based good practice, the vast majority of what we can do and what can make a difference to are simple changes and easy to implement initiatives. If you look at all of my suggestions in this chapter – which of these dramatically changes the face of your company, organisation or job? Or even your day-to-day work life? I'd guess at none. But for someone, they will be a positive day-to-day change, and I hope dramatically so.

* Commissioned by the Association of Accounting Technicians

** UK L&D report 2018

# When Things Are Good – Supporting The Good Days

Have a think about the days before you go on holiday and the faintly ridiculous things you start preparing to take with you.

Firstly, I guarantee you'll pack enough pants to cover yourself in the event you end up shitting yourself three times a day for a week, we all do that. But what else makes your suitcase? Paracetamols, obviously. Just in case you get a headache, even though painkillers will be buyable there. You'll probably take razors, shampoo and conditioner, even though you'll likely have these for free in the hotel. You've obviously got that big thick book you've wanted to read for a few months that's 700 pages long, but you'll also take two more just in case you finish them. Everyone needs a charger, but two are better.

We do this because we are worried a bad thing will ruin a good thing. We feel anxiety because we've spent so much time looking forward to the good thing, that the thought of a broken charger or a headache makes us feel we need to over prepare even though logic tells us we can sort those things easily and they are not at all major issues.

So, if you live with a mental illness sometimes you will swap 'anxious for going on holiday and ruining a good time' to 'anxious for going to the cinema/seeing friends/going on a day out/going for a walk/going to a sports match/going to a show/going absolutely-bloody-anywhere you may fancy and anxiety ruining a good time'. It's the same premise packaged differently.

I have a chapter on the other book titled 'The Bad Good Days' and it explores how for me, at my worst, I actually feared the good days more than I feared the bad. The bad days were par for the course and normality, a nugget of good didn't freak me out. But the genuinely good days, the ones where I felt like I was really living life, they petrified me. I was constantly on edge that things would capsize and I'd crash down and not only feel terrible but also lose a rare good day in the process – so sometimes, I just didn't bother with the good days.

The point of this chapter is for two reasons. 1) to illuminate or remind you that just because you're with the person you're supporting in a normally good environment or day, does not mean it does not have a potential for anxiety and 2) to explain what it can feel like and why.

My Dad taught me a great lesson about this growing up. He worked for the Environment Agency for a while and in his forties started developing panic attacks. He'd worked for years as a builder and always had to graft silly hours to provide, and then the boy that grew up with nothing had earned a serious job in something he was interested in and something he cared about, so was sitting in a dream job. My brother was seriously ill at this stage and receiving cancer treatment at Great Ormond Street and the pressure on Dad was enormous really.

He began to have to deal with anxiety in a serious way every day and dreaded the meetings he would need to regularly have with some pretty big time people. He would have to sit in rooms with several prominent superiors and they were formal, demanding audiences. This was his worst period. He would overanalyse escape routes if he felt lightheaded and planned the seating plan to allow him to sneak out if he needed and would generally love the work but hate these meetings. He liked all the people, he knew the subject matter intimately, he loved his colleagues but he hated these days.

One day, mid-meeting, he felt an unbearable wave of anxiety. His palms become sweaty, his heart rate ran away from him, the room spun, his mouth dried and he needed fresh air, quickly. He made it known he had to retrieve a specific document from the office and felt the crushing disappointment of hearing his boss say 'Don't worry Ian, I've got it here'. Busted. He didn't have his 'out' anymore.
To his eternal credit, Dad just came out with it and said 'I actually need to leave immediately, sorry. I'm feeling a bit unwell and anxious and I need to leave. I hope you understand' and left. He later explained the anxiety to colleagues and everyone got on board and understood and gave him respect for dealing with it.
From that day on, he never had anxiety about those meetings again. He didn't feel in anyway stuck in there and actually looked forward to them. He told me once the entrapment feeling had been taken out of the equation, everyone now knew and he had nothing to hide, he felt freed by their knowledge and that was enough to keep him feeling well enough.

This works similarly for supporting good days and keeping them or making them good days. Having an escape plan can be a really good thing. Just letting the person you are with have a way out if needed can often be enough to keep the day moving well. Simple things like a signal to leave if they'd like to leave, researching chilled out places nearby to go and have a calm period if needed, transport options to get home if they need to be made and so on. These will take 10 minutes to sort and agree and can have a huge impact. It allows the person you are supporting the opportunity to feel safe knowing they are able to seek refuge as and when needed.

It is important to not become overly reliant on them though and if they become a source of anxiety in themselves i.e. the person will simply not go out without a plan whereas previously they would, then it's worth discussing another option or other ways so it doesn't become counterproductive.

Another note to bear in mind is that your person may well turn down things they normally like due to this very issue with good days. They may have not gone off of the activity, person or day but just really feel like it's too much hassle. Encouraging them to find ways, or maybe to ask you for support to find ways to re-engage with their formerly favourite activities would be a good start here. As would discussing the amount they care about the loss of activity. Is this activity that they are avoiding one they have been passionate about for years or always done? If so, finding a way to make it happen again is a good reclamation of their health. If it is a pursuit they do not feel much loss of, maybe the battle here is not worth it – under certain circumstances. I actually believe ANY chance to fight your anxiety lying to you is worth the time, but this may not be the case always.

We, those of us living with a mental health condition, live with a mix of conflicting emotions and thoughts and the way good days can actually be intimidating before or during the event is possibly one of the most frustrating.

The pressure to enjoy the thing is so strong and demanding that we can very easily be tripped up by our symptoms and that can be a really lonely feeling. We all have FOMO, the Fear Of Missing Out from time to time, but this can be especially true for us. Having FOMO over an event you are logistically unable to attend feels rubbish – but imagine having it over an event you are already at! You're in the room and there, but you're not participating mentally due to illness. It's incredibly difficult and may explain some behaviours before or during a day that you'd understandable automatically consider to be a good one.

I believe with experience and support finding a way to make the good days remain as they are intended is possible for all of us. What I hope for this chapter is that it may go some way to explaining the thought process behind how they may currently feel tainted, frightening or useless to those seeking recovery.

# Mind Your Language

One of the first terrible lessons we are universally taught is that; 'sticks and stones may break my bones, but words cannot hurt me'.
Thankfully, we seem to have moved on from this rubbish, but there is still stigma in language. This is built upon centuries of misunderstanding of mental health leading to the normalisation of ostracising and demeaning terms when discussing mental illness that can have a profound impact on those living with conditions.

I have a particular interest in this because my own mental health condition, Obsessive Compulsive Disorder, has always been viewed publicly and socially as something completely different to what it actually is. And that's fine, because the doctors and the true sufferers know what it is, right? So there can't be any damage as long as they know? Nope.

The issue with language and public perception being altered to paint a condition to be something that it isn't is that, alongside a general lack of sympathy and empathy to the reality, those that have the condition will often develop a skewed understanding of what they themselves are actually going through exactly. They may not seek or may delay seeking help as they assume what they are feeling isn't the condition they've seen portrayed. If their symptoms feel severe and life altering yet the media and the public show a watered down and trivialised version, how are they to accept their own illness?

OCD, for example, has had a rough time of being repurposed as a personality trait. Think Monica from Friends, Obsessive Cat Disorder birthday cards, cleaning companies named 'OCD Clean' and the overused 'I'm a bit OCD about that'. A thing I hear all the time is that OCD is a spectrum disorder, and it is. For those that actually have the disorder. Not for everyone else. I have had people argue with me on TV, radio and in person about this. Neurotypical people saying with the sort of blasé confidence of Boris Johnson's hairdresser that; 'we all have it, just to different degrees' is both frustrating and possibly very damaging.

We are all obsessive, and we are all compulsive. But being 'Obsessive Compulsive' is a medical term. Having Obsessive Compulsive Disorder is an actual, diagnosed, and often very serious disorder that can have wide ranging consequences on your life. So much so the World Health Organisation lists it as one of the top 10 most debilitating conditions a human can suffer from.

So, we can see then why 13 year old teenagers, dealing with a whole host of other pressures in the modern world, find themselves experiencing severe symptoms and googling them to be presented with potential OCD – only to rubbish this suggestion as 'OCD isn't as serious as my symptoms' and thus, not seeking help. Those living with anorexia may not see the issue fully because tabloids 'accuse' celebrities of having anorexia that do not, or refer to a politician as 'having bipolar' because they flip flop an opinion. It slowly erodes the seriousness of the condition and when that happens it can go some way toward people not having an efficient enough recovery experience and that is outrageous.

That is why language matters. In itself it may seem isolated and of little damage, but every time we add a little more stigma in the world we get a little further away from where we need to be.

Conversely, the mental health revolution we are now starting to see has caused its own anxieties for people that do not live with a mental illness but are supporting a loved one that does. The reason being they are so petrified they are going to say the wrong thing. Firstly it is worth appreciating the fact that the conversation you have with your loved one is obviously a different thing to the public conversation about mental health.

It's difficult because ignorance is not a good thing but it is a very present and very real thing we need to learn to co-exist with a little better. I do not begrudge someone being ignorant about mental health, we are all ignorant in some ways. But I do begrudge them claiming understanding of something they haven't really invested any time into understanding. If someone makes an OCD joke to me that I think may be worth calling out, I will do and hopefully that lesson will stick with them forever and it's not necessarily their fault they didn't know. They were probably just never corrected. But when someone is told the truth and still speaks with stigmatising language that boils my piss.

My own belief is that we need to treat this ignorance as opportunities to learn and not use them as just opportunities to vilify. Once upon an angry time, I would actively seek out companies that were misusing OCD (it's not hard to find) and I would contact them, publicly shame them and try to make them feel about 2ft tall. It made me feel better for a few seconds but it stopped a genuine conversation occurring. There are a few great examples of companies and individuals being called out in the right way to then hold their hands up and say 'teach us' and from then on in they make a concentrated effort to be more mindful. That's how we need to view the subject when supporting someone with their mental health.

My advice would be to not panic and to be cautious and purposeful with your words, but accepting of the fact that mistakes are nearly unavoidable. It's unlikely, by the sheer fact you are reading this book, that you are the sort of supporter to not try and find better language and better ways to communicate. By investing your time in reading this you are evidencing a clear desire to be better – so if you are overly concerned about miscommunication, don't be. Use it to learn.

A sure-fire way to fast track your understanding is to go directly to the person and ask them 'Hey, I'm trying to be better, is there anything I or others say or do that makes you feel uncomfortable when it comes to mental health?'. It may not be as glamorous a conversation as you'll ever have, but it may be one of the most important.

Language develops, even generation to generation so understand we are all learning as we go too. I have a glossary section at the back of this book. Some terms on there are already up for debate and in 10 years' time it is highly likely I will look back and wish I hadn't used certain terms I have, so even I'm acknowledging I need to keep up. And I've written a book on mental health! (It's this one, actually. Good, aint it?) Don't be frightened of getting the language wrong, just consider the benefits of getting it right.

The key benefit to appropriate language is that it facilitates conversation in a much smoother way.
For example, if the person you are supporting is having a bad day or moment and has kicked off over something that you think may be an angry reaction to a symptom, you can approach this in two ways.

1) *'That was wrong. Don't do that again'* – is dismissive, has no open end to it and is possibly needlessly confrontational.

2) *'Did we have to do it that way, can you maybe try and do this another way next time? Is there a better way do you think?'* – is open ended, requires a response and is non-judgemental.

This is a very clean example and doesn't allow for tone or the way you naturally speak. If you wouldn't naturally say words like that, word it as you would. No one wants to feel patronised or like they are being dictated to. But it's a good starting point.
Also, it's worth noting that 1) might even be successful and it might be what the person needs to hear, but if we're looking for best case practice, here are a few suggestions I would make around language and communication that I think may be helpful;

1) Ask open ended questions.

2) Allow for the person to divulge as much or as little as they wish

3) Do so in a relaxed (or appropriate) environment. If you talk in the car, talk in the car. If you talk in a coffee house, stick to it.

4) Make sure you allow appropriate time so that the person does not feel you are clock watching.

5) Mirror their chosen language. If they prefer 'mental illness', use it. If they prefer 'unwell mentally', use it.

Ultimately, language (and communication) is an ever-evolving concept. One of the worst things you can do is to become so scared of saying the wrong thing that you eventually stop saying anything at all. Be honest about what you know and use any ignorance you have as an opportunity to be taught, not only in general but specifically to the person you support.

Using this opportunity to listen and learn will not only help you day-to-day and to keep up to date with what is and is not acceptable in the modern world and directly to the person you are supporting, it will also start some vital conversations in a safe, positive and enlightening way.

# Looking After Your Number One Priority.

You.

Right, hear me out! We all have people in our lives, our children, our spouses, our best friends – that we consider to be more important than us. People that we would choose to have our good health, choose to win the lottery over us, choose to be happy before we choose to be happy ourselves. That's a powerful motivator and a completely understandable position and I have people in my life I feel that way about too – but, ultimately, one of the best things we can do for those people is reverse the roles and understand that looking after ourselves first is a part of looking after them.

We should want to look after ourselves just for us – the benefits for positive selfishness are good for everyone, but if you want to prioritise your loved one, a really good way to do that is put yourself first.

Living with a mental illness is complex and comprehensive and difficult and where clarity and calmness can be achieved, that should always be an aim. So being unwell and then looking around you and seeing those around you becoming unwell due to, in part, your own condition and the stresses that can cause on others, can be truly devastating.

You'll have heard how 'you can't help someone if you can't help yourself!', and although a flawed argument it does have some truth in there and if that is a good motivator for you to keep yourself healthy then so be it. Use it.

For family members reading this book, particularly parents and siblings, you are very likely to be sharing the same socioeconomic factors as the person you are supporting and are therefore exposed to similar issues and environment, so it is unsurprising that you may also be struggling with some of the same factors that affect them.

How does looking after yourself look, though? Well firstly, as you will have read, this book is largely about honesty and about making motivation matter to achieve actions that ultimately benefit in the short to long term so let's start here.

Being honest with yourself and realising and accepting 'I am struggling to be a support today' is a very healthy and very positive step to take, because those days will come. Admitting this to yourself will help you police your own feelings and behaviour and allow you to spot when it is becoming overwhelming for you. Please remember you are a supporting cast member. The person you are supporting is the lead star and their professional, highly trained medical team are the directors. Your role is significant and can be life altering, but you cannot 'fix' a person and you are not in charge of leading everything.

There will be logistical examples where you DO have to put the person first. Maybe not watching certain films when they are around if they include something triggering, maybe adjusting a family diet, it could be a case of not inviting guests around without warning or being understanding enough to accept your loved one may cancel last minute, due to symptoms. Those examples of putting someone first are fine, but putting someone's health and wellness ahead of your own is not.

If you are maybe a little imbalanced in this regard and find your mental or physical health deteriorating and believe it may be in part due to the pressures of the support you are providing your loved one, do as they would do and visit your GP and discuss how you feel. Even the act of doing this may recharge you and keep you confident you have things under control. Alternatively, if you are close enough to speak with their social worker or secondary care team (psychologist, psychiatrist, counsellor, community psychiatric nurse) you may have an opportunity discuss how to be a better support (spoiler: it'll involve looking after yourself first and foremost!). There are also charities that offer fantastic support for supporters and these are often condition relevant charities (like OCD Action). Your local NHS providers, or the charities themselves, may be able to recommend a support group for you, which would be a place you can go and meet other loved ones of people living with a mental illness and discuss the trials and tribulations with people that understand where you are coming from.

Really seemingly simple measures like ensuring you are eating three meals a day (and sitting down, not rushing), sleeping correctly, resting appropriately, socialising when you can and want etc. may seem like basic functions – but can be quickly neglected if you are prioritising someone else. Right now, be honest with yourself, is your support of your loved one impacting regularly on any of these things in this paragraph? If so, maybe you are overstretching.

Offering or accepting to support a person living with a mental illness is a brave, noble and kind thing to do. I could not have more respect for you, however, it is of paramount importance you appreciate and understand that this is a massive stress on you mentally too, and keeping on top of it is good for both you and the person you support. Give yourself permission to accept that you need to water your own plants first. Be as effective as a supporter as you can be, as much as you can be, but never more so. Respect that part of the process. Knowing that you are doing something amazing for someone else is an unbelievable feeling – but treat yourself with the same love and care that you do for them and remember that doing something amazing for you, and putting yourself first, is worthy of your time and a non-negotiable.

# Thank you and good luck.

Sometimes when I'm feeling world-weary, and life feels like it's full of punches, villains and bad news, I remind myself to look around and remind myself that we are on the cusp of a Kindness Revolution.

It's easy to pick up a paper or scroll through social media and come to the conclusion that it is a good idea to close the curtains forever. We're inundated with the negatives and the positives get lost, and so do we. We have such a running commentary of bleak outlooks and dizzying information we can get stuck on pause when things aren't going right. A 'good news channel' isn't quite sexy enough to sell so more often than not, we're going to be blasted with the bad.

But, check around you. Really stop and check. People are talking about kindness like it is medication and in many ways it is. They are talking about it like it is religion even. People are completely disillusioned by everything we're being fed and it's no surprise just waking up and doing is so difficult for so many.

When I'm blinded by the dark it doesn't take long to be able to see that we as humans are inherently good. I've seen so much proof. We are social creatures and we understand the importance of community and making ours as strong as we can. It's biology. (Probably. I just made that up).

If I ever needed a reminder that the world is full of beautiful people I have it in the form of you holding this book. You have made an active choice to seek knowledge on how to better support someone in your life. That is fucking incredible.

As you'll have worked out by now this is not an A to Z, and nor would I say it is a 'How To'.

There is not one destination or one common goal to move towards, but there are signposts to aim for. It's a constantly moving journey. This is largely my story and I have tried to share it for good use, but it is my own. The person you are supporting has a whole other story to read and learn, so the way you use the lessons in this book are going to be entirely dependent on exactly who that person is. So use it as an idea starter, a brainstorm. My route will not be their route, but you'll have learned enough here to move forward. And if you haven't? No refunds.

To the young people that are reading this to support your peers of similar age, you are the reason I have no fear for where the world is headed. Your generation is the best of us and never let anyone convince you different. But please remember you, first. This is your youth as well. If your own adolescence isn't quite what you expected it would be and isn't living up to the films you've seen and the stories you've been told, that's absolutely fine. Don't rush it or judge it, just keep trying to make positive changes and look around you for the good. It is there. That's a promise.

For the parents that are reading this to better understand their children, at whichever age they may be, I salute you. No matter how you got here, be it as close as can be or with a splintered relationship, you are doing right by them by learning what they need. I hope it helps. Don't be scared to confront the bad things, you already know they exist. Closing your eyes and ears will not make them go away, but concentrated and educated efforts may just.

To the colleagues, employers, teachers, classmates, sports coaches or the generally curious – you may feel you are not in a position to help. You are. If you left the house today, you'll have met someone living with a mental illness. You may not even have had to leave the house to find them. Learning how to better communicate with those fighting